THE COMPLETE EQUINE
LEGAL & BUSINESS
HANDBOOK

THE COMPLETE EQUINE
LEGAL & BUSINESS
HANDBOOK

LEGAL INSIGHTS AND PRACTICAL TIPS
FOR A SUCCESSFUL HORSE BUSINESS

MILTON C. TOBY

ECLIPSE
PRESS

Lexington, Kentucky

Library of Congress Cataloging-in-Publication Data

Toby, Milton C.
    The complete equine legal and business handbook : legal insights and
practical tips for a successful horse business / by Milton C. Toby. -- 1st ed.
        p. cm.
    ISBN-13: 978-1-58150-157-5 (pbk.)
    1. Horse industry--Law and legislation--United States. 2. Horses--Law
and legislation--United States. I. Title.
    KF390.5.H6T63   2007
    343.73'07661--dc22

                                                        2007002442

Printed in the United States
First Edition: 2007

a division of
Blood-Horse Publications
PUBLISHERS SINCE 1916

CONTENTS

INTRODUCTION

Calling a book the "Complete" anything is both optimistic and risky. On the other hand, "Sort of Complete" doesn't inspire confidence in readers, and the "Complete Guide to Everything the Author Thinks Is Really Interesting or Possibly Useful" is awkward and unwieldy.

So, in the interest of full disclosure, an admission: *The Complete Equine Legal & Business Handbook* is not "complete," at least not in the absolute sense of the word. The book won't turn you into a lawyer, for example, nor should it. Some matters are best left to attorneys, and those things are identified throughout the text. There is no substitute for experienced counsel in many situations, and the old saying "a lawyer who represents himself has a fool for a client" applies with equal strength to non-attorneys who take on their own legal work.

You should have some familiarity with the legal issues relating to your problem, however, for your own peace of mind and to get the most value for your money when talking to an attorney or accountant. If the attorney or accountant has little equine experience, you may even have to educate the professional.

The Complete Equine Legal & Business Handbook is aimed at persons like yourself who want to know more about equine law, a savvy set who recognize that understanding the sometimes-complex interaction between law and business will allow them to operate more efficiently.

Anticipating a legal problem always is better than trying to solve the same problem after the fact. *The Complete Equine Legal & Business Handbook* will help you avoid unpleasant surprises by pointing out potential legal issues, along with some preventive medicine.

Ranging from the legal status of animals as property and the growing controversy over animal rights, to types of business ownership, dispute resolution, contracts, liability, sales, taxes, employment, and estate planning, this book covers areas of possible conflict for all horse owners and equine businesses, no matter the size, breed, or discipline. *The Complete Equine Legal & Business Handbook* also includes case studies that illustrate how legal principles are applied in the real world, resources for additional information at the end of most chapters, and an appendix with a glossary and citations to a variety of state statutes that directly affect the horse business.

Finally, a caveat. The information in this book is provided for educational and informational purposes only. Nothing here is intended by the author or publisher to be legal advice, nor should anything in this book be taken as such. Any questions about specific legal problems should be directed to an attorney, preferably one with expertise in equine law. References, either good or bad, from friends in the horse business can be valuable tools in locating a lawyer, and many state or county bar associations have referral services that can put you in touch with local attorneys. National listings of equine attorneys, updated annually, also can be found in *The Blood-Horse Source* and *The Horse Source* (both available at www.exclusivelyequine. com).

Milton C. Toby
December 2006

1

ANIMALS AS PROPERTY

A nimals are property. Simple on its face, this characterization is a far-reaching legal concept that forms the foundation for virtually all equine law and business principles. The law divides property into two general categories: real property (land and all things growing or built on the land) and personal property (everything else). Although it may surprise people who treat their animals like family members, or sometimes better, animals are considered personal property in all fifty states.

Like other property, animals are considered "goods" under the Uniform Commercial Code. This body of law, adopted in some form in every jurisdiction, governs business transactions. Disputes involving animals are resolved in the same way as disputes involving other types of property, without regard to any "rights" the animal might possess. Animals' owners, not the animals themselves, are plaintiffs and defendants in the event of a lawsuit. Damages for harm to an animal generally, but not always, are limited to economic damages — the animal's fair market value.

Because they are considered personal property, animals can be bought, traded, sold, or given away; leased; bred commercially with undesirable animals being culled; raced and exhibited, all without their owners running afoul of the law. An animal that becomes sick or injured can be euthanized, with neither the owner nor the government under any legal obligation to provide medical care.

There are some ethical considerations when euthanasia is being considered. The American Association of Equine Practitioners (AAEP) guidelines state that euthanasia should be based on medical factors, not economic considerations, regardless of the horse's age, sex, or potential

9

value. The guidelines set out four questions that should be answered in the affirmative before euthanasia is appropriate:

1. Is the horse's condition chronic and incurable?
2. Is there a hopeless prognosis for life?
3. Is the horse a hazard to itself or to its handlers?
4. Will the horse require continuous medication for the relief of pain for the rest of its life?

As personal property, animals have no legal rights — at least at the time of this writing. Animals do enjoy some legal protections in recognition of their status as living creatures, however, which arguably creates for them a special classification falling somewhere between humans and nonliving property such as computers and automobiles.

A comprehensive review of the rapidly growing areas of animal law and animal rights is beyond the scope of this book. This chapter will focus on the legal status of animals in three areas:

1) the grassroots movement to change the status of animal owners to guardians and its implications for the horse industry,

2) animal protection and related criminal statutes,

3) damages for harm to animals.

GUARDIANS AND OWNERS

There can be no real controversy over the fundamental idea that animals are entitled to proper care and that they should be protected from intentional mistreatment and abuse or negligence. The dispute arises over how the legitimate interests and well-being of animals can be protected. Confusion over "animal rights" and "animal welfare" contributes to this dispute.

Animal welfare means just what the words suggest: a concern for the health and welfare of animals within the existing legal framework. For the traditionalist, the road to protection of animals is paved with better owner education, availability of veterinary care, more well-equipped and well-funded shelters, harsher penalties for animal cruelty convictions, and vigorous enforcement of existing anti-cruelty laws. The basics of animal welfare include adequate shelter, food and water, veterinary care, and companionship.

The animal rights movement, on the other hand, often reflects nontraditional and oftentimes radical efforts to protect animals. At one end of the spectrum, animal rights activists stage marches and urge boycotts of companies accused of mistreating animals. At the other end of the spectrum, extremists launch violent attacks on commercial animal operations and facilities where animals are used in research, destroying property and releasing animals.

The Animal Liberation Front (ALF) and the Earth Liberation Front (ELF), for example, are considered part of a "serious terrorist threat," according to James F. Jarboe, Domestic Terrorism Section Chief of the FBI's Counterterrorism Division. Testifying before Congress in February 2002, Jarboe reported that ALF and ELF members committed some six hundred criminal acts in this country during the preceding six years, with damages in excess of $43 million.

A moderate approach, more middle-of-the-road than the actions of ALF and ELF but still outside the mainstream, is a legal restructuring of the traditional owner-property relationship between humans and animals. Advocates are urging state and municipal lawmakers to rewrite their rules, substituting the word "guardian" for "owner" wherever possible in laws that affect animals. The purpose of the change in wording, according to its advocates, is to instill a greater sense of respect and compassion for animals. This, proponents argue, could lead to a reduction in animal abuse.

The guardian movement had its genesis in 1995, at the eleventh annual Summit for the Animals held in St. Louis, Missouri. Representatives from forty-seven national organizations approved several resolutions there, including one styled "Adopting Language that Recognizes Animals as Individuals and Not as Property or Things." This resolution put forward the proposition that "animals are not property to be used for the benefit or whim of humans." In Defense of Animals, a California-based, non-profit animal rights advocacy organization headed by veterinarian Dr. Elliot Katz, soon took up the cause with its nationwide guardian campaign: "They are not our property ... we are not their owners."

The first serious attempt to effect a regulatory change from "owner" to "guardian" failed in San Francisco, but a similar measure was adopted shortly thereafter, in July 2000, by the city council in Boulder, Colorado. Rhode Island followed suit in 2001, becoming the first (and so far, only) state to amend its laws to recognize human guardianship of animals. Cities in California and Arkansas adopted similar legislation the same year. By the end of 2006, In Defense of Animals identified Rhode Island; Marin County, California (encompassing more than two dozen cities); and some fifteen individual cities as jurisdictions recognizing animal guardians.

Rhode Island General Law Section 4-1-1(4) is typical. After being amended, the statute provides that a "Guardian shall mean a person(s) having the same rights and responsibilities of an owner, and both terms shall be used interchangeably. A guardian shall also mean a person who possesses, has title to or an interest in, harbors or has control, custody or possession of an animal and who is responsible for an animal's safety and well-being."

Adding the word "guardian" to a state or municipal law, especially when the law allows "guardian" and "owner" to be used interchangeably, sounds innocuous enough. After all, many animal owners already treat their animals more like family members than as property, and being called guardians rather than owners is not likely to make them more responsive to their animals' needs.

AT A GLANCE

- Animal welfare vs. animal rights: Animal welfare is concern for health and welfare of animals within a legal framework. Animal rights advocates often use more extreme measures to protect animals from perceived harm.
- Proponents of "guardianship" do not consider animals as property.
- The law considers animals as personal property and "goods" under the Uniform Commercial Code.

Some activists argue that the change in language will reduce the incidence of animal abuse, simply by making owners feel more responsible for their animals. This may be wishful thinking, however, considering that child abuse continues at an alarming rate despite the unquestioned legal and moral responsibility parents and legal guardians now have for the welfare of children.

Strong criticism of the policy shift has emerged from seemingly unlikely sources. In May 2003, for example, the executive board of the American Veterinary Medical Association approved a position statement opposing guardianship language. The official AVMA position reads:

Ownership vs. Guardianship

The American Veterinary Medical Association promotes the optimal health and well-being of animals. Further, the AVMA recognizes the role of responsible owners in providing for their animals' care. Any change in terminology describing the relationship between animals and owners does not strengthen this relationship and may, in fact, diminish it. Such changes in terminology may decrease the ability of veterinarians to provide services and, ultimately, result in animal suffering.

The board of directors of the American Kennel Club adopted a similar resolution in 2003, stating, in part, that the "AKC believes that the term guardian may in fact reduce the legal status and value of dogs and thereby restrict the rights of owners, veterinarians, and government agencies to protect and care for dogs. It may also subject them to frivolous and expensive litigation. The term guardian does nothing to promote more responsible treatment of dogs." Other groups voicing similar opposition include the Cat Fancier's Association, the Pet Industry Joint Advisory Council, the National Animal Interest Alliance, the Responsible Pet Owners Alliance, and the American Veterinary Medical Law Association. Equine organizations appear to have remained silent to this point.

"What's the problem?" you might reasonably ask at this point. Anything that makes people more conscious of the fact that an animal is not a disposable commodity and should not be abused must be a good thing. What could go wrong? So far, nothing.

Laws in Rhode Island and in the cities that have adopted guardianship language generally appear to be cosmetic and allow "owner" and "guardian" to be used interchangeably. The same rights and obligations generally are attached to each term. None of the revised laws have been in force long enough to know for certain whether the change is cosmetic or actually substantive. There is no doubt, however, that such mixed usage fails to recognize that owner and guardian have legally distinct and very different meanings.

The owner of property, according to *Black's Law Dictionary* and an enormous body of legal precedent, has the right to "enjoy" the property and to "do with it as he pleases, even to spoil or destroy it, as far as the law permits." It is this bundle of rights, and the potential for harm, that make necessary laws that recognize the unique status of animals and that protect them from cruelty, abuse, and neglect.

A guardian, on the other hand, is a horse of an entirely different color. Strictly speaking, again according to *Black's Law Dictionary* and the courts, a guardian is a person who has both the legal right and legal responsibility to take care of another person who is incapable of taking care of himself or herself. Adults who are incompetent for some reason and children are examples of individuals who require guardians. The subject of a guardian's care is the guardian's "ward."

So far, so good. It does not sound unreasonable to compare an animal that depends on an owner for its care and well-being with a child who depends on a parent for the same things.

A guardian also may have a fiduciary duty to the ward, however. This simply means that a guardian has a legal responsibility to act in the ward's best interest, even at the expense of the guardian's interests. Guardians and owners, in other words, are fundamentally different, mutually exclusive entities. Owners own property, guardians protect the rights of incompetent individuals, and a law that uses the terms interchangeably is a legal contradiction.

The potential ramifications of this clear legal distinction between "owner" and "guardian" are enormous. Assume, for a moment, that "guardian" is not merely another name for "owner" and that a person actually can become the guardian of an animal in the strict legal sense. Implicit in this assumption must be the fact that the object of the guardian's care and responsibility, an animal, now becomes the guardian's ward, with associated legal rights that must be protected.

Any meaningful change in status from an animal owner to an animal guardian must, at some point, also encompass a change in the status of the animal from property to ward. Under the current state of the law, which recognizes only property and persons, the animal thus would assume the same legal rights as a child or incompetent adult.

If an animal is property, the animal can be bought and sold, a simple legal transaction that results in a change of owner. If, on the other hand, the animal has the legal status of a ward with specific rights that must be protected, it is difficult to imagine a situation in which the animal legally could be sold (or even given away) by its guardian. Animal adoptions would become far more complicated and expensive, as human adoptions already are.

Under current law it is possible, in some situations, to justify the euthanasia of an animal for strictly economic reasons, such as an illness requiring lengthy and expensive veterinary care that an owner either cannot afford or will not pay. Euthanasia in this circumstance almost certainly would no longer be an option if the caretaker is a guardian and the animal enjoys the legal status of a ward.

After Barbaro suffered a catastrophic breakdown in the 2006 Preakness Stakes the colt's owners had the resolve and the resources to send him to the New Bolton Center in Pennsylvania for extensive and expensive veterinary care. The heroic efforts to save Barbaro's life should be applauded. Typically, though, a horse with Barbaro's injuries would have been euthanized, an option that would not be available if horses had legal rights similar to those of a child.

It also is easy to imagine an argument that it is not in the best interest of a Thoroughbred to be raced as a two-year-old, or at all, or that dogs should not be exhibited at shows or used in field trial competitions, or that zoos violate the legal rights of their inhabitants. Commercial animal breeding in any form certainly would violate the legal rights of an animal ward, as would human consumption of animals for food and the unrestricted use of animals in medical research.

CRIMINAL STATUTES

Status as property does not mean an animal is nothing more than the legal equivalent of a refrigerator or an automobile or a computer, however. Although generally defining animals as personal property, the law also recognizes that animals represent a particular class of property and imposes attendant obligations on an animal's owner. In recognition that animals are living creatures generally dependent on their owners for care, a legal niche is carved out to provide them with additional legal protection.

Animal protection laws generally are enacted and enforced at the state level, resulting in substantial variations in penalties from jurisdiction to jurisdiction. One notable exception is the Horse Protection Act (HPA), which was passed by Congress in 1970 and amended in 1976. The HPA was enacted in response to public outcry against "soring," a practice in which chemical or mechanical irritants are applied to a horse's forelegs to create or accentuate a high-stepping gait. The HPA is applicable to all breeds, but trainers of Tennessee Walking Horses are the most frequent offenders. The HPA provides for criminal and civil penalties for soring. The former includes up to two years of prison time and a maximum fine of $5,000 for a conviction at trial; the latter includes disqualification from classes in which an affected animal competed, suspension from competitions for trainers and owners, and fines imposed through administrative hearings.

The legislation has teeth. The final night of the 2006 Tennessee Walking Horse Celebration in Shelbyville, Tennessee, was cancelled after federal inspectors disqualified a majority of the horses entered in the World Championship class prior to showing.

While the HPA is aimed at one particular abusive practice and one particular species, state animal abuse statutes are more comprehensive. State laws generally require an animal owner to provide adequate food and water, basic shelter, and some veterinary care, although the specific requirements vary. Neglect, cruelty, and abuse of an animal are criminal offenses everywhere, although the penalties also vary.

Although most state laws allow at least some kinds of serious animal neglect or abuse to be prosecuted as a felony rather than as a misdemeanor, this is not the situation everywhere. The Animal Legal Defense Fund (ALDF) surveyed animal abuse statutes in all fifty states and reported in 2006 that eight states have no felony animal cruelty laws on the books. Those states are Alaska, Arkansas, Hawaii, Idaho, Mississippi, North Dakota, South Dakota, and Utah.

The ALDF identified California, Illinois, Maine, Michigan, and Oregon as states having the strictest animal cruelty laws. In those states, according to the ALDF, cases of animal cruelty can be prosecuted as felonies, animals may be confiscated from their owners prior to trial, veterinarians have a legal obligation to report suspected cases of animal abuse, and courts can order persons convicted of abuse to undergo counseling. An attorney familiar with the criminal laws of your jurisdiction should be consulted for up-to-date state-specific information.

Not surprisingly, the laws of most states fall somewhere in the middle. In Kentucky, for example, the owner of an animal is guilty of cruelty in the first degree if he or she uses the animal for fighting, a Class D felony

CASE STUDIES

Burgess v. Taylor, 44 SW3d 806 (Ky App 2001)

Kentuckian Judy Taylor owned two registered Appaloosa horses nicknamed Poco (whom she acquired as a foal) and P.J. (whom she bred). There was undisputed testimony at trial that Taylor considered the horses as members of her family. Following a divorce and serious illness, Taylor reluctantly decided that she no longer could care for Poco and P.J. by herself. She entered into a "free-lease agreement" with Jeff and Lisa Burgess, under which the Burgesses agreed to provide pasture and care for the horses in return for the use of the animals. Such agreements are common, and no money changed hands.

The Burgesses further agreed that Taylor could visit Poco and P.J. whenever she wished, and that if conditions changed and they could no longer care for the horses, they would be returned to their owner. Taylor never transferred ownership to the Burgesses, and she never gave any indication that she did not want the horses returned at some unspecified time in the future.

Poco and P.J. arrived at the Burgess farm on August 31, 1994, and shortly thereafter Lisa contacted a horse dealer well known for buying animals for slaughter. He purchased Poco and P.J. for $1,000, then resold them to Ryan Horse Company, a business that provided horses to slaughterhouses. Poco and P.J. subsequently were shipped to Texas and slaughtered in late September, less than a month after Taylor had turned the horses over to the Burgesses.

The court determined that Lisa Burgess repeatedly lied about the sale of Poco and P.J. to Taylor and also encouraged an acquaintance to lie about the whereabouts of the animals. Taylor eventually discovered the grisly fate of her beloved horses with help from members of a humane association.

A year later Taylor filed a lawsuit against the Burgesses for the loss of her horses. Other defendants, including the individual who had lied to Taylor at the urging of Lisa Burgess, the person who bought the horses from the Burgesses, and the Ryan Horse Company were dismissed from the lawsuit for procedural reasons.

Following a one-day trial, a jury found that the Burgesses had breached their agreement with Taylor and had intentionally inflicted emotional distress on Poco's and P.J.'s owner. Taylor was awarded $1,000, representing the fair market value of Poco and P.J. The jury could have stopped there and should have done so under a strict application of the animal-as-property theory. It was undisputed that Taylor could have replaced Poco and P.J. for that sum.

Instead, the jury also awarded Taylor $50,000 in compensatory damages and an additional $75,000 in punitive damages. The compensatory award was due to the Burgesses' "outrageous conduct," and the punitive award was intended to deter similar conduct in the future. The verdict and award were affirmed by

(Continued on next page)

the Kentucky Court of Appeals in 2001.

The appellate court did not acknowledge that the large jury award was proper simply because Poco and P.J. were animals and thus were entitled to some special protection under the law. In fact, the Court of Appeals specifically determined that one of the elements that must be proven for a claim of intentional infliction of emotional distress is the "offender's conduct" (the breach of the agreement and subsequent sale of Poco and P.J.) rather than the "subject of said conduct" (the animals themselves). This might suggest that the fact that Poco and P.J. were animals was irrelevant to the award of damages.

A year later the Kentucky Court of Appeals appeared to affirm that analysis. In *Ammon v. Welty*, 113 SW3d 185 (Ky App 2002) the court took up the question of damages resulting from the destruction of a family pet dog by a county dog warden. The court denied the claim, noting that it was undisputed that Hair Bear, "an unregistered mixed breed with no particular training or skill other than as a companion, had no market value ... The affection an owner has for, and receives from, a beloved dog is undeniable. It remains, however, that a dog is property, not a family member ... The loss of love and affection from the loss or destruction of personal property is not compensable." *Id.*, at 187-88.

Nevertheless, in *Burgess v. Taylor* the Court of Appeals clearly recognized and took into account both the strong emotional bond that existed between Taylor and her animals and the severe emotional distress she suffered when she learned what had happened to Poco and P.J. It is highly unlikely that a similar analysis would be used to resolve the loss of other items of personal property such as an appliance or automobile, regardless of the circumstances. It is reasonable to suggest that the defendants' conduct was outrageous not in spite of, but *because*, Poco and P.J. were animals.

Petco Animal Supplies Inc. v. Schuster, 144 SW3d 554 (Tex App 2004)

In this case the Texas Court of Appeals considered the types of damages that were appropriate when a purebred Schnauzer escaped from a Petco groomer, darted into traffic, and was run over and killed. The court explained that Texas law "classifies dogs as personal property for damage purposes, not as persons, extensions of their owners, or any other legal entity whose loss ordinarily would give rise to personal injury damages." The court then reversed lower court awards of $10,000 as compensation for the owner's mental anguish and emotional distress, $10,000 as compensation for the dog's "intrinsic value" and the "loss of companionship," $10,000 in exemplary damages, $160 in counseling costs for the owner, and $857.68 as compensation for lost wages while the owner searched for the dog.

The Court of Appeals left in place damages for the replacement value of the dog, reimbursement for the dog's obedience school fees, reimbursement for microchip implantation, and attorney fees.

In *Roemer v. Gray*, a trial court judge in Seattle, Washington, took a different tack in a case involving a pet cat that was killed by a neighbor's dog. The court entered a default judgment awarding the cat's owner $30,000 as compensation for the animal's "intrinsic value," $15,000 for "emotional distress" relating to the cat's death, a $90 cremation fee, $80 for the owner's medical bills, and $24.12 in interest.

(A note about legal citations: Throughout this book cases are referenced using standard legal citation format. In the above example, Burgess is the last name of the party initiating the appeal [the Appellant] and Taylor is the last name of the party responding to the appeal [the Appellee]. The next portion of the citation indicates that the full text of the court's opinion can be found in Volume 44 of the Southwestern Reporter, third series, starting on page 806. Appellate decisions are reported in regional volumes covering courts located in several states. The final part of the citation indicates that the opinion was rendered by the Kentucky Court of Appeals in 2001. Law school libraries maintain current collections of reporters, as do the law libraries found in most county seats. Decisions also are available through a variety of subscription or free online services.)

with a maximum punishment of five years in prison. There also is a legal obligation to provide adequate food, water, and shelter for animals, and a prohibition against torture, mutilation, neglect, and other mistreatment.

There are numerous exceptions to the laws in Kentucky — hunting and fishing, food processing, veterinary care, and bona fide medical research — and most cruelty offenses that do not involve animal fights are charged as misdemeanors. A recent change in state law elevates the punishment for second and subsequent convictions of torturing a dog or cat to a felony. The ALDF ranks Kentucky's anti-cruelty laws as among the weakest in the nation.

DAMAGES

Another consequence of animals' legal status as personal property is a general limitation on an owner's potential monetary recovery when an animal is killed or injured. If the death of an animal results from an intentional act or through the negligence of another person, the owner generally must seek compensation in a civil lawsuit for the destruction of property, rather than for wrongful death, which is the usual legal remedy for a person's death.

Winning a wrongful death lawsuit can result in a panoply of damages for the plaintiff, ranging from emotional distress to lost earning potential to loss of consortium to punitive damages in a particularly egregious case. On the other hand, if a lawsuit alleging intentional or negligent destruction of, or injury to, an animal succeeds in court, recovery generally is limited to the fair market value, or the replacement value, of the animal.

In a few states, however, statutes specifically allow recovery for so-called non-economic damages following the death of an animal. A recently enacted Tennessee law, for example, allows the owner of a pet to recover up to $4,000 beyond the economic value of the animal if certain conditions are met. To recover, the owner must establish that the animal's death was the result of another person's actions that were both unlawful and intentional or negligent and that the death occurred while the animal was on the owner's property or under his or her supervision.

Illinois also allows pet owners to recover for non-economic damages, including emotional distress, for the death of an animal in certain limited circumstances. Similar legislation has passed or is pending in a few other jurisdictions. Generally, though, an owner's ability to recover something in a civil lawsuit beyond economic damages remains the exception rather than the rule.

Even without specific laws, however, juries occasionally go beyond an animal's actual replacement value to compensate an owner.

RESOURCES

Animal Law, Cases and Materials (3rd ed., Waisman, Frasch, and Wagman, Durham, N.C.: Carolina Academic Press, 2006) contains a wealth of information about various animal law topics. That the book is in its third edition is indicative of the rapid growth in animal law courses at the nation's law schools.

Organizations with information about animal law include the Animal Legal Defense Fund (www.aldf.org) and the Humane Association of the United States (www.hsus.org).

2

DISPUTES

High profile criminal and civil cases command endless newspaper headlines and top billing on national and local news broadcasts. The number of television courtroom reality programs, such as *The People's Court* and *Judge Judy*, seems to increase every year, and it is difficult to watch television for more than a few minutes without seeing an ad or two for personal injury lawyers. An infamous billboard for a Florida personal injury law firm reportedly proclaimed: "If you've been injured, someone, somewhere, owes you money."

The only sensible conclusion is that every dispute, no matter how important or how trivial, eventually winds up in court. However, most disputes are resolved without the direct involvement of a judge or jury, either through non-judicial administrative proceedings, some type of alternative dispute resolution, or informal negotiations between the parties.

This chapter outlines the state and federal court systems, addresses public and private administrative proceedings, and introduces alternative dispute resolution.

THE COURTS

Each state has its own system of courts to resolve civil disputes and criminal charges. Kentucky's state court system is typical. Each of Kentucky's 120 counties has three levels of trial courts: a small-claims court (for civil matters when the amount of money or damages in dispute is $1,500 or less); a district court (for civil matters when the amount in dispute is $4,500 or less, for the trial of criminal misdemeanors, and for preliminary hearings in more serious felonies); and a circuit court (with general jurisdiction over civil cases and for the trial of felonies). Some counties also have specialized family and drug courts. A trial by jury is not available in small-claims court, where a judge is the decision maker, but is a legal right in district and circuit courts.

Kentucky, like other jurisdictions, also provides for appellate review of trial court decisions. Decisions from small-claims court are reviewed by the district court, district court decisions are reviewed by the circuit court, and circuit court decisions are reviewed by one of two appellate courts, either the Kentucky Court of Appeals or the Supreme Court of Kentucky. Any party dissatisfied with the results of a civil or criminal trial has the right to appeal the decision only once to a higher court that will review the trial proceedings. Any subsequent appeals are at the discretion of the next higher court.

Appeals generally address only procedural errors in the trial — whether evidence was properly admitted, for example — and *not* whether the trial decision itself was correct or incorrect. A court decision is not final until all avenues of direct appeal have been exhausted.

In any trial, civil or criminal, the party making the claim has the burden of proving all the facts necessary to his or her case. In civil cases the plaintiff is the individual or entity who initiated the complaint. In criminal cases the plaintiff is the state and not the victim of the offense.

A civil plaintiff can win by proving that the allegations are more likely than not true. This standard of proof, called "preponderance of the evidence," merely means that more evidence supports the plaintiff's case than the defendant's. The margin can be narrow; 51 percent to 49 percent is good enough.

The standard of proof in a criminal case is much higher, rising from "more likely than not" to "virtual certainty." A criminal defendant is presumed innocent and can only be convicted of an offense if there is evidence of guilt "beyond a reasonable doubt." This standard is substantially higher than the "preponderance" standard in civil trials.

It is this difference between civil and criminal burdens of proof that allowed O.J. Simpson to be exonerated in his criminal trial for the murders of his wife, Nicole Brown Simpson, and her friend, Ron Goldman, but later be found guilty in a civil wrongful death trial for the same killings. The first jury found the evidence of guilt did not rise to the level of "beyond a reasonable doubt," while the second jury later determined that similar evidence did satisfy the less-demanding "preponderance of the evidence" standard.

Operating in parallel with each jurisdiction's state court system are federal courts. Each state has one or more federal district trial courts (there are ninety-four judicial districts in all) that can hear some, but not all, civil and criminal disputes. The judicial districts are organized into twelve circuits for appellate purposes, with a federal circuit court hearing appeals from each of the district courts in the circuit.

Some disputes can be raised in either state or federal court; others cannot. State courts, for example, generally have exclusive jurisdiction over family law matters such as divorce, child custody, and adoption; probate matters; real estate questions; and juvenile criminal cases. Federal courts, on the other hand, have exclusive jurisdiction over matters such as bankruptcy and copyright or trademark claims.

AT A GLANCE

- Most disputes are resolved without going to court.
- A typical state court system includes three types of trial courts: a small-claims court, a district court, and a circuit court.
- Alternative dispute resolution (ADR) includes mediation and arbitration.
- Advantages to ADR include speedier resolution than a lawsuit, greater privacy, and fewer costs.

Civil claims, the primary focus of this book, are initiated when one party files a complaint with the clerk of the appropriate court setting out the allegations of wrongdoing. Depending on the jurisdiction, the complaint also may have to include supporting facts. The parties generally represent themselves in most small-claims courts, but more serious complaints should be drafted by counsel familiar with the laws in your particular jurisdiction. After a complaint is filed with the appropriate court, it is delivered to the defendant in a process known as "service." Personal delivery of the complaint and summons (demanding a response to the complaint) always is adequate while service by mail or some other method may or may not be allowed, depending on state law.

A person on the receiving end of a summons and complaint will have a set period, usually about 21 days, to respond. Ignoring the complaint will not make it go away, and a failure to respond within the provided time may result in a default judgment in favor of the plaintiff. This means a court will decide the plaintiff wins simply because there was no response, with no regard to the actual merits, or lack thereof, of the claims set out in the complaint.

Equine law disputes can be, and have been, brought in both state and federal courts. Anyone considering a lawsuit should confer with a local attorney to determine where the complaint should be filed. There are advantages and disadvantages to filing in either federal or state court, and starting in the wrong court can lead to unnecessary delay or in some instances to outright dismissal of the complaint if the court lacks jurisdiction to hear the matter.

Cases move ponderously through the court system, with the time between filing a complaint and final resolution after appeals usually measured in years rather than in months. Even when court cases are settled prior to trial, which happens more often than not, the legal process can be very expensive and time-consuming. The inherent shortcomings of the process have led to growing acceptance of various kinds of alternative dispute resolution (ADR) — non-judicial methods of resolving disputes. ADR can be cheaper, faster, and far more user-friendly than a traditional lawsuit.

ALTERNATIVE DISPUTE RESOLUTION

Although no reliable statistics are available, it is likely that the vast majority of disputes between individuals are resolved informally, without taking the matter to court and without the aid or intervention of a third party. This informal resolution is the simplest kind of alternate dispute resolution. Some risks are involved, however, including the possibility that statements made by one party to facilitate the negotiations might later be considered admissions of fault or responsibility in the event of litigation. In some states, even an apology might be considered an admission of fault.

Facilitated ADR generally takes the form of either arbitration or mediation. The two are similar but with some important differences.

Arbitration, the more formal of the two, closely resembles a conventional trial. An impartial third party, the arbitrator, serves as the "judge" to whom both parties present their arguments. There may be other witnesses, including experts, and a substantial amount of documentary evidence. At the close of the proceeding, the arbitrator makes a decision that generally is binding on the parties.

Arbitration is considered a voluntary process, but many common situations mandate arbitration. Good examples are the compulsory arbitration provisions found in the conditions of sale of many public auction companies. At the Keeneland horse sales in Lexington, Kentucky, for example, a buyer and seller involved in a dispute regarding a horse's physical condition, such as wind (air capacity), are *required* by the conditions of sale to submit the matter to an arbitration panel comprising three veterinarians. By participating in the auction, the buyer and seller have agreed to be bound by the conditions of sale, and going to court if a party is dissatisfied with the outcome is not an option.

An argument that a party should not be bound by the conditions of sale because he or she didn't read them almost always will fail. Courts presume a signed contract was read by the parties involved. The seller became bound by the conditions when he or she contracted with the sales company to sell the horse; the buyer became bound by the conditions by signing the acknowledgment of purchase.

The process works like this: If a buyer discovers a potential problem within a set period (typically quite short) after the fall of the auctioneer's hammer, the buyer notifies the sales company. The auction company provides to the parties a list of veterinarians, giving the parties some limited veto power over who sits on the arbitration panel. The veterinarians examine the horse and make a determination about the alleged problem. The panel decision is binding on everyone.

You can include a mandatory arbitration clause in your own contracts, with language similar to the following:

> While we make every effort to provide services that meet the prevailing standard of care for the industry, it is possible that disputes may arise. If the parties are unable to resolve the dispute in a reasonable amount of time, the parties agree to submit the dispute to mediation. If the parties cannot agree on an impartial mediator, or if the mediation is unsuccessful, the parties agree to

binding arbitration conducted pursuant to the rules of the American Arbitration Association. The arbitration shall be conducted by an impartial third party, either an AAA-certified arbitrator or a non-certified arbitrator, agreeable to both parties. The parties agree to abide by the arbitrator's decision and specifically waive their right to seek judicial resolution of the dispute. The winning party may recover reasonable attorney fees and costs.

This generic clause may not be appropriate for any particular contract situation. The advice of an attorney is needed to decide whether an arbitration clause should be included in business contracts, and if so, how that provision should be drafted.

Mediation, unlike arbitration, is less formal and is more truly voluntary. Although a court may occasionally order mediation, the disputing parties generally must agree to submit the dispute to a mediator. A mediator, unlike an arbitrator, does not make a decision. Instead, the mediator listens to both sides and then tries to facilitate the parties' own efforts to come to a resolution. Mediation thus occupies a middle ground between informal negotiations and binding arbitration.

The advantages of ADR are numerous:

ADR generally resolves a dispute faster than a lawsuit. This can be particularly important when the subject of the dispute is a living creature with a limited number of productive years. ADR also can be more convenient than a legal proceeding because the parties and the arbitrator or mediator can set their own schedules without reference to a judge's always-crowded docket.

ADR should be cheaper than a lawsuit, at least in theory, because lawyers often are not involved and because there generally is not extensive discovery or testimony by costly experts. There are fees associated with ADR, however, and expected savings may not materialize.

ADR generally provides more privacy for the parties, for a couple of reasons. First, ADR usually doesn't include "discovery." After a lawsuit is filed, the parties have a legal right to discovery, a process through which the parties can obtain information from each other on a wide range of topics. Discovery includes written questions, sworn depositions, examinations by doctors or other professional experts, and in many instances the process can be very intrusive.

Second, with few exceptions, court records, documents, and the trial itself are matters of public record, open to anyone with curiosity about the case. This public access to records and information could cause problems. The owner of a breeding stallion, for example, reasonably might prefer to keep a dispute about the fertility of the horse out of the public eye as much as possible. This would be much easier to accomplish with ADR, where the parties can agree to keep the proceedings and the terms of any resolution private.

A further advantage of ADR is the possibility of having an arbitrator or mediator with expertise in the horse business. A qualified arbitrator or mediator should be able to function effectively in an area in which he or she has no expertise, but persons in the horse business are likely to be more comfortable dealing with someone who has some familiarity with the industry.

One of the often-cited virtues of the American jury system is trial by a jury of one's peers, which means a decision by a representative cross-section of the community. It doesn't mean a jury comprising horse people, and your jury might or might not understand the issues at the heart of the dispute. While there is no guarantee that an arbitrator or mediator will have knowledge of the horse business, the parties at least have input into the selection process.

Some disadvantages are associated with ADR, which is not suited for resolution of all disputes and may not be the best choice for the parties.

Limited or no discovery generally is a point in ADR's favor, for example, but there may be some disputes in which extensive disclosure is necessary for a full and fair resolution. For example, a dispute arising from the alleged negligent handling of a boarder's horse by a farm employee may depend on information that shows a pattern of similar occurrences at the facility. The discovery necessary to obtain such information probably is unavailable without filing a lawsuit. Testimony of witnesses or production of documents can be compelled by a court but sometimes will be unavailable during mediation or arbitration.

It also is possible that the insurance carriers for the parties might have an interest in the outcome of the dispute and would object to ADR. If the dispute involves liability, personal injury, property damage, or anything else that might involve an insurance claim, ADR should be discussed with the insurance carrier(s) *before* the parties suggest or agree to the process.

ADR provides a quick, easy, and inexpensive way to resolve many, but certainly not all, disputes. Advice from an attorney about whether to file a lawsuit or pursue ADR would be money well spent.

AGENCIES AND ORGANIZATIONS

Less visible than judicial resolution of disputes are administrative hearings arising from alleged violations of rules promulgated by public agencies and private organizations.

On the public side, for example, state racing commissions govern horse racing; state departments of transportation license farm trucks and trailers; local zoning boards dictate whether a person can keep horses on the owner's property; the Occupational Safety and Health Administration establishes safety standards for employees on farms and in other workplaces; the Food and Drug Administration approves medications and treatments for animals; state licensing boards determine who can provide veterinary care; and the Environmental Protection Agency may have something to say about manure disposal practices.

On the private side, the governing body for each discipline drafts rules for competitions, and breed registries maintain extensive breeding and ownership records. The list goes on.

Although administrative bodies are pervasive, they also tend to be invisible, unless you run afoul of their rules — or at least appear to do so. When this happens, a person's livelihood and reputation may be put at risk, and the proper response is essential. It always is important to be familiar with the rules that control an activity; it is essential to know the rules and all the options when a violation is alleged. Consider the following scenarios:

1) A Thoroughbred trainer receives notice that one of his horses tested positive for a prohibited substance after winning an important race.

2) An owner receives notification from the United States Equestrian Federation that she has been charged with a serious violation of association rules at a recent hunter show where she was an exhibitor.

3) A breed registry informs a mare owner that a foal cannot be registered because there are questions about its parentage or because one or more of

the foal's owners has been suspended by the association.

In each example an administrative body (a state racing commission in the first, private groups in the second and third) is alleging a violation of its rules. Depending on the circumstances, the penalties for such violations can be severe: disqualification of a winning horse, loss of a purse or prize money, return of a trophy, suspension or revocation of a license and the resulting loss of income, non-registration of a horse and a subsequent precipitous drop in value.

What is the proper response to such charges? Each administrative body has its own rules and procedures, and it is impossible to offer specific advice about a particular organization or rules violation here. There are a few considerations common to most situations, however.

For example, fundamental due process of law requires that anyone charged with a violation receive both notice of the alleged violation and an opportunity to be heard before any action is taken. The required notice should inform the party of the specific infraction being charged, and if the individual is not already familiar with the rules, this would be a very good time to review them. It is impossible to defend against an alleged violation if the person charged lacks a full understanding of the rules relating to the supposed infraction.

Also, keep in mind that an express agreement to be bound by the rules of a public or private regulatory body generally is not required. Either membership in an organization or participation in a regulated activity nearly always will be sufficient to make a person subject to the applicable rules.

For example, the general rules of the United States Equestrian Federation (successor to the American Horse Shows Association as the governing body for equestrian sports in the United States) provide that "every recognized competition and every person participating at the competition including exhibitor, owner, lessee, manager, agent, rider, driver, handler, judge, steward or technical delegate, competition official or employee is subject to the Constitution and Rules" of the organization. It is a person's participation in a recognized horse show, rather than membership in the federation, that brings that person under the umbrella of the organization's rules and regulatory authority.

Entry blanks for recognized horse shows also include an express agreement to be bound by the federation's rules. Even if an entry blank is not signed, participation in the horse show constitutes an implied consent to be held accountable for any and all violations of the rules. In like manner, owners and trainers agree either expressly or implicitly to be bound by the rules of a state racing commission by choosing to compete in a recognized race meeting. Application to register a horse carries a similar implied consent to be bound by the registry's rules and regulations.

The required notice also should indicate how and when to respond to the allegations. This requirement is similar to the time limit for responding to a lawsuit discussed earlier in this chapter. A response to the allegations must be submitted in the manner required, within the specified time limit. This is true even if the person charged with a violation has absolutely no doubt he or she is innocent of the alleged violation. Failure to respond in a timely manner might result in a decision by default against the person charged. While there may be a procedural way to address such a default, it is an unnecessary hurdle that easily can be avoided by responding to the allegations in a timely manner.

An important decision at this point is whether to retain an attorney to assist with the response and to represent you through the rest of the proceedings. Most organizations allow, but hardly ever require, that a party be represented by counsel, either when making or defending against an allegation of misconduct. (In the United States Equestrian Federation scheme, an allegation made by one member against another member, or against the organization, is called a "protest" while an allegation made by a representative of the organization itself against a member or non-member is referred to as a "charge.")

One general rule is to decide whether to retain an attorney based on what ultimately is at stake in the disciplinary proceeding. If the worst penalty that can be imposed if the agency prevails is a small fine, it might be difficult to justify the expense of an attorney, whose legal fees would be greater than the fine. If, on the other hand, the punishment is a possible suspension from competition or a hefty fine, it would be foolish to proceed without counsel. An attorney familiar with equine law and administrative procedures can provide guidance through the process and also provide impartial advice about the best course of action.

Following the initial response, the organization might ask for additional information. If so, it should be provided in a timely manner. The person charged also should start assembling evidence to support a defense. If there were witnesses, affidavits (statements given under oath) should be obtained. It seems that everyone has a video camera or cell phone camera these days, and a videotape or photographs of the incident also may be available. Reports from show stewards and other show officials should be obtained and reviewed.

If the alleged violation involves a positive test for a prohibited substance, the person charged should request the testing laboratory report and consider asking for a second test. Most public and private administrative bodies that test for prohibited substances provide in their rules for a "split sample," a procedure in which blood and/or urine samples are divided into at least two identical parts. The first sample is submitted for testing after the competition. If the result of that test is negative, the second sample generally is destroyed.

If, on the other hand, the first test result is positive, a rules violation can be charged. At this point the person charged should have the option of requesting that the second sample be tested, to confirm or refute the first positive result. Rules vary from one organization to another regarding the method for selection of a second laboratory and other procedures for this testing, but the second test usually must be requested within a specified and generally fairly short period of time. The right to request a second test might be lost due to a failure to make a timely request.

Depending on the applicable rules, there may be a hearing before a decision is made regarding the allegations. Most administrative bodies, including the United States Equestrian Federation, The Jockey Club, and most state racing commissions, will conduct a hearing at the request of a party alleged to be in violation of the rules. An administrative fee may be required. Many organizations also can order a hearing on their own initiative if one is not requested. If no hearing is held, a decision will be rendered based on the evidence submitted by the parties.

An administrative hearing is similar to a trial but with several important differences. A hearing officer, or hearing committee, rather than a judge will be in charge of the proceeding and may have the assistance of the administrative organization's legal counsel. There will not be a jury. The parties will have the right to call and cross-examine witnesses and to present evidence, and the hearing officer or committee also can ask questions. The usual rules of procedure and evidence will be relaxed, and, in general, the

CASE STUDIES

Kentucky State Racing Commission v. Fuller, 481 SW2d 298 (Ky 1972)

The most infamous disqualification in the history of Thoroughbred racing occurred in the 1968 Kentucky Derby, when first-place finisher Dancer's Image was disqualified after a urine sample tested positive for the analgesic phenylbutazone or a derivative. Calumet Farm's Forward Pass was declared the winner, and the legal wrangling began in earnest.

Stewards at Churchill Downs held an administrative hearing a few days after the race, disqualifying Dancer's Image. Owner Peter Fuller appealed to the Kentucky State Racing Commission (now the Kentucky Horse Racing Authority), which affirmed the decision of the stewards.

Kentucky's rules of racing provide for judicial review of a final agency decision, in this case the disqualification of Dancer's Image by the racing commission, and Fuller appealed the order to the Franklin County Circuit Court. Late in 1970, some twenty months after the contested Derby, the court tossed out the commission order and ruled that Dancer's Image was the winner after all. The racing commission, not surprisingly, appealed the circuit court decision to a higher court.

After some preliminary discussion of procedural questions, the court reached the principal issue before it. This was *not* whether the initial urine tests for phenylbutazone were accurate or whether Dancer's Image should have been disqualified. Instead, the appellate court considered only whether there was sufficient evidence in the record to support the racing commission decision disqualifying Dancer's Image.

Generally, when a court reviews the decision of a government agency, the court is bound by the agency decision if there was "substantial evidence" to support it. In the Dancer's Image case the appellate court found "an abundance of substantial evidence supporting the findings and rulings of the Kentucky State Racing Commission." Four years and two months after the 1968 Kentucky Derby, Forward Pass became the official winner.

Allen v. Kentucky Horse Racing Authority, 136 SW3d 54 (Ky App 2004); Casse v. New York State Racing and Wagering Authority, 517 NE2d 1309 (NY 1987); Fogt v. Ohio State Racing Commission, 210 NE2d 730 (Ohio Ct App 1965); Sandstrom v. California Horse Racing Board, 189 P2d 17 (Cal 1948)

Depending on your generation, your understanding of the legal process probably comes from television programs such as *Perry Mason*, *L.A. Law*, or

Law and Order. A common thread running through all three is "innocent unless proved guilty," a fundamental right accorded all criminal defendants by the U.S. Constitution. "Absolute insurer rules" or "trainer responsibility rules," common in horse racing and other equine sports, turn the old adage on its head. These rules presume that trainers are responsible when their horses test positive for illegal substances, in effect making the trainers guilty unless proved innocent.

The effect of this presumption is to shift the burden of proof from the governing body to the trainer, who must prove innocence by showing that he or she did not administer the prohibited substance to the horse or did not negligently allow someone else to tamper with the animal. The result can be imposition of a penalty without actual proof of guilt.

Courts have uniformly upheld absolute insurer rules, despite what might appear on the surface to be a clear violation of due process of law. The *Casse* Court, at page 1312, summarized the situation:

> Moreover, the trainer responsibility rule is a practical and effective means of promoting these State interests-both in deterring violations and in exercising sanctions. The imposition of strict responsibility compels trainers to exercise a high degree of vigilance in guarding their horses and to report any illicit use of drugs, medications or other restricted substances by other individuals having access to their horses. Additionally, the rebuttable presumption of responsibility facilitates the very difficult enforcement of the restrictions on the use of drugs and other substances in horse racing. Indeed, it would be virtually impossible to regulate the administering of drugs to race horses if the trainers, the individuals primarily responsible for the care and condition of their horses, could not be held accountable for the illicit drugging of their horses or for the failure either to safeguard their horses against such drugging or to identify the person actually at fault. It is not surprising, therefore, that trainer responsibility rules have been upheld almost without exception, in other jurisdictions.

American Horse Shows Association v. Ward, 718 NYS2d 593 (Supreme Court of New York, 2000)

Courts also have upheld the right of private organizations to establish and enforce their own rules. Following a 1996 guilty plea to one count of conspiracy to commit wire fraud relating to a bizarre scheme in which horses were killed to obtain insurance proceeds, noted show-jump rider Barney Ward was expelled by the American Horse Shows Association (now the United States Equestrian Federation). He also was permanently barred from attending any recognized competition as a participant or spectator.

Ward took the AHSA to court, arguing that even if he could not compete himself he wanted to watch his son participate in horse shows. He argued among other things that he already had resigned from the AHSA and that the organization had no authority to discipline a non-member. The Supreme Court of New York found that argument meritless, ruling that Ward's membership in the AHSA at the time of his criminal conduct, plus his promise to be bound by the organization's rules, authorized the AHSA to discipline him, regardless of his current membership status. The court also implied that the organization could discipline anyone who violated AHSA rules, even if the person never had been a member.

hearing will be much more informal than a trial. Following a decision by the hearing officer or committee, the rules may allow for a judicial review, a challenge of the finding in court. Most agency and organization rules do.

A case involving prominent Thoroughbred trainer Bob Baffert illustrates the workings of a disciplinary proceeding. On May 3, 2000, a horse trained by Baffert, Nautical Look, won the seventh race at Hollywood Park. Blood and urine samples were obtained from the horse, with one-half of each sample (the "official sample") sent for initial testing. The official sample of urine and the second portion (the "split sample") of the urine sample both were positive for trace amounts of morphine, a prohibited substance. The official blood sample subsequently was destroyed due to an internal agency policy, and the split blood sample was destroyed when no request for retesting was made within a specified time limit.

Following a stewards' hearing during which an extensive amount of evidence was presented, Baffert's training license was suspended for sixty days. Baffert appealed the suspension to the state racing commission within the required time limit. He also obtained a "stay" of the suspension, the effect of which was to postpone imposition of the penalty until the ultimate resolution of the appeal. This is a common practice.

Before the appeal to the state racing commission was decided, however, the trainer also filed a civil lawsuit in federal court claiming a violation of his civil rights because the blood samples had been destroyed before they could be tested by experts for the defense. A federal district court in California sided with Baffert, but the Ninth Circuit Court of Appeals reversed the lower court and ordered Baffert's complaint dismissed. The Ninth Circuit did not decide the merits of Baffert's complaint, only that the timing of the federal lawsuit was premature because the state racing commission appeal was pending.

After Nautical Look tested positive for a prohibited substance following the May 2000 race, the rules entitled Baffert to a hearing before the stewards made a decision. State procedures then gave Baffert an opportunity to appeal his suspension from the track stewards up the administrative food chain to the California Horse Racing Board.

More importantly, especially for a trainer whose livelihood depends on an ongoing ability to saddle horses for races, Baffert was able to postpone his sixty-day suspension until the final resolution of his appeal. The dispute finally was resolved in 2005, nearly five years after Nautical Look won the race in question, when the California Horse Racing Board dismissed the charges.

Although it might seem that Baffert manipulated the rules simply to avoid punishment, such a conclusion would be unfair. Administrative rules and regulations are in place to protect both the interests of the parties involved and the integrity of the activity being regulated. These are lofty goals, and they can be achieved only when everyone involved in any sort of horse-related activity understands his or her rights and obligations under the rules of the governing body. Exercising your rights under the rules is an essential part of that protection.

RESOURCES

Information about ADR can be obtained from the American Arbitration Association, 335 Madison Avenue, Floor 10, New York, NY 10017-4605, (800) 778-7879; www.adr.org; and the Association for Conflict Resolution, 1015 18th Street NW, Suite 1150, Washington DC 20036, (202) 464-9700, www.acrnet.org.

Other useful Internet sites for rules and regulations include www.usef.org for the United States Equestrian Federation; www.jockeyclub.com for The Jockey Club; and www.aqha.com for the American Quarter Horse Association.

3

OWNERSHIP

Owning horses can be a serious business for some people or a pleasant hobby for others. (The Internal Revenue Service may have something to say about that choice, a topic that is addressed in a later chapter.) There is no legal requirement that a horse operation must be classified as a "business," but if you plan to operate a commercial boarding stable, give riding lessons, breed or race Thoroughbreds, sponsor an Olympic hopeful, or get favorable tax treatment, establishing your horse operation as a business is the first logical step.

There are a variety of ways to own and operate a horse business, from the very simple to the very complicated. The process can be as straightforward as setting up shop on your own as a sole proprietor or as complicated as forming a "C" corporation with officers, directors, investors, and a maze of attendant paperwork. There are advantages and disadvantages to each type of ownership, and your first step should be to consult an attorney and an accountant for advice on the most suitable course of action. There is no one "best" way to own a business, and the approach you choose will depend on the facts and circumstances unique to the situation.

This chapter introduces several common types of business structures and assesses each based on five factors: (1) availability of capital for running the business, (2) operational control of the business, (3) business and personal liability, (4) federal income tax implications, and (5) "red tape." A summary is included in chart form at the close of this chapter. You should keep in mind that this chapter adopts a very broad definition of "business." A single horse, for example, can be the owner's entire business.

THE BASICS

Determining the best way to operate a horse business is not a task to be undertaken lightly. Some of the basic questions that should be asked and answered *before* deciding on an ownership structure include:

1. Is the business property located within one state? If not, it may be necessary to take into account the laws of multiple jurisdictions in planning a business.

2. Who will own the business?

3. In what state(s) do you intend to do business?

4. How many people will make day-to-day management decisions? Who are these people?

5. How much hands-on participation does the owner, or owners, along with others who may invest or join in the business, want to have in operations? Does that vary at all according to the tasks being considered? For example, is one person more interested in or suited for leading trail rides? Providing physical care for the horses? Financial record keeping? Communicating with the public about the business?

6. If the owner has children, are they adults? Will they participate in the business for a short while or do the children want to stay in the business for a long period?

7. Have you identified anyone else with a similar business from whom you might be able to gain advice (preferably not a direct competitor)? Have you actually consulted such a person?

8. Will adding this business to an existing farm operation require an initial investment of capital on your part? How much can you afford to invest initially in this new business? Are investors necessary?

9. What are the long-term goals for the business and for the owners personally? Does everyone involved share the same goals? Have you talked about these things, or have you just assumed everyone has the same goals? Are the goals attainable? Do they also provide some measure of challenge?

10. How risk averse are you and any relevant others, such as your spouse and potential investors? Do you agree on the amount and types of business risk you are willing to accept?

11. Have you given any thought to a business plan?

12. Have you established a business relationship with a veterinarian and a farrier? Will they be available on a regular basis to provide care for horses your horses?

13. Have you opened a separate bank account for the new business?

14. Have you applied for the appropriate federal employer identification number (EIN) for the new business? Do you already have an EIN for an existing farm operation?

15. Have you applied for account numbers with any relevant state and local taxing authorities?

16. Will the added business affect in any way your obligation to participate in federal and/or state unemployment or worker's compensation programs?

17. Have you obtained or developed a satisfactory method or system for keeping track of the time you spend on the business, as well as the revenue and expenses?

18. Do you have any plans to expand the scope of the business in the future? For example, do you anticipate getting into areas such as breeding or racing? If you anticipate getting into breeding, have you considered the market you want to reach? Are you talking about breeding horses for pleasure riding or ranching, or to compete/race?

AT A GLANCE

- The main factors to consider when deciding which business structure to choose:
1) How much capital do you have?
2) Who will have operational control of the business?
3) How much business and personal liability do you want to risk?
4) How will you handle federal income taxes?
5) Do you want to deal with legal and corporate "red tape"?

19. If you have considered getting into the business of racing horses, how will you acquire such horses? Do you understand the mechanics of claiming race purchases in your state? Do you know how auctions work? At this point, have you considered the possibility of joining or forming a partnership for the specific purpose of buying a share of a racehorse?

20. Are you familiar with the concept of syndicates, in which you can participate as co-owners with others by contractual agreement as to capital to be raised; interests in the specific horse to be sold; method of decision-making; responsibility for income, expenses, and tax consequences; and

liability of investors (which is unlimited)?

With answers to these questions as background information, the next step should be preparation of a sound business plan.

THE BUSINESS PLAN

Economists generally agree that failure to have sufficient capital in hand at start up is the most common reason small businesses fail. This risk can never be eliminated. It can be reduced substantially by coming up with a sound business plan, including a realistic assessment of anticipated income and expenses *before* launching a business. A comprehensive business plan should be a necessary requirement for any business. No matter what the business or the ownership entity selected, the more advance planning, the better.

Optimism and a positive attitude are valuable attributes for a business owner — up to a point — but a business plan should be realistic. A business plan is more than wishful thinking about the success of a new venture. The business plan should be a sensible assessment of your goals, along with an objective and detailed outline of how you are going to attain them.

A well-drafted business plan doesn't dictate every decision, nor should it. A business plan should direct a business, not micromanage it. The plan should reflect your goals and general business philosophy, however. Consider a business plan as a road map with the main routes and hazards well-marked but with sufficient flexibility to allow for a few hopefully pleasant side trips.

Your business plan should include, at a minimum, the following:
• How the business will be owned
• How the business will be financed
• Projected income and expenses
• Tax considerations

Some other considerations for a business plan might be:
• Is it in writing?
• Does it adequately identify the business goals and objectives? The purpose of the business?
• Is the business form you've chosen allowed in your state? Have you spoken to any advisers about this yet?

• Does the business plan list types of advisers to be consulted? This could be an important tax-planning issue.

• Does it explain where you will obtain the initial capital needed to begin the investment? Does it state how much capital you need to invest?

• Does it identify how you will find and secure the business of clients? Does it explain how and where and how often you will advertise the availability of your services?

• Does it give you a time-line of some sort, so that you can compare your intended progress to your actual progress?

• Does it estimate projected income and expenditures for the next year? Two years? Three years?

• Does it specify how long the business will last? Common choices are "in perpetuity," meaning that the business will continue indefinitely, or "for a term of years," such as ten or twenty.

Although the type of ownership logically should be the first item listed in a business plan, it should not be the first planning decision made before starting a new business. Instead, questions about financing, projected income and expenses, liability, and taxes should be resolved first. The answers to those questions may point to the best or in some cases the only practical ownership option.

SOLE PROPRIETORSHIP

A sole proprietorship is exactly what the name implies, a business owned and operated by a single individual — the proprietor. It is the simplest way to operate a business and by far the most common.

Capital

"Undercapitalization" is a term for that uncomfortable condition when a business has more bills than money to pay them. A lack of operating capital can be an annoyance in the short term and the downfall of a business if the negative cash flow continues.

In a sole proprietorship, responsibility for gathering the necessary capital falls entirely on the shoulders of the individual business owner. Sole proprietors are quintessential entrepreneurs, and individuals uncomfortable in that role might need to rethink the decision to go it alone.

Putting together sufficient financing can be a significant problem for a sole proprietor, whose access to capital probably will be limited to his or her own funds or to money that can be borrowed from family members or from friends. For the majority of sole proprietors who are not lucky enough to be independently wealthy, the unavailability of capital can be a serious problem, one that can doom a business before it ever starts.

Bank loans and credit cards may be alternative sources of financing, but neither is an attractive option. Banks are notoriously reluctant to risk money on small businesses in general and on horse ventures in particular. Financing a business with credit cards should be avoided except in the direst of emergencies because of the high interest rates usually charged for purchases and for cash advances.

A home equity loan or a line of credit also is a possible source of financing for your business. Most lenders offer attractive interest rates for these loans, at least initially, primarily because the borrower is putting up his or her house as collateral. Defaulting on a home equity loan puts your house at risk of foreclosure, however, and staking your home on the success of a new, untried business is a risky venture.

Control

A sole proprietorship can be an attractive option for an individual who wants to call all the shots for the business. A sole proprietor has no partners to report to, no investors to satisfy. As a sole proprietor, you take full credit for all of your successes, but you also shoulder all the blame for your mistakes.

Liability

Concomitant with complete control over the operation of the business is sole liability for all the debts it incurs. Depending on the nature of the business, those debts can be substantial. Keep in mind that by establishing a sole proprietorship you are putting your personal assets on the line if the business gets into a financial bind and the business assets are not sufficient to cover the debt.

The assets of a business, which are all the property owned by the business, are at risk no matter what ownership structure is selected. Some ownership structures discussed later in this chapter protect an owner's personal assets in many situations; some do not. Because a sole proprietor *is* the business, there is no practical distinction between business and personal assets for a one-owner operation.

The ultimate effect of this is that a creditor who obtains a court judgment against a sole proprietor can attack both the assets of the business (such as horses, tack and other equipment, a horse trailer and truck, and business bank accounts) and the personal assets of the business owner (such as a house, an automobile, personal property, and personal bank accounts) to satisfy a business debt. This realization can come as a very unpleasant surprise to a sole owner who doesn't understand the ramifications of setting out on his or her own.

In the context of owner responsibility, it is important to understand the distinction between liability for a debt and liability for injury to a person or to property. A debt is a legal obligation on the part of an individual or business to pay for something received, either goods or services. An obligation to pay the feed store for a delivery of grain is a common example of a debt incurred by a boarding farm owner.

Liability for injury, on the other hand, is financial responsibility that results from some action that has harmed an individual or his or her property. A business owner can, and certainly should, have adequate insurance coverage to protect against personal injury or property damage claims. Insurance cannot protect a business owner from debt, however.

Taxes

Profits and losses from the business are reported on the sole proprietor's individual federal and state tax returns. Tax is assessed at the owner's individual tax rate. The business is not a taxable entity generally although some localities may require payment of licensing or other fees.

Red Tape

Some jurisdictions may require registration of the business name. Beyond that, there usually are no formal legal requirements for setting up a sole proprietorship. Upon the death of the owner, a sole proprietorship simply ceases to exist. If the owner has a will — and everyone should — the business assets are distributed along with the rest of the estate according to the owner's wishes. If the owner dies intestate (without a will), the business assets are distributed according to the inheritance laws established by the state. Federal or state estate taxes may be due.

PARTNERSHIPS, GENERAL AND LIMITED

Partnerships have played an important role in the horse business throughout the years, both in the ownership of businesses and in the ownership of horses. In many instances, the "business" is the horse or horses.

General Partnerships

A partnership is formed when two or more individuals come together to operate an unincorporated business for a profit. Implied in the formation of a partnership is an ongoing business relationship. If two or more individuals join forces for a single business transaction, such as the purchase of a particular horse, the business entity formed more properly is called a joint venture rather than a partnership. Both partnerships and joint ventures are treated the same by the IRS, and for the sake of simplicity "partnership" will be used to describe both entities throughout this book.

Capital

Adding general partners increases the potential operating capital of the business, either directly through contributions of money or other assets by the partners or indirectly through increased borrowing power or through the contribution of services such as training, boarding, or veterinary care. It is important to match the contributions of services to the nature of the business, however. A licensed trainer might be a valuable addition to a racing partnership, for example, but probably would have little to offer a partnership formed to operate a boarding stable or to buy broodmares.

The availability of additional operating capital does not eliminate the need for a comprehensive business plan, however. Whatever the level of involvement and investment of the partners, a sound business plan provides direction for the operation and gives potential partners valuable insight into what can be expected from the partnership.

Control

While a sole proprietor maintains complete control over the operation of a business, general partners share the management decisions for a partnership unless the partners have agreed to some other arrangement. Unless the partners agree to a different plan, such as an allocation based on the partners' respective contributions, profits and losses are distributed equally.

Liability

General partners share "joint and several liability" for the debts incurred by a partnership. This means that each general partner is individually responsible for the partnership debts. A creditor seeking to collect a debt may choose to sue all of the partners, some of them, or only one for the full amount. As in a sole proprietorship, the general partners are personally liable for partnership debts, with business and personal assets at risk.

> ### AT A GLANCE
>
> - Have a business plan in place *before* launching a new venture.
> - The main business structures to consider when setting up your business are sole proprietorships, partnerships (general and limited), corporations, and limited liability companies.
> - Sole proprietors are responsible for gathering all the necessary capital for their business. They also incur all losses.

Closely related is the concept that each partner acts as an agent of the partnership. Agency is discussed more fully in a later chapter. For our purposes it is sufficient to know that each partner has the ability to make decisions for the partnership and to obligate the other partners. An individual partner can borrow money for the partnership, for example, thereby obligating the entire group to repay the loan. The potential for abuse is obvious, and it should go without saying that you should know your partners before starting a business with them.

Taxes

Partnership profits and losses are distributed to the partners on a regular basis, either equally to each partner or according to an allocation plan agreed to by the partners. The profits or losses are reported on each partner's individual tax return, and if tax is due it is paid at the taxpayer's individual tax rate. Like a sole proprietorship, a general partnership is not a taxable entity. A partnership generally is required to file informational federal and state tax returns annually even though no tax is paid by the business.

Red Tape

A written partnership agreement is advisable to reduce the potential for misunderstandings among the partners, but a written agreement generally is not legally required to establish a general partnership. If a general partnership is based on an oral agreement, the "handshake deal" common in the horse business, legal disputes are resolved by reference to terms set out in the Uniform Partnership Act (UPA) or the Revised Uniform Partnership Act (RUPA). Both are model partnership agreements, and one or the other version has been adopted by law nearly everywhere.

The UPA was drafted in 1914. Despite some amendments and state-by-state modifications upon adoption, the UPA failed to address some important aspects of modern business ownership. A significant revision was done in 1994, and RUPA was born. Three years later another set of revisions reflecting changes in limited partnership law was added. A review of the revisions in partnership law is beyond the scope of this book, and a local attorney should be consulted. To date, according to the National Conference of Commissioners on Uniform State Laws, some thirty states and territories have revised their partnership laws to mirror RUPA.

They include the following: Alabama, Alaska, Arizona, Arkansas, California, Connecticut, Colorado, Delaware, District of Columbia, Florida, Hawaii, Illinois, Idaho, Iowa, Kansas, Kentucky, Maine, Maryland, Minnesota, Mississippi, Montana, Nebraska, Nevada, New Jersey, New Mexico, North Dakota, Oklahoma, Oregon, Puerto Rico, South Dakota, Tennessee, Texas, U.S. Virgin Islands, Vermont, Virginia, West Virginia, Washington, and Wyoming.

RUPA has been generally well received, but the changes can create problems for partnerships, some of which will be governed by old law and others by the revised law. For example, a partnership in existence in a state *before* the partnership laws were revised will continue to be governed by old partnership law *unless* the partners elect to be governed by the new statutes. That may or may not be a sound business decision, and advice from an attorney should be sought before that decision is made.

The danger of proceeding without a written partnership agreement depends on whether the partners intend to operate the business in a manner different from the generic terms of UPA/RUPA. The further afield the partners plan to operate, with unequal profit and loss distribution, for example, the less likely it is that the standard terms of the UPA/RUPA will achieve the partners' intentions.

A written partnership agreement should include, at a minimum, the rules under which the partnership will operate (such as distributions), the contributions of each partner, and the rights and obligations of the partners. If one or more partners are contributing assets other than money or services, a monetary value for the assets should be established.

The partnership agreement also should address what will happen to the business if a partner dies or wants to sell his or her interest. A partnership generally terminates upon the death or disability of a partner, but the agreement can provide options to keep the business going if a partner dies. Purchase of the deceased partner's interest in the business by the other partners is a common solution, and life insurance policies can be acquired to finance the transaction.

Limited Partnerships

A general partnership has only one class of partner. Limited partnerships have two classes of partner — at least one general partner and at least one limited partner. The general and limited partners have different roles and obligations in the operation of the partnership.

Limited partnerships were popularized by Dogwood Stable owner W. Cothran Campbell in the 1970s as a way to involve people in the ownership of Thoroughbreds while limiting the new owners' economic risk. Campbell would buy a well-bred horse, usually a yearling, and then offer limited partnership shares in the horse. He would serve as the general partner, making all management decisions for each partnership while the limited partners essentially went along for the ride, enjoying tax breaks and the excitement of racehorse ownership.

Campbell quickly became a major player at major Thoroughbred auctions, and horses carrying the Dogwood colors won a number of important races.

Limited partnerships lost some popularity during the mid-1980s when sweeping changes in the country's tax laws made such arrangements less attractive as tax shelters, but they remain important today.

AT A GLANCE

- If you buy a horse with a friend, the business entity formed is called a joint venture and it is treated the same as a partnership by the IRS.
- Limited partnerships usually have a general partner who manages the business and limited partners with little to no operational role.
- C corporations are subject to double taxation under the IRS but also can have unlimited investors.

Capital

A limited partnership has the same advantage of numbers as a general partnership when it comes to raising capital. The more partners who are involved, the more potential capital, other assets, or services are available for the business.

Control

Decision making for a limited partnership rests with the general partner, or partners. Limited partners, on the other hand, have no role in management of the business. One of the selling points for limited partnerships is that the arrangement allows newcomers to invest in the horse business without having any particular expertise. Becoming a limited partner obviously is less attractive for an individual with expertise who wants to play a role in how the business is run.

Liability

The general partner, or partners, in a limited partnership have unlimited personal liability for the debts incurred by the business. As in a general partnership, their personal assets are at risk along with the assets of the partnership to satisfy business debts.

Limited partners, as the name suggests, have limited liability for business debts. While the business assets always are at risk for payment of a debt incurred by the partnership, the liability of a limited partner cannot exceed his or her investment in the business. The tradeoff for a limited partner who gives up operational control of the business is protection for the partner's personal assets. If a limited partner does become actively involved in decision making for the business, the status as a limited partner, along with protection for the partner's personal assets, generally is lost.

Taxes

Limited partnerships receive the same tax treatment as general partnerships. Profits and losses are distributed to the partners and reported on their individual tax returns. The partnership files an informational return but pays no taxes itself.

A potential tax complication for limited partners is their inability in some circumstances to use a partnership loss to reduce taxable income from other sources. This subject is covered more fully in a later chapter. For now, keep in mind that participation as a limited partner nearly always will be considered a "passive activity" by the IRS. A passive activity is one in which the taxpayer does not have material participation (does not play an active role), and current law allows a passive loss to be counted against only passive income from other sources. Depending on an individual's financial situation, this restriction may make a limited partnership an unattractive business ownership option.

Red Tape

The Uniform Limited Partnership Act (ULPA) underwent significant revisions in 2001, and to date it has been adopted by only a handful of states. As with general partnerships, limited partnerships formed prior to a state's adoption of ULPA will be governed by prior state law.

Limited partnerships can be an effective way for a general partner to raise capital without surrendering control of the business, but there are complications not found with a traditional general partnership. A limited partnership agreement must be in writing, and the partnership generally must be registered with the secretary of state or similar office in the jurisdiction where the partnership is formed.

An individual, usually a general partner, must be designated as the registered agent for the partnership to accept service of legal documents on behalf of the business. The limited partnership agreement also must be drafted carefully to avoid violating the regulations of the Securities and Exchange Commission, which may classify solicitations to join the partnership as the sale of unregistered securities.

CORPORATIONS, "C" AND "S"

Unlike a sole proprietorship and general and limited partnerships, a corporation is a legal entity standing alone. (This distinction may be blurred somewhat in states that have adopted a version of RUPA.) A corporation is separate from its owners, called shareholders, and the law considers a corporation as a "person" that can sue and be sued. A corporation's status as a separate legal entity generates both advantages and problems for the owners. A "C" corporation is formed and taxed under Subchapter C of the Internal Revenue Code; an "S" corporation is formed and taxed under Subchapter S. ("C"omplicated and "S"impler is one way to remember many of the differences between the two entities.) Both types of corporations are discussed together, with the few differences noted.

Capital

A vastly increased availability of capital is one of the most obvious appeals of a corporate business structure. While a partnership may attract a few individual investors, a corporation has the possibility of drawing in hundreds of investors, with sales of different classes of stock generating a substantial amount of money for the business. This advantage is restricted somewhat if an S corporation is elected because the applicable tax laws restrict the number of investors to seventy-five. An S corporation also can offer only one class of stock for sale to shareholders. C corporations, on the other hand, can offer multiple classes of stock and have unlimited investors.

The ability to generate a truly significant amount of operating capital by establishing a C corporation generally has not been realized in the horse business, however. Horsemen's reluctance to "go public" may be a result of the disastrous attempt to incorporate Spendthrift Farm in the early 1980s, which is discussed more fully in the case studies portion of this chapter.

Control

Control of a corporation is vested in the officers and directors, who make decisions about how a business is run. Other shareholders have no say in the day-to-day operation of the corporation although they may have the ability to influence the business, albeit indirectly, through the election of officers and directors. In the case of a closely held corporation, one that has one or very few owners or shareholders, the directors and officers also may be the only shareholders. They both can control the operation of the business and directly benefit from their decisions.

Liability

Shareholders in both C and S corporations, like limited partners, have limited liability for debts incurred by the business. When shareholders invest in a corporation through the acquisition of stock, they put their investment at risk if the business fails. Investors' personal assets, again like the personal assets of limited partners, generally cannot be forfeited to satisfy debts of the corporation.

Anyone considering a corporation — or as we will see later, a limited liability company — solely on the basis of limitations on liability should realize that the protections afforded by the business structures may be illusory. Lenders and businesses that provide goods or services may require a personal guarantee for loans before extending credit, effectively destroying any limitations on liability inherent in corporate ownership. The requirement for personal guarantees may be more likely for new businesses or for endeavors perceived as especially speculative and risky, such as the horse business.

Taxes

Aside from a limitation on the number of shareholders and classes of stock for an S corporation, the principal difference between C and S corporations is how the IRS treats them.

A C corporation is subject to double taxation. Because the business is a legal entity separate from the shareholders, the corporation has separate tax liability for the profits earned. This corporate-level taxation is the first tier of double taxation and effectively reduces the amount of current or accumulated earnings available for distribution to the shareholders as dividends.

The second tier of double taxation occurs after corporate earnings are distributed to the shareholders as dividends. This distribution typically is made on a pro rata basis according to percentage of stock ownership. For example, an investor who owns 10 percent of the stock in a corporation would receive a dividend of $100 for each $1,000 of earnings distribution. The shareholders must report their dividends as income on their personal tax returns, thereby increasing their tax liability.

Double taxation sounds especially onerous, like giving Uncle Sam two bites at the tax apple, but it is not always a bad thing. Corporations and individuals pay income tax at different rates. Consider a closely held corporation, where one individual owns all the shares, for example. In that situation, paying taxes on corporate profits prior to distribution of the reduced earnings as dividends, where they are taxed a second time, may result in a lower overall tax bill if the corporate tax rate is lower than the owner's individual tax rate.

If this sounds complicated, it is. The facts of each situation are different and judging whether double taxation helps or hurts any particular taxpayer is well beyond the scope of this book. An accountant or tax attorney familiar with the horse business should be consulted before settling on a corporate structure for a horse business.

Unlike C corporations, S corporations are not taxed at the corporate level. Instead, corporate profits are passed through to the shareholders, who must report the dividend earnings as ordinary income on their personal tax returns.

Losses suffered by a C corporation are not passed along to the shareholders as happens in a partnership but may be claimed only by the business. Losses incurred by an S corporation generally can be passed through to the shareholders, but the shareholders' ability to actually use the losses to reduce other income is restricted by the amount of time they have owned stock in the company and other factors.

Red Tape

A corporation, whether organized under Subchapter C or Subchapter S of the Tax Code, is the most complicated way to own a business. Articles of incorporation and bylaws must be drafted and filed with the proper state authorities; formalities such as annual meetings, minutes of those meetings, the issuance of stock certificates, and quarterly reports must be met; and general administrative expenses, including bookkeeping and accounting, almost certainly will be higher for corporations than for any other type of business.

One of the advantages at least indirectly related to the formality of a corporate structure is the ability of the business to continue beyond the death of its owners.

LIMITED LIABILITY COMPANY (LLC)

Limited liability companies, which combine many of the attractive features of both partnerships and corporations, have been in existence for only twenty years or so. They are a creation of state law, and problems initially resulted because only some states recognized the form of ownership. That ceased to be an issue as more and more states accepted LLCs.

Capital

An LLC, like a partnership or corporation, generally provides more access to operating capital and other assets than a sole proprietorship, simply by virtue of numbers of participants. In most states a single individual can establish an LLC, however, and in that situation the increased ability to raise capital is lost.

Control

The owners of an LLC are called "members" rather than partners or shareholders. The LLC can be managed by the members collectively, by only some of the members, or by a non-member manager retained for that purpose. The scheme of operational control is decided by the members and set out in the operating agreement for the business. Unlike a general partnership, however, where management authority goes hand-in-hand with unlimited personal liability, a member can participate in the management of an LLC without suffering unlimited liability for business debts.

Liability

Members of an LLC, like limited partners, have limited liability for debts incurred by the business. The assets of the business are at risk as always, but the members' personal assets cannot be attacked to satisfy business debts. As noted earlier, this protection can be lost if the members of an LLC personally guarantee a debt.

Taxes

An LLC combines the limited liability enjoyed by the shareholders in a corporation with the ability to participate in the management of the business and the flow-through taxation of a general partnership. An LLC generally is not a taxable entity (although some states have tried to change this status), and business profits or losses are passed through to the members who report them on their individual tax returns. There is no double taxation.

Red Tape

Establishing an LLC is more complicated than setting up a sole proprietorship or a partnership but is far less complicated than getting a corporation off and running. Specific requirements vary from state to state, but generally an LLC must be registered with state authorities by filing a relatively simple form and paying a small fee. A simple annual report usually is required, but the members of an LLC do not have the substantial filing and reporting requirements imposed on corporations.

The filing requirements for LLCs and corporations are a limited source of income for states, but they also provide some protection for businesses that deal with the registered entities. State records can be searched, either via the Internet or manually, and information about limited personal liability for the owners of a business can be obtained. The availability of

CASE STUDIES

Marsh v. Gentry, 642 SW2d 574 (Ky 1982)

A sole proprietor has only himself or herself to answer to for business decisions, but that is not the case when people go into business together. An officer or director of a corporation, for example, has a legal requirement to act in good faith, to act in the best interests of the corporation, and to make decisions on an informed basis. The Uniform Partnership Act (UPA) imposes a fiduciary duty on general partners, which means that a partner must place the best interests of the partnership above his or her own personal interests.

During the 1970s Tom Gentry and John Marsh formed a partnership in Kentucky to buy and sell horses. Among the horses owned by the partnership were the Thoroughbred mare Champagne Woman and her foal Excitable Lady.

The partnership purchased Champagne Woman at auction in 1976 for $155,000, then consigned her to the 1978 fall sale of breeding stock at Keeneland in Lexington, Kentucky. Gentry decided to buy Champagne Woman, but he did not inform Marsh. Acting through an agent, Gentry acquired Champagne Woman for $135,000. Marsh did not know that Gentry was the buyer, and he did not bid on the mare himself.

Gentry also told Marsh that Excitable Lady had been sold privately at a price specified by Marsh to a buyer in California, but he refused to disclose the name of the purchaser. Marsh did not learn that Gentry had purchased Champagne Woman until a year later, and he did not find out that his partner was the sole owner of Excitable Lady until the filly won a race at Churchill Downs in 1981. Marsh stated that he would not have sold his half-interest in either horse if he had known that Gentry was the buyer.

Understandably upset, Marsh sued. He alleged that Gentry withheld relevant information, misled his partner, and violated his duty to act in the best interest of the partnership. The UPA requires that:

"Every partner must account to the partnership any benefit and hold as trustee for it any profit derived by him without the consent of the other partners from any transaction connected with the formation, conduct, or liquidation of the partnership or from any use by him of its profit."

The court found it "instantly apparent" that Gentry had not complied with the requirements of the UPA when he "misled his partner concerning the sales of Champagne Woman and Excitable Lady."

Regarding the sale of Champagne Woman, the court explained that the UPA required that Gentry inform Marsh that he would be a prospective bidder at the Keeneland fall sale. Regarding the latter private sale, the court said that "a partner has an absolute right to know when his partner is the purchaser" of property owned by the partnership. This was true, the court added, despite the fact that Marsh obtained the price he wanted for Excitable Lady. The problem was that Gentry did not disclose the fact that he was the buyer and not that the sale generated less money for Marsh than a sale of the filly to a third party.

Gentry argued that Marsh could not complain about the auction sale of Champagne Woman because it was an accepted practice at auctions for one partner to secretly purchase a horse to buyout the partnership. The court did not accept this argument, stating that "where an 'accepted business practice' conflicts with existing law, the law ... is controlling."

The Spendthrift Farm Experience
McGonigle v. Combs, 968 F2d 810 (11th Cir 1992)

Spendthrift Farm near Lexington, Kentucky, at one time was one of the largest Thoroughbred breeding farms in the world and by a wide margin the most successful consignor of yearlings to the Keeneland select yearling sale. In 1983 Leslie Combs II and his son Brownell decided to incorporate Spendthrift and offer shares in the historic farm to the public. They decided to offer $35 million in stock in a private placement (a sale of securities offered directly to selected private investors) that was followed by a public offering of Spendthrift Farm stock.

Of some five hundred potential investors contacted, thirty-four agreed to participate in the private placement. Prior to investing, each individual signed a document indicating that the investor had carefully reviewed the lengthy private placement proposal; had a net worth of $5 million or more; possessed either alone or with an investment adviser sufficient knowledge and experience to understand and evaluate the potential risks of the investment; and understood that despite Spendthrift's past success the investment constituted a substantial risk.

The private placement closed in August 1983, with investors paying $7.50 per share. The initial public offering (IPO) took place three months later, at an opening price of $12 per share. Leslie and Brownell Combs retained a controlling interest (approximately two-thirds of the stock) in the farm.

It must have looked good on paper — sell one-third of a famous and successful Thoroughbred breeding farm to the public and raise millions of dollars for expansion. In reality, the plan was doomed almost from the start. Sale of stock requires registration with the federal Securities and Exchange Commission, which imposes a high degree of regulation on the enterprise. Requirements include the filing of quarterly, public business reports.

To anyone familiar with the cyclical nature of breeding farm income, the reports looked like they were expected to look: very low or non-existent profits during the first, second, and fourth quarters, and spectacular profits in the third quarter when the summer and fall yearling sales traditionally are held. To investors unfamiliar with the business of selling auction yearlings, however, the quarterly reports were a disaster and a clear and immediate indicator of a bad investment.

Confidence in Spendthrift stock fell, from the opening price of $12 per share to around $3 per share. Investor lawsuits against Leslie and Brownell Combs and almost everyone else involved with the stock sales were initiated, and the first Thoroughbred breeding farm ever listed on a stock exchange moved into bankruptcy. It is not surprising that people in the horse business remain wary of large public offerings of stock in their farms as a way to generate operating capital.

this information allows a potential creditor to learn whether a debt will be secured by the assets of the business and the personal assets of the owner or by the business assets alone. Extending credit in a situation where business owners have personal liability for debt may be more attractive than loaning money to a company where the owners have limited personal liability.

By the same token, corporations and LLCs are required by law to identify themselves with "Inc." or "LLC," respectively, to give potential creditors notice of the organizational status of the businesses.

Whatever choice you make about how to operate your business, the decision does not have to be permanent. As a general rule, though, it is easier to make changes upward on the continuum of complexity, from a partnership to a corporation, for example, than in the other direction.

COMPARISON OF OWNERSHIP ENTITIES

	Sole Proprietorship	General Partnership	Limited Partnership	"C" Corporation	"S" Corporation	Limited Liability Company
CAPITAL	Limited to the capital that can be raised by sole proprietor	Increased access to capital in proportion to the number of partners	Increased access to capital in proportion to the number of partners	Increased access to capital in proportion to the number of shareholders	Increased access to capital in proportion to the number of shareholders	Increased access to capital in proportion to the number of members
CONTROL	Sole proprietor has complete control over the business	General partners share operational control of the business	General partners share control; limited partners do not participate	Officers and directors share control; shareholders do not participate	Officers and directors share control; shareholders do not participate	Controlled by members or by manager
LIABILITY	Sole proprietor is responsible for all business debts, liabilities, and obligations	General partners share joint and several liability for partnership debts	General partners share joint and several liability; limited partners' liability limited to investment	Owners' liability limited to amount of investment; no personal liability for business debts	Owners' liability limited to amount of investment; no personal liability for business debts	Members' liability limited to amount of investment; no personal liability for business debts
TAXES	Business profits and losses are reported on the owner's personal tax return	Business profits and losses are reported on the partners' personal tax returns; business is not taxed	Business profits and losses are reported on the partners' personal tax returns; business is not taxed	Double taxation at corporate level and at individual shareholder level	No double taxation; treated like partnership	Business profits and losses are reported on the members' personal tax returns; business is not taxed
RED TAPE	Virtually none; name registration may be required	Few legal requirements; written partnership agreement recommended	Written partnership agreement required; must be filed	Complicated	Complicated	Written operating agreement required; must be filed; annual report

RESOURCES

The following provide information about selecting the proper business entity:

Horse Owners and Breeders Tax Handbook (current edition), Thomas A. Davis, American Horse Council, 1616 H Street NW, 7th Floor, Washington, D.C. 20006. www.horsecouncil.org

Legal Aspects of Horse Farm Operations (3rd ed.), James H. Newberry Jr., University of Kentucky College of Law, Office of Continuing Legal Education, Suite 260 Law Building, Lexington, KY 40506.

Copies of uniform partnership laws can be found at the Web site for the National Conference of Commissioners on Uniform State Laws: www.nccusl.org.

RECORDS AND ACCOUNTING

The paperwork requirements for starting a business vary from almost none (a sole proprietorship) to extensive (a corporation). And once the business is up and running, the owner or owners must maintain a variety of records.

Record keeping can be a lot of work even for a simple business, and it may be tempting to let the task slide in favor of more interesting pursuits such as going riding or attending the races. For some people, mucking out stalls might be more enjoyable than filling out tax records and filing receipts.

Keep this in mind: At some point, in response to an audit, for example, it may be necessary to prove to the IRS that your horse activity really is a business entitled to deductions for business expenditures. You also may be required to prove the level of your participation in the activity. One of the tests always used by the IRS and tax courts is whether an activity is conducted in a businesslike manner, and a frequently cited indicator is whether the owner kept good records. The more your activity looks like a real business on paper, the more likely the IRS will decide that you really are operating a business.

Two questions frequently asked by people starting new businesses or by owners trying to make an existing business more efficient are "What records should I keep?" and "How long should I keep them?" Neither of these questions has a simple, one-size-fits-all answer, but this chapter will provide some general guidance. This chapter also will address some accounting basics for business owners.

RECORDS OF TRANSACTIONS

Always err on the side of keeping more records than you think you actually need, but keep them organized. If you have lots of records that cannot be found when needed, it is the same as not having the records at all. The length of time that records should be kept will vary, depending upon the type of document and the purpose for which it is held.

Business transactions include bills and receipts for feed, veterinary and farrier care, utilities, vanning, training, and so on. If you pay all bills by check or credit card, you will have an additional record of the transaction — the check or credit card receipt. If you pay with cash, *always* get a signed receipt.

Paying by check or credit card gives you a measure of control, as well as knowledge of where your money goes. Cash tends to disappear quickly and is difficult to tie to any particular receipt or item of expense. At tax time you must be able to document your expenditures to claim them as business deductions.

Open a separate bank account for your business, even if the business is very small. Many taxpayers get into difficulty by starting a small business while continuing to use their family or personal checking account. If the business owner is audited, it will be difficult to satisfy the IRS that all claimed expenses actually are business expenses. Never mix household and business purchases from the same account, even if it means separating items and writing two checks at the store.

Whenever possible, pay by check. Make full use of the memo section of each check you write for your business. This will provide an extra source of information about the nature of the payment you made. Keep all canceled checks (or the duplicate copies if your bank does not return checks), your bank statements, and check registers. Arrange them in numerical order for easy reference.

Keeping canceled checks may be easier said than done, however, as many banks no longer routinely return anything other than a monthly statement to customers. It nearly always is possible to get copies of canceled checks from a bank, but the process can be expensive and time consuming.

Banking online, along with the general shift toward a "paperless office," balances convenience with risk. Computers crash, nearly always at the most inopportune time, and the necessity for backing up any important business data should go without saying. Many business owners keep multiple copies of records, stored either electronically or on paper, with at least one set of records stored off-site.

Be sure to put complete beginning and ending dates on the fronts of check registers. If you later need to compare the register to a bank statement or check, it will be much easier if you can tell at a glance whether you should expect to find a particular check listed in a particular register. Keep these records as long as necessary to ensure they will not be subject to billing or payment disputes, contract claims, injury or damage claims, or tax audits. A certified public accountant (CPA) can offer advice.

The time factor for potential billing and payment disputes tends to be fairly short, as compared with the time you might have to keep records that could apply to contract claims, injury or damage claims, and tax audits. Each state has its own statutes of limitations for various types of legal claims that can be raised, and a comprehensive summary is beyond the scope of this book.

> **AT A GLANCE**
>
> - Keep more records than you think you'll need and keep them organized.
> - Maintain a separate bank account for your business.
> - Keeping good records can help in the case of a business dispute.
> - Property titles or deeds must be kept indefinitely — and in a safe place.
> - Sole proprietors should keep personal income tax records for at least three years, preferably 10 years.

In Kentucky, for example, a personal injury claim can be brought to court for one year from the date a person knew or reasonably should have known of an injury. A contract claim can be brought for fifteen years. Your state will have its own rules about how long a business owner might be exposed to potential claims. Check with an attorney about the statute of limitations periods that may apply to situations in your state.

Each party to a contract should receive and keep a signed, original document. This requires you to execute at least two originals, as all contracts involve at least two parties. Never write or make notes on the original after it has been executed. If you have a need to make notations, make a photocopy first, and write only on the copy. Keep your original for at least as long as any potential legal action could arise as a result of the contract.

Records pertaining to a transaction might also include a telephone log or even a diary or log of discussions. These can be helpful in the event a dispute over the terms of an agreement later arises. You should make it an ongoing part of your business procedures to write down at the time of the discussions, or very shortly thereafter, a summary of what you understood about a business agreement at the time.

It is not necessary to do this for every transaction or contract or agreement, but err on the side of caution for any large or expensive project, as well as any project that could end up in court if things go badly. While most individuals may be "good people" and most transactions present few real problems, a business owner has a very real interest in protecting himself or herself in those few situations where things don't go well. Unfortunately, no one knows until after the fact which situations will go awry.

Do not wait until after a dispute arises and then attempt to reconstruct what was said or done. For one thing, memory fades over time. For another, if the dispute resulted in any sort of court action, you might be able to use, in support of your position, a log or diary that you routinely kept and in which you made contemporaneous, dated entries. If you simply write down your recollection long after a discussion actually occurred, you may be prevented from using the document as evidence and, in any event, you will be less credible.

RECORDS OF PROPERTY TRANSFERS

Records regarding transfer of any property by title or deed should be kept indefinitely, in a safe place. If you own or purchase real estate as part of your horse business, you should keep a copy of the deed in a safe place. Keep in mind that while an oral contract may be valid in some situations, the statute of frauds requires that the transfer of real property (land, not horses) *must* be memorialized in writing to be enforceable in court should a dispute arise.

Title documents for automobiles and trucks, mobile homes, and trailers also should be kept in a safe place. Keep with those documents any notes, or mortgages, or records of tax liens or judgment liens, and releases of liens pertaining to any property you own. Should you need quick access to any documents, organize them in an easily identifiable manner.

PAYROLL RECORDS

Keep all records regarding payroll for your employees. These records include W-4s on which your employees indicate how many withholding allowances they intend to claim. You will then use this information throughout the year as you withhold taxes from their paychecks. You also should keep employer copies of the W-2s, on which income and withholding are reported to the IRS. You also may have substitute W-2s, such as 1099s, for independent contractors.

Other payroll records you should keep include I-9s, which are necessary to establish an employee's right to work legally in the United States (These are discussed more fully in Chapter 12.); wage and tax transmittal statements; state and local tax withholding records; unemployment insurance records; and worker's compensation records. If you provide employee benefits, be sure to keep records of these. Check with your attorney about the length of time to keep payroll and benefits records in your jurisdiction.

Each employee should have a separate file in which his or her forms and records are kept. Make sure you know when to update such records. The IRS allows you to assume that information provided to you on a W-4 remains the same from year to year, unless an employee informs you otherwise. It is a better practice to offer employees each year the opportunity to review their withholding allowances and make changes as appropriate.

Some of the payroll records, such as the wage and tax transmittal records, receipts for payments of taxes withheld, contributions to unemployment insurance, and so forth, do not relate to any one individual employee. Instead, they summarize the payroll taxes paid by the business for all employees. Keep these separately, along with the other tax records of the business.

LEGAL DOCUMENTS THAT ESTABLISH YOUR BUSINESS

Even if you operate your business as a sole proprietor, you may be required to register your business in your state, county, or town. As a sole proprietor, you would not require a separate income tax identification number, but you might require a tax account number for sales or services provided to customers. Check with your attorney to determine business registration requirements if you are operating as a sole proprietor. There may not be any, but if filings are necessary, keep copies of any documents necessary to operate your business. If you subsequently decide to terminate the business, hold onto the records until, under your state's limitations periods, no one could have any claims against you because of the business.

A general partnership may be required to file documents with the state and with the county clerk that lists the name of the partnership, identifies at least one general partner, and lists the partnership's mailing address, as well as the address for service of process in case someone decides to file a lawsuit against the partnership. Filing is *required* for a limited partnership. Generally, the service of process address will be a street address because a complaint cannot be served to a post office box, even though such a box may be used for most other business matters.

Each business partner should receive and maintain an original copy of the partnership agreement. The partnership agreement specifies the name and terms of the business relationship, tells how the agreement can be changed, and states the conditions under which the partnership will automatically terminate. The partnership agreement explains how partners will receive distributions and the responsibilities of the individual partners for liabilities of the business. In the event the partnership terminates, this document provides the mechanism for allocating assets and debts among the partners.

Corporations, once their existence is established by satisfying state registration requirements, are separate legal entities. To exist, each corporation will have to file, usually with the secretary of state, an initial corporate charter, or articles of incorporation, and bylaws. Basically, the corporate charter or articles of incorporation identifies the name of the business, the name of the person who is filing the papers (the legal mechanisms for this vary from state to state), the value of initial stock issued, and the business and street addresses of the business.

The bylaws identify the initial officers and directors and specify procedures for electing and/or appointing subsequent officers. Procedures for voting and establishing committees, duties of officers, and so on also will be found in the bylaws. Originals of these documents, as well as any documentation that these documents have been properly filed, should be kept by the person in the business charged with the responsibility for keeping the corporate records.

Corporations are accountable to their shareholders. The larger the number of shareholders, the more complex this can become. As a general matter, all minutes of stockholder and directors' meetings should be maintained in a separate minutes book and made available for inspection by the shareholders. This is more than good practice — it is often a legal requirement established by states. Check with your legal adviser to find out whether your state has requirements as to the form of the information to be kept with the minutes book.

Many attorneys who practice in this area not only will help you establish the business but also can help you obtain a corporate minutes book, stock certificates, and a corporate seal. In addition to minutes books, corporations must maintain a record of all stock outstanding, including names and addresses of shareholders, numbers of shares held, classes of stock, and the values of each share. All corporate records must be maintained as long as the corporation exists or has any potential for liability to shareholders or any other person or entity.

TAX RECORDS

A sole proprietor must keep all personal income-tax records for at least three years. Ten years is better practice. A sole proprietor who sells products subject to state sales tax also must develop and maintain records of any money collected on behalf of the taxing authority.

A partnership, like a sole proprietor, pays no federal income tax at the entity level. Rather, the partnership obtains a federal tax identification number for use in reporting tax information on the partnership return and then files the informational return and gives to each partner a tax document showing his or her individual share of net ordinary income and certain other income and expenses that pass through to the individuals. Each general partner should receive a copy of the income tax informational forms filed on behalf of the partnership each year. For federal purposes, this is a Form 1065. Your state probably has a similar informational form, and local taxing authorities also may require informational reports.

The information from Form 1065 is then included in the partners' individual income tax returns. Partnerships also report this information to their states. In some local taxing authorities, more than an informational return is required. Some Kentucky counties, for example, require payment of a tax on the net profits of the partnership, *prior* to distribution to the individual partners. A local tax-identification number is required for payment of these taxes. These records should be kept for at least as long as any tax records must be kept and perhaps longer for a long-term partnership.

A corporation is a separate entity and will be taxed as such. It must, therefore, have its own tax identification number at all levels of taxation. All tax records and tax-identification numbers should be maintained in the same manner as other business entities keep such records.

INSURANCE POLICIES

Keeping copies of your insurance policies handy may sound obvious, but a surprising number of business people don't, at least not in a way that anyone could find the information quickly. At least one other person should know the location of *all* insurance policies and related documentation. Keep the original policies and any changes of which the insurer informs you in a single location. This includes property insurance, life insurance, disability insurance, liability insurance, health insurance, and any other policy you may have that is in any way intended to protect your business from loss, to provide income or pay bills during periods of disability, or to provide for your family in the event something happens to you or the business. These documents should be kept for as long as the policies are in force or could be reinstated.

ESTATE PLANNING DOCUMENTS

A power of attorney lets someone else act for you when you are unavailable to act for yourself. The document that identifies the person or persons holding such powers should be maintained in a safe place and in a manner that makes it easily accessible to at least one other person.

Suppose, for example, that you are a sole proprietor. For some reason you are unavailable or unable to sign an important document or pay a bill when it comes due. You have appointed someone to have power of attorney, but no one knows where the document is because you like to keep your privacy and don't want to risk that the person with authority to sign for you will take advantage of the power of attorney. The person you have appointed cannot act without the power of attorney, properly executed and filed with the state or county if necessary, that says he or she can act for you.

Your business also may be affected by the contents of your last will and testament or a trust agreement. These also should be maintained in a manner easily accessible to those who need them. Also remember that you can usually dispose of shares of stock in your corporate business, and you can pass on assets from a business operated by you as a sole proprietorship through your will.

If you have a partnership, however, it is the partnership agreement that will specify the terms for distribution of your partnership interest at your death. Often family members may not even know the form of ownership in which the business is held, making it critically important to keep all these records together.

ACCOUNTING

Many of the records business owners should create and maintain involve accounting in one way or another. Going to the races or a horse show nearly always will be more interesting than doing accounting work, but record keeping is a necessary part of operating a business. Unless the horse operation is large enough to employ a bookkeeper, the job will fall on the owner's shoulders.

Even if you use an accountant to prepare tax returns, that person must receive financial information about the business in a usable form. It will save a substantial amount of money if you present business records to your accountant in an organized manner rather than as loose receipts in a shoebox. In addition, you must be able to discuss business decisions with the accountant. If you intend to prepare tax returns without professional assistance, which almost never is a good idea, it becomes even more critical to understand certain basic accounting terminology.

You will need to be able to prepare and read financial statements so that you can compare how your horse business is doing from year to year. This will enable you to see what your business has accomplished and assist you in planning for the future. The sections that follow should give you some of the information you will need.

COMMON FINANCIAL REPORTS

Cash or Accrual?

Accounting is just a way to record financial transactions. One of the first business management decisions you must make is whether to use the cash method or the accrual method of accounting. The cash method of accounting is familiar to most people. Individual taxpayers, for example, use the cash method of accounting. They report income to the IRS, as a general rule, in the year in which the money is actually received and claim allowable deductions in the year in which the expenses are actually paid.

Professional service businesses, other small firms that maintain no inventory and have few long-term assets, and farms also may use this method of accounting. To qualify for the cash method of accounting, however, the business cannot be one that requires an inventory. Also, you must use the cash method of accounting for your business unless you keep account books.

With the accrual method of accounting, you report income when it is earned, even if you do not actually get paid then. You report expenses when you incur them, even if you do not pay them at the time they are incurred. Records of these types of transactions — purchases and sales "on time" — are maintained in the "account books" of the business.

Also, if you sell equipment or supplies as part of your horse operation, items that would be classified as "inventory," you may be required by the IRS to use the accrual method of accounting. This means that you would be required to keep account books. To help you understand the practical differences between the cash and accrual methods, consider the example of Jackson Farms.

Roger Jackson owns a three-hundred-acre farm on which he boards horses, maintains riding trails for use by the public, and offers horseback riding lessons. He likes his privacy, and the only partner of any kind that he wants is his wife, Alice. She helps with the books. He has chosen to operate as a sole proprietor.

Existing contracts for the year total $12,000, with various beginning and ending dates. Most people but not all, unfortunately, pay these monthly. A few people paid in lump sums at the beginning of their contracts, with those contracts totaling $4,000. This was a rare treat for Jackson, because he certainly needed the money and welcomed the unexpected and unusual security this gave him.

In addition, a new boarder has just signed a one-year contract to keep her horse on the farm, with monthly payments over the twelve-month period. One doting grandparent gave a year of weekly riding lessons as a birthday gift to her grandchild this year and paid for the lessons all at once. Plus, Jackson expects to earn about $6,000 from the extensive riding trails he has developed on the farm.

Jackson has had a difficult time, despite having a valid contract, collecting for veterinarian expenses he incurred in an emergency situation on behalf of a horse owner. As is typically the situation, the veterinarian expected, and received, payment from Jackson, who then had to seek reimbursement from the horse owner. Rarely will a service provider such as a veterinarian or farrier agree to bill a horse owner directly.

AT A GLANCE

- The two most common accounting methods are cash and accrual.
- The cash method is what most people use for their personal accounts. Income is reported in the year it is received and deductions are claimed in the year expenses are paid.
- With the accrual method, income is reported when earned even if actual payment has not been received, and expenses are reported even if they are not paid at the time they are incurred.

Another customer had not paid all of her boarding fees and was in arrears when she moved her horse to another stable. Jackson has decided to write off the losses as bad debts rather than pursue them in court. He has had various other ordinary business expenses totaling $3,600 so far this year.

As a sole proprietor, Jackson simply includes business income and expenses, and the resulting profit or loss information, on Schedule C of the federal form 1040 income tax return. So, what difference does it make if he uses the cash method or the accrual method of accounting?

On the facts given here, let's assume first that Jackson uses the cash method of accounting. With this method, he will claim as income on Schedule C all of the income from the existing contracts, riding lessons, and use of riding trails that he actually receives during his tax year (typically the calendar year from January 1 to December 31). If he doesn't receive part of it until next year, then he will not report the income until then. He will report as income the full $4,000 lump sum payments for boarding contracts as well as the money received from the grandparent because he received it this year.

Jackson may claim as expenses the regular operating expenses, which are $3,600 so far this year. The bad debts are another matter, however. He can only write off as a bad debt those items that were from sales or services previously included in income and definitely known to be worthless. Jackson would have to meet very strict IRS requirements in order to satisfy these criteria. As a cash-basis taxpayer, it is more difficult for him to do this. If he doesn't pursue all his legal remedies, which probably would cost more than he would collect taking attorney fees into account, he does not know for certain that the debt is worthless.

If Jackson chooses the accrual method of accounting, on the other hand, several things will be different. Although he received $4,000 in lump sum boarding contracts, he doesn't actually earn the money until the horses are boarded for the week or month. The one-time payment from the grandparent, likewise, is not earned until the lessons are given. Jackson can defer reporting these sums as income until they are actually earned. This may reduce his taxable income for the current year.

With respect to the boarding fees that were in arrears, as an accrual method taxpayer, he probably claimed the boarding fees as income when they were due, not when he actually received the money. This would satisfy the first part of the IRS test allowing Jackson to deduct the bad debt on his tax return. He must still be able to demonstrate to the satisfaction of the IRS that the debt is worthless, which can be difficult.

For Jackson, even operating as a sole proprietor, the accrual method of accounting may give some tax benefit not available to cash-basis taxpayers. The greater the complexity of the business, in terms of numbers of owners, form of ownership chosen, etc., the more likely the accrual method will be of tax benefit. Remember, however, that the accrual method *requires* account books be kept.

Formal records and careful documentation are necessities. Perhaps because accrual method bookkeeping is less familiar to many individuals, business owners sometimes improperly record the timing of income and expenses. The cash method, while still requiring good records, is simpler. You cannot change accounting methods from year to year, in an attempt to lower your tax bill. Once you have begun your business and filed your first income tax return, you must get permission from the IRS to change your accounting method. Ask your accountant for advice before you start!

Balance Sheets = A Photograph of Your Business

One of the reasons for generating financial reports is obviously to document income and expenses for tax-reporting purposes. Some horse businesses also may have to worry about sales taxes, especially in states where such taxes are imposed on services. Equally important, however, and frequently overlooked, is the benefit of having good financial reports for planning the future direction of your horse business.

The balance sheet provides a simple snapshot of the company at a given time. Sometimes it is referred to as a net worth statement. The first part of the balance sheet lists the assets or resources of the business. Assets include cash and property treated as cash, such as checking and savings accounts, certificates of deposits, etc., as well as the value of property and equipment. Accounts receivable are also assets, but these may not appear on the balance sheets of cash-basis taxpayers.

The second part of the balance sheet contains a list of business liabilities and owner equity in the business. Liabilities generally include accounts payable or bills due as of the date of the document, taxes due, and debt. Owner equity is a combination of capital contributions made by owners and undistributed earnings.

Take a look at the Jackson Farms balance sheet on page 72. After consulting with his accountant and attorney, Jackson decided to consider his entire farm part of the business. Although he recently added the riding trails and horseback riding lessons, he has not started separate businesses for these activities. He is using a calendar year.

Notice that the balance sheet is "as of" a particular date. As a sole proprietor, Jackson wants to keep things simple, but he could provide even more detail by specifying the various accounts in which he has his

---

Jackson Farms
Balance Sheet
As of December 31, 2006

Assets

Cash, cash equivalents	$8,400
Equipment	$89,000
Buildings	$75,000
Farm land	$300,000
Total Assets	**$472,400**

Liabilities

Feed bill due now	$3,400
Fertilizer, etc. due now	$8,100
Equipment loan balance	$17,000
Land, bldg. loan/note	$54,000
Total Liabilities	**$82,500**

Equity

Opening Balance Equity	$370,857
Net Ordinary Income	$19,043
Year-End Equity (Net Worth)	$389,900
Total Liabilities and Equity	**$472,400**

---

funds and by distinguishing current assets and liabilities from non-current assets and liabilities. Current assets are those that will be received as cash or converted to cash within one year. Current liabilities are those due and payable within one year. Everything else is non-current.

As sole proprietor, Jackson's year-end equity equals the net worth of the horse farm operation. You will notice that the total liabilities and equity equals total assets. This is always the case. If Jackson had partners or shareholders, he would have to calculate the equity share for each one. Each owner's equity is that owner's opening balance equity, plus his or her investments during the year, less any distributions made during the year to that owner. The totals of the liabilities plus the total equity of all owners always will equal the total value of the assets, just as it does for Jackson as shown here.

Because Jackson has chosen to reinvest his net ordinary income back into the business and because he is a sole proprietor, it appears as part of his equity. If he had taken some of the earnings for family living expenses, that amount would appear as a reduction in his equity.

Profit and Loss Statements Gauge Your Progress

The profit and loss statement, sometimes called a P&L or even an income statement, shows the net earnings of a business over a specific period. The standard period is one year, though the year may be tied to something other than a calendar. The fiscal year for your business might be tied to the date on which your business began or to a key time in your business. For example, a horse breeder might tie the end of a fiscal year to the completion of yearling sales held each year so that all revenues received from the sales fall in a particular reporting period.

Unlike the balance sheet, which is a statement of the net worth of the business at a particular point, the profit and loss statement tells a business owner if the business has increased or decreased over time. The

Jackson Farms*
Profit and Loss

	Jan. 1, 2006 through Dec. 31, 2006	Jan. 1, 2005 through Dec. 31, 2005
Ordinary Income		
General farm operations	$64,000	$70,000
Horse boarding	$16,000	$10,000
Trail use fees	$3,200	$0
Riding lessons	$4,400	$2,550
Total Income	**$87,600**	**$82,550**
Ordinary Expenses		
Bank service charges	$57	$57
Legal fees	$1,500	$1,500
Supplies	$3,900	$6,330
Equipment purchase	$13,000	$7,000
Interest expense	$12,000	$4,800
Veterinarian fees	$6,000	$9,000
Payroll	$18,000	$16,000
Tax preparation fees	$300	$300
Misc.	$7,400	$11,250
Taxes	$6,400	$6,400
Total Expenses	**$68,557**	**$62,637**
Net Ordinary Income	**$19,043**	**$19,913**

*These numbers are not intended to resemble costs on an actual farm. They merely serve to show how such a document might look and the kinds of information one might gain from an examination of the documents from year to year. Check out the balance sheet to see where else the net ordinary income appears.

profit and loss statement shows a summary of the income from all sources and the expenses by each category of expense. After subtracting the expenses paid or credited during the period from the income received or earned during the period, you will see the net income for the period reflected by the statement.

After you have been in business for more than one year, you can compare income and expenses from year to year, using the profit and loss statement. You can track the sources of your income to see if, for example, your income from any particular source is increasing or decreasing as a percentage of your total income. You can see if expenses are as expected or if one or more categories are greater or less than anticipated. This information can be helpful in planning for the next year. The Jackson Farms profit and loss statement at the end of this chapter gives an example of how a simple version might look.

An examination of the Jackson Farms profit and loss statement shows that income from general farming operations decreased from 2005 to 2006 while income from other areas increased. Jackson should ask himself whether this was intended or if he needs to make changes, such as hiring additional help for either the new areas or the general farm operations. He also should look at the expense items. Were they as expected? Should some of the items in the miscellaneous expense category be listed separately? Should some categories be further reduced to increase net income? Should a category be increased or added to assist in the production of net income?

Use Cash-Flow Projections To Anticipate Cash Needs

A cash-flow projection is strictly that, a forecast based upon assumptions you have made of the cash expected or needed at some time in the future. The purpose of a cash-flow projection is not to set targets or goals for the business but to anticipate cash needs. It should be revised as often as necessary, and even if you have a tendency to be optimistic, force yourself to be just a little pessimistic in making your projections.

Money owed to your horse business may never arrive, even from a customer with a timely payment record. Expenses to renovate your barn may be larger than expected. To make matters worse, when doing cash planning, you may even need to consider some things that do not even show up on your balance sheet. If you are using the cash method of accounting, for example, an order for feed will not appear on the balance sheet until you have paid for it.

An executory contract, one in which you have agreed to do something in the future, such as breeding a horse, may not appear on the balance sheet until money changes hands. A pending lawsuit in which your business may become liable for payment of money will be necessary to include in your cash-flow forecast but will not appear in your balance sheet. An example of this might be a claim for negligence that an injured rider has made against your business. You might suddenly need cash if the jury decides your business was at fault.

Jackson Farms
Cash-Flow Projections/Assumptions

First Quarter 2007

	January	February	March
General farm operations	$1,000	$1,000	$1,500
Horse boarding	$1,200	$1,200	$1,200
Trail use fees	$100	$100	$300
Riding lessons	$200	$200	$400
Total Revenue	**$2,500**	**$2,500**	**$3,400**
Bank service charges	$0	$0	$28
Legal fees	$0	$0	$500
Supplies	$325	$400	$400
Equipment purchase	$1,083	$1,083	$1,083
Interest expense	$1,000	$1,000	$1,000
Veterinarian fees	$500	$1,000	$1,000
Payroll	$1,500	$1,500	$1,500
Tax preparation fees	$50	$0	$0
Misc.	$620	$620	$600
Taxes	$1,600	$0	$0
Total Expenses	**$6,678**	**$5,603**	**$6,111**

In Jackson's case, his cash-flow chart shows he will not make it through the winter without careful advance planning. If his assumptions about the first three months of the year are reasonably correct, he needs to be sure to have savings on hand or a line of credit upon which he can draw until that time of year when his revenues exceed his expenses.

Develop a Budget

All businesses need a budget. All businesses need a budget. All businesses need a budget. Get the point? Few people really enjoy developing a budget because it is often perceived as some sort of straitjacket to prevent creativity or because it is based upon unrealistic goals. Such a budget is badly designed or poorly implemented. Your balance sheet and profit and loss statements tell you something about where your horse business has been and what it has already done. A good budget helps a business owner take control of the future.

A well-conceived budget helps you get your business where you want it to go. It spells out the goals, breaks them into manageable pieces, allocates resources, and assigns responsibility for performance of various aspects of it. The written budget does not need to be elaborate but should specify the period to be covered by the budget. It should clearly state the goals for which resources are being allocated. If goals will take longer than the budget period to be accomplished, the budget should state what part will be accomplished during the budgeted time period. Whenever possible, specific individuals should be assigned to complete tasks that will promote accomplishment of the goals.

In small horse businesses, a properly developed budget may be used primarily as a road map for attaining goals. In larger businesses, it also may be used for control of expenditures. In both situations, short-term and long-term goals are broken into chunks that can be accomplished within a given period. The goals are prioritized, and resources are then allocated to goals in accordance with the priorities. In examining the Jackson Farms profit and loss statement, it is clear that income from general farming has declined from 2005 to 2006.

If this was the result of a decision by Jackson to commit fewer resources to general farm operations in hopes of increasing income from the other three areas, then he may not need to worry that net income as a whole also declined. He should ask, however, if the goals he set for his horse business were reasonable. If they were not, then he should use that information to revise his budget for the next time period.

The cash-flow projection also gives Jackson a picture, based upon assumptions that he hopes are realistic, about the cash flowing in and out of his business during a particular time frame. If all goes well, the items of outgoing cash are previously budgeted items for which Jackson is amply prepared. If so, that is one indication that the budget was realistic. If some items on the cash-flow projection were not budgeted at all or if an item is much higher or lower than expected, then either the assumptions that went into the cash flow were wrong or the budget was unrealistic, or both.

Devise a System of Internal Control

Business owners need some sort of system to prevent and detect errors in the recording of information about the business. It might be as simple as always paying bills and expenses by check then reconciling the check register to the statement you receive from the bank each month. You might add to that process recording expenses in a separate ledger, using receipts as your guide, and comparing the balances in the checkbook. Take steps to safeguard your records physically in the event they are needed for a tax audit or to prove the terms of a contract.

If you own a large horse business, you will have additional needs for an internal system of controls, including protection against errors, theft, and other losses. One means of accomplishing this is to divide the financial accounting and record-keeping tasks.

One partner, for example, might perform data entry for your horse business' various sources of income and expenditures while another writes checks and reconciles the checkbook. Or perhaps one of you writes the checks and the other reconciles the checkbook. If you sell supplies in your business, a third partner might periodically compare actual inventory to that listed on the books.

The more elaborate your business operation and the greater the number of owners or investors to whom you must report, the more important it will become to physically protect the data you generate about your business and to prove that the information is error free. Computer software can streamline the record-keeping and accounting processes, but working and back-up copies of the data should be maintained. Many experts advise that a complete set of accounting data should be kept in a secure off-site location for added protection.

RESOURCES

Small Business Association: One of the best sources of information about all aspects of business operation. SBA Answer Desk, 6302 Fairview Road, Suite 300, Charlotte, N.C. 28210, (800) 827-5722. www.sba.gov.

5

CONTRACTS

If you take away only one thing from reading this book, it should be this: *Get it in writing!* Horse business traditionally has been conducted with nothing more than the strength of a handshake binding the parties. That is not, and never has been, sound business practice. The following rule of thumb should govern your business dealings: If a particular outcome to a business transaction is important (getting to breed a mare to a certain stallion, for example) or if the effect of an unexpected problem would be unacceptable (such as a costly injury to a boarder or her horse), you should insist on a written contract with the other party.

The usual objections to requiring written contracts should sound familiar to everyone:

"It is too much trouble to use a written contract."

"No one else around here does it that way."

"I don't know how to write a contract, and lawyers are too expensive anyway."

"My customers will think that I don't trust them if I make them sign a contract before I board their horse or before I let them ride on my land."

"My boarders will go to another farm where they don't have to sign a contract."

"I don't want to make (insert name of merchant here) mad."

These are all legitimate concerns. No one wants to add complication and aggravation to a business or pleasure activity, and many horse enthusiasts view the use of written contracts as far more hassle than benefit. After all, you may think, nothing bad has happened yet. What is the worst thing that can happen to me if I continue to do business as usual, without written agreements with my customers? The possibilities are almost endless.

Using written contracts will not protect you from everything that might go wrong, of course; nothing can do that. A well-drafted written contract should cover the problems most likely to occur and make it easier to predict the outcome when something unexpected happens. That predictability is the real value of getting agreements in writing. You might enjoy a surprise treat on your birthday, but the fewer surprises you have to face where your farm and horses are concerned, the better off you are.

A contract is nothing more than a set of promises between the parties. Usually this amounts to a promise by one person to do something in return for a second person's promise to do something else, called a bilateral contract. Less common are unilateral contracts, in which one party makes an offer and another party accepts by actual performance rather than by a reciprocal promise.

A valid contract can be either written or oral, although written is better, and it can be as simple as an agreement between two people outlined on a cocktail napkin, or as complicated as a multi-page, multi-party document crammed to the four corners with incomprehensible fine-print legalese. A valid contract creates legal obligations between the parties and allows for enforcement in court if the contract is broken.

WRITTEN OR ORAL?

We met the Jacksons in the previous chapter. They have been involved in the horse business for several years, as competitors at local shows, as horse owners, and as small-scale breeders. They presently own two horses, which they keep on their farm a few miles outside town. One of Mrs. Jackson's co-workers, a secretary, just bought her first horse, a gelding intended for trail riding, and she wants to board the animal at Jackson Farms. Although not in the business of boarding horses, the Jacksons agree because the extra money will come in handy.

The Jacksons and their new boarder come to a mutual understanding. After a lengthy chat on the telephone, the new boarder agrees that while the horse is in the care of the Jacksons, she will be responsible for several specific expenses: board, including feed and a safe stall; veterinary care; and blacksmith services. The Jacksons agree to notify the horse's owner before incurring any non-emergency expenses.

Without anything else happening, an oral contract has come into being. The Jacksons have promised to provide certain boarding services, for which the owner has promised to pay. Their boarder also has agreed to pay for specific out-of-pocket expenses. This type of bare bones agreement, unfortunately, is fairly typical in the horse business. Although it is a good start, the contract is incomplete and several important terms are not addressed.

A few months later, while making a final check of the barn before turning in for the evening, Mrs. Jackson notices the new horse is showing some signs of colic. He appears nervous, and he is sweating and nipping at his flanks. The situation does not appear critical, though, and as agreed, Mrs. Jackson attempts to contact the horse's owner before calling the veterinarian.

The owner is not available, however, and the horse's condition appears to worsen. Jackson contacts the farm's regular veterinarian, who comes for an after-hours emergency call. He diagnoses the condition as a potentially serious colic and recommends immediate surgery. Still unable to contact the horse's owner, the Jacksons reluctantly authorize the surgery, relying on the oral agreement negotiated earlier. The bill for the surgery, which saves the horse's life, and postoperative care amounts to several thousand dollars, which the veterinarian bills directly to the farm, a common practice.

AT A GLANCE

- *Get it in writing!* A written contract provides greater protection in case of dispute.
- Oral contracts are common in the horse business, but they can be difficult to enforce in court if the parties can't prove the contract existed.
- There is no such thing as a "one size fits all" contract. Work with your attorney to prepare the best contract for a given situation.

At this point, one of two things will happen. The horse owner reimburses the farm owner for the veterinarian's bill (either with or without attendant grumbling) or she refuses. In either case the veterinarian will look to the Jacksons for payment. The farm owners, after all, actually authorized the surgery. The ultimate outcome may rest on the fact that the Jacksons and their boarder never executed a written boarding contract.

This common situation illustrates two important points about contracts.

First, if everything goes as expected, the Jacksons incur unauthorized expenses on behalf of the owner in an emergency, and the boarder pays the bill when it arrives — whether there was a valid contract will have no practical impact. Because the expectations of both parties were satisfied, neither party should have any complaints. In other words, although neither party anticipated the problem, the outcome surprised no one.

If, on the other hand, one of the parties fails to perform as promised, the value of a contract becomes obvious. Consider, for example, what happens if the boarder balks at paying what she calls a "ridiculous" veterinarian bill for unnecessary and unauthorized surgery, a not unlikely reaction from a first-time horse owner with limited disposable income. The veterinarian, naturally, looks to the Jacksons for payment as they authorized the surgical procedure in the first place. They pay the bill to preserve a good relationship with the veterinarian, who happens to be the only veterinarian with equine expertise within fifty miles and then seek reimbursement from the boarder. If the boarder balks at reimbursing the Jacksons, their only recourse for getting paid is to take the boarder to court.

The oral boarding agreement between the Jacksons and the horse owner sets out some, but not all, of the responsibilities and obligations of both parties. In this example, the Jacksons have a responsibility to attempt to notify the owner before incurring expenses in a non-emergency situation, but the possibility of the owner being out of touch when there is an emergency was not discussed. The boarder agreed to pay the veterinarian's bill, but whether that agreement was contingent on prior notification is unclear.

If the Jacksons go to court in an attempt to force the owner to reimburse them for the bill, the judge or jury will have some basis for allocating the cost of the surgery. Here, the terms of the contract suggest that the owner of the horse probably is responsible for the veterinarian bill although the question of prior notification may become an issue. Without an agreement of some kind, however, the chances of forcing the reluctant owner to pay are small.

This leads to the second important principle regarding contracts. While an oral contract is better than no contract, a written contract is best. Having an agreement memorialized in writing and signed by the parties does not guarantee that the parties will abide by the agreement. The advantage of a written contract is that neither the existence of the contract nor its terms is in doubt. However, in the case of an oral contract, the first step to enforcing the agreement in court often involves simply proving that the contract actually existed, and if it did, that the terms of the agreement are as one or the other party claims. This can be difficult when, months or years after the fact, memories have faded and interests may have changed.

No matter how reasonable the Jacksons' actions in the above example were, they may find themselves on the paying end of a large veterinarian bill for someone else's horse if they must rely on an oral agreement to prove the owner really is responsible for the emergency care they authorized on her behalf.

Although an oral contract can be as binding on the parties as a written contract, there is an important caveat. Some contracts *must* be in writing and *must* be signed by the parties to be enforced in court.

Every jurisdiction has a statute of frauds in one form or another. Statutes of frauds require that certain contracts must be in writing. They include contracts for the transfer of real estate, contracts to answer for another person's debt, contracts whose terms make it impossible to complete the contract within one year, and contracts for the sale of some goods. Your attorney can provide guidance on the statute of frauds in your state.

A written contract provides little protection if it isn't read by the parties. Courts assume that a person who has signed a contract only did so after reading and understanding the document. "But, Judge, I didn't read it" almost never will be a successful defense to a breach of contract claim.

There is no such thing as a "one size fits all" contract. Each contract represents a particular business transaction, and the terms of the contract should be tailored to the transaction's individual circumstances. A properly drafted boarding contract should address different concerns than a contract for leasing a competition horse, for example, and the respective contracts should be drafted with the particular transaction in mind. A contract for breeding a mare to a particular stallion will be different from a contract for purchasing frozen semen for artificial insemination.

This does not mean that you cannot have a standard contract for boarding, or leasing, or for lessons; you can, and should, have standard contracts for common situations. The practice is simpler and less expensive than having new contracts drafted for each transaction. Even a comprehensive standard contract may have to be modified to fit a particular situation, however.

CONTRACTS 101

Not every agreement constitutes a contract that can be enforced in court. The requirements for a valid contract include offer and acceptance, consideration, capacity of the parties, and a lawful purpose.

Offer and Acceptance — Every contract starts with an offer of something by one party and an acceptance of that offer by a second party. Communicating to a feed dealer that you want a thousand bales of alfalfa hay delivered on July 1 of the current year and that you'll pay $5 a bale is an offer that the merchant can either accept of refuse. If the feed dealer accepts the offer and promises on-time delivery of the hay at the specified price, the first steps toward formation of a bilateral contract have been taken. The parties have made mutual promises to perform, and they have assumed mutual obligations. In other words, a valid offer made by one party allows a second party to accept and by so doing create a binding contract.

The terms of the offer should be as specific as possible. If you accept an offer to buy one thousand bales of hay, with the variety unspecified, you will not be able to complain if the hay that is delivered is timothy rather than alfalfa.

Depending on the circumstances, a person also may be able to accept an offer by performance. "I'll pay you five hundred dollars if you paint my fence" is an offer that can be accepted by promising to paint the fence (an exchange of promises that creates a bilateral contract) or by actually painting the fence (an exchange of a promise to pay and actual performance that creates a unilateral contract).

In either situation, a "meeting of the minds" is an essential part of contract formation. A meeting of the minds means just what it says. The parties must agree that there is a contract and on the substance of the terms of the agreement. Without a meeting of the minds, there is no contract.

Not every statement made by one person to another is an offer. A statement of intent, such as "I think I'll sell my horse for a thousand dollars," is not an offer, and the person making the statement cannot be forced to sell the horse by someone who shows up at the barn the next day with a check for a thousand dollars. Nor is an opinion such as "I think I'd like to have my fence painted" an offer specific enough for another person to accept.

A solitary question such as "Are you interested in selling me that horse?" does not constitute a valid offer either. While the inquiry might lead to negotiations that result in the eventual sale of the animal, the initial question is not an offer another person can accept. This is true for most preliminary negotiations.

Only the individual to whom an offer is directed can actually accept the offer. An offer to sell a horse for a thousand dollars, made to a particular person, cannot be accepted by a third party who overheard the conversation. The status of an advertisement or flier directed at the general public offering to sell the same horse is less clear although most courts treat ads and fliers as invitations to make an offer rather than as offers themselves.

In that case an individual who sees the ad offering a horse for sale technically is making an offer to the horse's owner when he shows up at the stable with a check. The owner of the horse then can accept or reject the potential buyer's offer. The same generally is true for price stickers on merchandise in a store.

An offer also should state how long the other party has to respond. If no time limit is specified in the offer, courts generally allow a "reasonable time" for response. What is reasonable in one situation might be unreasonable in another, and the party making an offer should either include a set time or specify that "time is of the essence" in any offer.

Finally, an acceptance must exactly mirror the offer. If the acceptance terms differ from the offer, the roles of the parties are reversed. The

---

AT A GLANCE

- A valid contract must include offer and acceptance, consideration, capacity of the parties, and a lawful purpose.
- In a "meeting of the minds" the parties in a contract agree that a contract is needed and what the terms should be.
- Consideration represents the bargaining between the parties to arrive at the contract's terms.
- With few exceptions, a minor cannot legally enter into a binding contract.

"acceptance" actually is a counter offer that can be accepted or rejected by the person who made the original offer. If the offer is to sell a five-year-old Hanoverian dressage horse for $25,000, for example, the acceptance cannot be for a selling price of $20,000. In that case, the owner of the horse can either accept of reject the $20,000 counter offer.

Consideration — This can be the most difficult concept of contract formation to understand, but it also is one of the most essential. There cannot be a valid contract without consideration.

Each party to a valid contract gives up something to get something else. Those are the inducements to enter into the contract in the first place, and they are the consideration underlying the agreement. If the contract is for Party A to sell a horse to Party B for a thousand dollars, Party A's consideration is giving up the horse in return for the money and Party B's consideration is giving up the money in return for the horse. Consideration represents the bargaining that went on prior to the offer and acceptance by the parties, and without those elements the contract is not enforceable.

The following is a gratuitous promise that cannot be enforced in court: "I'm going to buy a new horse, and when I do, I'm going to give you this one." If I decide not to give you my horse after I buy a new one, a court is very unlikely to make me do so because there was no consideration on your part. I made a promise, which might carry with it a moral obligation to act. There was no bargaining, though, and you didn't give up anything. The contract is not valid because of a lack of consideration.

This, on the other hand, is a contract that *can* be enforced in court: "I'm going to buy a new horse. If you board my current horse at your farm without charging me anything while I'm looking, I'll give you the horse when I find a new one." In this situation there was bargaining, and both parties gave up something to receive something. I promised to give up my horse in return for free board; you promised to provide free board in return for my horse. If I renege on the deal, you stand a very good chance of having a court force me to do what I said I would do.

Legal Capacity — The age of majority is the age at which an individual becomes an adult for legal purposes and assumes responsibility for his or her actions. It is not necessarily the same as the age at which a person can marry without parental consent, vote, or drink legally. In nearly all jurisdictions the age of majority is eighteen, but an attorney familiar with the laws in your state can provide current local information.

The age of majority matters here because with few exceptions a minor lacks the legal capacity to enter into a binding contract. A party deals with a minor at his or her own risk in any business transaction. If the business is giving riding lessons, for example, a written contract signed by a minor student will provide little legal recourse if the minor refuses to pay for the lessons. If the nature of the business makes written liability waivers a good idea for participants in equine activities, a waiver signed by a minor will provide little or no protection in the event of an accident.

This isn't meant to suggest that you'll never get paid if you give riding lessons to a minor or that you'll always be sued if a minor is injured on your farm. More often than not business transactions with minors proceed as expected, with both sides satisfied with the outcome. In those cases it is irrelevant whether a valid contract was in force. For everyone's protection, however, both the minor *and* a parent or legal guardian should sign any legal documents.

Like minors, persons who are drunk or under the influence of drugs lack the legal capacity to enter into a valid contract. This may make deals struck at a post-race party somewhat problematic, for example, and it is a good business practice to review the terms of the contract after the celebration when everyone involved has full control of their faculties. Individuals who are mentally incompetent also lack the capacity to enter into valid contracts, and the signature of a legally responsible person such as a parent or guardian should be required on all contracts.

Lawful purpose — It should go without saying that a contract with an unlawful purpose is not valid. An agreement to fix a horse race, which is a criminal offense everywhere, will not be enforced by a court, even if all the other requirements for a valid contract are met.

ANATOMY OF A CONTRACT

No single contract can cover every conceivable business transaction. There are too many variables, and each situation is very fact-specific. For this reason it is dangerous to rely on so-called "form contracts," fill-in-the-

SAMPLE BOARDING CONTRACT

A. THIS AGREEMENT is made and entered into as of the _____ day of _____ ____, 200_____, by and between _____ Farm, of _____ (hereinafter the "Farm") and _____, of _____ _____(hereinafter the "Owner").

WITNESSETH:

In consideration of the following premises and mutual covenants, the parties hereto agree as follows:

B. **1. Agreement to Board.** The Farm shall board the horse or horses owned by Owner that the Owner shall deliver to the Farm on or about _____, 200_____, subject to the terms and conditions of this Contract. Owner shall provide to the Farm information concerning the horse or horses to be boarded by separate letter, a copy of which is attached hereto and incorporated herein by this reference.

C. **2. Board Rate.** Owner agrees to pay the current monthly board rate charged by the Farm as set out below. This rate may be changed upon one month's written notice to the Owner.

$_____	pasture/horse
$_____	stall & turnout/horse
$_____	broodmare with foal
$_____	other (must be specified below)
_____	

The Farm agrees to provide normal and reasonable care and agrees to provide the following services: _____ _____ _____

Special instructions _____

In addition to the board rates shown above, Owner agrees to pay all expenses incurred in the proper care and maintenance of each horse, including such veterinarian, blacksmith, transportation, and advertising charges as may be incurred for each horse.

3. Billing. The Farm shall furnish to Owner on a monthly basis a statement of the board and expenses incurred with respect to each horse. Owner hereby agrees to pay the amount due as indicated on each monthly statement within 15 days of the date of such statement. A one and one-half percent (1 1/2%) per month interest and bookkeeping charge will be added to any amount due that is not paid within 30 days of the billing date. Any bill that has not been paid in full within 30 days of the billing date shall be deemed to be in default.

D. **4. Insurance.** Owner is solely responsible for maintaining any and all insurance on each horse. The Farm does not provide insurance coverage on boarded horses.

If the horse is presently insured, Owner shall provide that information on the boarding letter. If the horse is not presently insured, Owner shall immediately notify the Farm in writing of insurance coverage for the horse if such is later obtained. If Owner fails to provide such information, the Farm shall assume that any horse boarded pursuant to the terms of this Contract is uninsured.

E. **5. Risk of Loss and Indemnity.** The Farm shall not be liable for accident, injury, disease, theft, or death of any horse while in its custody. Owner agrees to release and hold the Farm harmless for any and all losses resulting from accident, injury, disease, theft, vandalism, lightning, flood, earthquake, or other act of God, whether foreseeable or not.

The Owner agrees to be solely responsible for the behavior of the horse or horses being boarded and specifically agrees to indemnify and hold the Farm harmless for any and all damages resulting in any way from the boarding of the Owner's horse or horses. The Owner agrees to reimburse the Farm for reasonable attorney fees and costs that arise from defending a lawsuit related to injuries or damage caused by, or related to, the horse or horses being boarded.

WARNING
Under Kentucky law, a farm animal activity sponsor, farm animal professional, or other person does not have the duty to eliminate all risks of injury of participation in farm animal activities. There are inherent risks of injury that you voluntarily accept if you participate in farm animal activities.

F.   **6. Duties, Rights, and Authority.** The Farm shall have all reasonable authority and discretion with respect to the keep, maintenance, care, management, and supervision of each horse. In addition, the Farm shall have the authority to choose the veterinarians to treat and care for each horse, and further authority to take whatever action the Farm, its agents, and employees deem best for the care of each horse, including, but not limited to, surgical procedures and all other veterinary treatment it elects to authorize. The Farm agrees to attempt to contact Owner at the telephone numbers shown below regarding extraordinary veterinary decisions or actions to take. It is specifically understood, however, that failure to contact Owner shall in no way abrogate the authority hereinabove granted.

7. Dangerous Condition/Illness. The Farm reserves the right to refuse to accept for boarding or to keep any horse if the Farm determines that the horse may be dangerous to life or property. Owner agrees to immediately remove any and all horses upon notice of such condition. The Farm reserves the right to refuse to accept for boarding any horse if the Farm determines that the horse is ill at the time of delivery to the Farm.

G.   **8. Term.** This contract shall remain in force unless and until it is terminated by either party upon one month's written notice. The terms and provisions hereinabove stated shall apply until each horse leaves the care of the Farm. Owner agrees to promptly remove any horse or horses upon the termination of this Agreement. A party in material breach of this contract shall reimburse the non-breaching party for reasonable attorney fees and costs directly resulting from the breach.

9. Assignment. This Agreement cannot be assigned by Owner without the express written consent of the Farm.

H.   **10. Security Interest.** Owner hereby grants and conveys to the Farm a security interest in the horse or horses being boarded to secure the payment of all costs (including attorney fees) associated with the horse or horses and hereby appoints _____ as his irrevocable attorney-in-fact to file any and all necessary financing statements to perfect said security interest. This contract may serve as a financing statement. The parties specifically agree that the Farm may exercise any and all rights of a secured party under Article IX of the Uniform Commercial Code.

I.   **11. Agister's Lien.** This Agreement does not affect and is in addition to the rights of the Farm which arise pursuant to Kentucky Revised Statutes (hereinafter "KRS") 376.400 and KRS 376.440.

12. Controlling Law. This Agreement shall be governed by and construed under the prevailing law of the Commonwealth of Kentucky, and venue for any action shall be _____ County, Kentucky.

13. Attorney Fees. In the event the Farm is required to institute litigation to collect any sums due it hereunder, the Farm shall be entitled to recover its reasonable attorney fees and costs expended, in addition to any other remedies.

J.   IN WITNESS WHEREOF, the parties have set their hands as of the day and year first above written.

FOR THE OWNER :   FOR THE FARM:

_____   _____

_____   _____

(TITLE)

_____

_____

_____

blank documents that can be found in a number of books aimed at the do-it-yourself horse owner. The money saved by using a generic contract may be small compared to the potential loss if a form contract fails to provide the anticipated protection for a specific business.

Form contracts can be a valuable starting point when drafting a contract. It is essential, however, that you understand your individual needs and how to modify the form contract to meet the desired goals. Mistakes are easy to make, and they can be costly!

Every contract should include several common elements, and you should be familiar with them, whether you are working with your attorney in drafting a contract, attempting to customize a generic fill-in-the-blanks contract from a book, or simply considering whether to sign a contract prepared by someone else. One of the more common uses of written contracts is for boarding horses. The sample boarding contract on pages 88–89 is provided for informational purposes only and is not intended to meet the specific needs of any particular horse business. It would be prudent to consult with an attorney before attempting to adapt this contract, or any other generic document, for your own business.

Also you need to keep in mind that boarding contracts generally are prepared by, and for the benefit of, farm owners, but this is not always the case. Many boarding farms do not use written contracts, and in those situations it is the responsibility of the horse owner to insist on a written contract. Boarders have a right to be protected by a written agreement, and they can — and should — insist on one. If the boarding establishment does not have a written contract, boarders should be prepared to offer contracts of their own.

Finally, contracts are about negotiation. Every term in any contract, whether a fill-in-the-blanks form contract or a custom document, is negotiable. When you are offered a contract, you should carefully read the agreement and object to any term that is problematic.

Several of the more important provisions in a sample boarding contract for a farm located in Kentucky are explained in the following pages. (The letters in front of each section refer to the corresponding section in the sample contract on pages 88–89.)

EXPLANATION

A. *Identify the Parties*

Every contract should identify by name, address, telephone numbers (land line and mobile), and e-mail the persons or businesses that are parties to the agreement. If one, or both, of the parties is a business, the contract also should include a statement that the person executing the contract actually has authority to act for the business he or she represents. The effective date of the contract also should be included somewhere in the document, and adding it to the first section is common.

B. *Identify the Horse/Horses*

Any time a horse is the subject of a contract, whether for boarding, leasing, sale or purchase, or breeding, the written agreement should clearly identify the animal. The horse can be identified in the body of the contract itself, or, in this example, by reference to a separate document that identifies the horse or horses being boarded. Using a separate identifying document may be simpler if movement of horses is anticipated because it may be easier to modify the boarding letter than the contract.

The reasons for this identification requirement should be obvious, because misidentifications can, and do, happen. The description should be sufficient to easily identify the horse in question and should include color, markings, breed, sex, age, any registration number tattoos or freeze brands, and scars or other distinctive points. A photograph can be attached to the contract and can make it easier to separate one "bay, no white" from another.

It also is important to record in detail the physical condition of the animal and any indications of previous injury. The horse owner may provide similar information, but the animal's condition should be assessed upon arrival by the farm owner. Any discrepancies with the information provided by the horse owner should be resolved immediately to avoid later claims that a pre-existing injury was suffered while the horse was being boarded. This should be done before you assume responsibility for the animal, for the same reason that prudent customers carefully examine a rental car for dents and scratches and report them to the rental agent before driving the car away from the lot.

Any tack or other equipment accompanying the horse also should be listed and identified to avoid later disputes about ownership of those items.

C. Who Pays What, When, and How Much?

Board charges can be calculated on a "per day" or "per month" basis. The latter is more common because the monthly bill is not dependent on the number of days in the month and less bookkeeping is required. "Per day" charges, on the other hand, make it easier to prorate a bill for a boarder who arrives or leaves in the middle of a month.

The contract should show when the farm will provide a bill to the boarder (every month is standard), and when the boarder must pay the bill. A board bill usually becomes due on the first of every month, with a grace period of a few days before the bill becomes overdue. For the farm's protection, the contract should include a provision allowing the farm to charge interest on overdue bills. The interest rate on overdue bills, such as 1.5 percent per month, also should be stated.

The contract should specify which out-of-pocket expenses the owner is responsible for. Out-of-pocket expenses might include veterinary and farrier services; vaccinations and deworming; transportation to shows, the racetrack, or the breeding shed; and any other special requirements. Also stated in the contract should be whether out-of-pocket expenses will be paid by the farm and then billed to the owner or billed directly to the owner by the person providing the service. The latter is more convenient for the farm owner, but a supplier might prefer to bill the farm rather than risk non-payment from an unknown horse owner.

Finally, the contract should explain the nature of each bill. For example, the bill due on May 1 could include the board charges for the coming month (requiring a boarder to pay in advance protects the farm), plus any out-of-pocket expenses that were incurred during the preceding month.

Many boarding contracts include the phrase "In consideration of $_____ " or similar language. In this context, "consideration" is a legal concept that refers to the money paid by the boarder to the farm owner. It represents the inducement for the farm owner to provide the promised boarding services. Consideration of some kind is necessary for a valid contract.

The contract should state that the farm will provide normal and reasonable care, and it should explain in detail the services and facilities the farm is agreeing to provide as part of the board. These can include stall or pasture board, turn-out service, exercise, grooming, training, and anything else about which the parties can agree. Whether you are the farm owner or the boarder, it is important to understand what will and will not be provided. Any special instructions relating to the horse's care also should be explained in detail.

D. Are You Insured?

Most horses are not insured. If an animal is covered by mortality or loss-of-use insurance, the owner in the boarding contract should note that fact. Most insurance carriers require the company be notified when an insured animal is injured or dies, and the contract should state whether the farm has a responsibility to notify the insurance company.

A statement that the farm does not carry insurance covering boarding horses (as is usually the case) and that the owner of the horse understands and agrees to board the animal under those circumstances also should be included in the contract.

E. The Exculpatory Clause

Most attorneys recommend including in boarding contracts an exculpatory clause in which the boarder agrees to a waiver of the farm's liability for personal injuries or injuries to the horse. (Liability is discussed in greater detail in Chapter 7.) This is important because of the nature of a boarding transaction.

When one party (here the horse owner, or bailor) delivers property to another (the farm owner, or bailee), the legal result is a "bailment." A bailment generally does not create a fiduciary relationship between the parties, such as that of a trustee or guardian, in which a duty to act for the benefit of the horse owner would be imposed by law on the owner of the farm. A bailment does impose upon the person accepting the property (the farm owner) the duty to exercise ordinary care.

The common-law rule in nearly every state is that when a bailment is created, the farm owner into whose care the boarded horse is entrusted is presumed to be responsible for any harm suffered by the horse. If a lawsuit arises, the presumption that the farm was at fault can be overcome by evidence that, more likely than not, the farm exercised ordinary care. This can be difficult to prove.

Kentucky has adopted a farm-friendly statute that shifts the burden of proof from the farm owner (who most everywhere else must prove that reasonable care was exercised) to the horse owner (who must prove that the injury was the result of negligence). Also, in recent years many states have imposed limitations on liability (generally for personal injury) for harm suffered while engaging in equine activities. Such laws frequently require inclusion of statutory language in contracts, and this example includes the warning language required in Kentucky. An attorney familiar with the laws of your state can advise whether such statutes should affect the decision to include an exculpatory clause in your boarding contract.

There is no required wording for an exculpatory clause. The parties should agree that while the contract is in force, the horse owner assumes all risk of loss for the animal. The boarder also should agree to hold the farm harmless for any and all injuries to the horse. The exculpatory clause should include a waiver for negligence although a court in your state may be reluctant to allow a party to eliminate liability for negligence by contract.

Depending on the state in which your farm is located, exculpatory clauses may not be strictly enforceable. Exculpatory clauses can be valuable nevertheless. Your farm liability insurance carrier may require such a clause as a prerequisite for coverage, and the fact that a boarder has agreed to a waiver of liability might discourage a lawsuit.

A boarding contract should include a "hold harmless" clause for the farm's protection. When executing a hold-harmless clause, the horse owner agrees to hold the farm owner without responsibility for damage or injury caused by the horse while it is being boarded. Hold-harmless provisions typically require the owner of the horse to pay any legal fees or other expenses incurred by the farm owner in defending a lawsuit based on harm caused by the boarded horse.

A typical situation would be where a farm visitor is kicked or bitten by the horse being boarded. If the injured party decides to sue the farm owner, the horse owner has agreed to be responsible for the injury and for any legal fees that arise because of the litigation.

A hold-harmless clause is not all encompassing, however. Public policy concerns generally prevent a farm owner from contracting away liability for his or her own negligence. A hold-harmless clause probably would not eliminate liability for a farm owner who negligently leaves a gate open, allowing a boarder's horse to escape to the highway and cause an accident.

F. Call 911!

Horses have a peculiar affinity for getting sick or hurt, and, paradoxically, emergencies in the horse business can become almost routine. One of the most important clauses in a boarding contract deals with authorization for emergency veterinary care, both for the physical welfare of the horse and the economic welfare of the parties.

The farm owner obviously should attempt to contact the horse's owner before authorizing major veterinary procedures, but if the owner is out of reach, the contract should give the farm authority to contact a veterinarian on the owner's behalf and to authorize appropriate veterinary care. If the boarder wishes to use a veterinarian other than one routinely employed by the farm, that veterinarian should be identified in the contract, and the boarder should provide contact numbers.

The farm owner and boarder also should agree on how any bill for emergency care will be handled. Will the farm owner pay and then bill the boarder, for example, or should the bill go directly to the horse owner?

G. All Good Things Must Come to an End

A boarding contract should anticipate a time when the parties no longer wish to be bound by its terms. A contract term of one year is common. The contract should require written notice at least thirty days in advance if either party intends to terminate the contract. The contract also should provide for termination if either party violates the terms of the agreement, called a "breach of contract," and the party not in breach should be allowed to recover attorney fees and court costs, if any, resulting from the default.

H. Consensual Security Interest

Dealing with unpaid bills for board and out-of-pocket expenses is one of the most frustrating tasks for the owner of a boarding farm and, like the question of liability, warrants a separate chapter in this book. An obvious remedy, selling the horse to recover the bill, may not be as straightforward as it sounds. Remember that a horse is the personal property of the owner, and an attempt to sell the animal without legal authority to do so may be considered theft (a criminal offense) or conversion (a civil tort that can give rise to a lawsuit).

One way to address the problem is to include in the boarding contract a provision granting the farm a security interest in the horse. The contract should state that the farm has a secured interest in the horse to guarantee payment for services provided by the farm and for unpaid out-of-pocket expenses, and that the farm may sell the horse in a commercially reasonable way, either at a public auction or privately, to recover the unpaid balance. Those are among the rights guaranteed to a secured party under Article IX of the Uniform Commercial Code, which has been adopted in some form in nearly all the states. An attorney familiar with the laws in your state can provide advice about the proper wording.

The contract also should state how long an overdue bill must be delinquent before the farm owner can resort to self-help. If the horse must be sold, and the sale price obtained is greater than the amount owed, any excess must be returned to the horse's now former owner.

I. Statutory Liens

Many states have statutes that give a farm owner a security interest in a boarded horse when bills are not paid, and many farm owners prefer to rely on these agister's liens rather than ask for a security interest in a boarding contract. (Agister is legalese for a person who boards livestock.) Unlike a consensual security interest, which depends on the written contract and agreement between the parties, a statutory lien arises as a matter of law when a horse is boarded. The reference in the sample contract is to the statutory lien in Kentucky.

While statutory liens can be helpful, the procedures that must be followed are complicated and generally require the farm owner to file a lawsuit, win a judgment, and then proceed against the owner of the horse as a judgment creditor. The contract also should include a provision allowing the farm to recover attorney fees in the event legal assistance is required to recover a delinquent bill. Whether you choose to include a security interest provision in your boarding contract, you should require the horse owner to identify any existing liens already lodged against the horse.

Liens and security interests are discussed in greater detail in Chapter 6.

J. Signatures

Each party to a contract should sign the document but only after reading it, making certain nothing has been left blank and being satisfied that the document actually reflects the agreement. It is a good practice to provide a signed original for each party.

Not included in the sample contract, but certainly worth considering, is a clause requiring arbitration or mediation for dispute resolution.

A BREEDING CONTRACT

Some terms, such as identification of the parties, should be included in every contract. Most terms will be dictated by the nature of the transaction, however. Consider a contract for breeding a mare to a stallion. This common contract is an essential but frequently overlooked part of the process. After putting in an often substantial amount of time and effort picking a stallion, then getting an initial commitment from the stallion manager, it is tempting simply to give the breeding contract a cursory reading, sign it, and drop the document in the mail.

Haste often truly makes waste in situations like these, however, and time spent familiarizing yourself with the terms of the contract *before you sign* will be well spent. The intent of this section is to present an overview of some, but certainly not all, of the important provisions and concepts you might encounter in a breeding contract, from the perspective of the mare owner.

When reviewing any contract, it is important to understand that few documents are truly neutral. A contract generally is drafted in favor of the party offering it. This doesn't mean that such a contract is unfair, but it does mean that the advantages conferred by the agreement will favor the party that had it written. A boarding contract drafted for a farm owner probably might show liability shifted to the horse owner, for example, and may allow only a very short period before an account is considered in default. An agreement for the same boarding transaction drafted in favor of the horse owner, on the other hand, might shift liability to the farm and keep an account out of default longer.

Contract terms are negotiable. If an offered contract truly is unfair, you can ask for the terms to be changed. Or you can elect to do business with someone else.

Stud Fees

The amount of the stud fee, and the circumstances under which it must be paid, are vitally important to the owners of both the mare and stallion. The amount of the stud fee is straightforward and should be set out in the contract; the circumstances under which the fee must be paid vary from contract to contract.

The majority of breeding contracts specify that the stud fee is payable on a "live foal" basis. Under a live-foal contract, the mare owner is responsible for the entire stud fee if, and when, the mare produces a live foal. The term "live foal" generally is understood to mean a foal that is able to stand and nurse without assistance, but the term should be defined in the contract. With a live-foal guarantee, the stallion owner assumes the risk that the breeding will not produce a live foal. Without a live-foal guarantee, the mare owner bears the risk of the mare failing to produce a live foal. Insurance, discussed in Chapter 8, should be considered in these cases.

Depending on the contract, a mare owner may be required to pay the full stud fee in the fall of the year in which the mare is bred, with a refund if the mare does not produce a live foal the following spring, or the stud fee might not be due until the mare actually produces a live foal. A veterinarian's certificate attesting to the fact that the mare did not produce a live foal

AT A GLANCE

- Key provisions in a typical breeding contract include the stud fee arrangement, statements regarding the mare's and stallion's breeding soundness, and a security agreement.
- Read the contract thoroughly and understand the provisions *before* signing.
- Contracts are usually written in favor of the party offering it. If you don't like the terms, negotiate or go elsewhere.

must be submitted to the stallion owner or manager, either to receive a refund of the stud fee if already paid or to avoid responsibility for the stud fee if not paid the previous fall. The contract can also specify whether the owner of a mare that does not produce a live foal is entitled to a return breeding to the stallion at no cost rather than a refund of the stud fee.

Most breeding contracts will require that the mare owner submit the veterinarian's certificate within a set period, sometimes as short as fifteen days, after the mare fails to produce a live foal. If the mare owner misses the prescribed deadline, the obligation to pay the stud fee remains, regardless of whether the mare produced a live foal.

It is possible that the breeding contract will simply make payment of the stud fee contingent on a live foal, with no other explanation. Presented with such an ambiguous contract, a mare owner should insist that "live foal" be defined and that the payment schedule is set out in detail. The contract also should specify whether the birth of twins constitutes production of a "live foal" for stud fee purposes.

A variation of the live-foal agreement is a "guaranteed in foal" contract. If your breeding contract contains this provision, the stallion owner assumes the risk that your mare will get in foal from the breeding, but you assume the risk that the mare will produce a live foal eleven months later.

Under such an agreement, the mare owner is responsible for the full stud fee if the mare is in foal at some specified time (typically forty-five to sixty days) after she is last bred to the stallion. If the mare loses her foal after that date or fails to produce a live foal, the stallion owner is not obligated to refund the stud fee. Once again, a veterinarian's certificate attesting to the fact that the mare is not in foal on the specified date is necessary to avoid responsibility for the stud fee.

A less common type of stud fee arrangement is the "no guarantee" or "non-refundable" contract. Here, the stallion owner assumes none of the risk, and the mare owner is responsible for the stud fee regardless of whether the mare ever conceives. No-guarantee contracts are most common for well-established, proven stallions whose reputations and popularity allow their managers to call all the shots when negotiating with mare owners.

Finally, a few breeding contracts attempt to split the responsibility, designating a portion of the stud fee as non-refundable, while making payment of the rest of the fee contingent on production of a live foal.

Health of the Mare

It is understood, and most breeding contracts specifically require, that any mare sent to a stallion must be in good general health and in sound breeding condition. The contract may require that a veterinarian's certificate accompany the mare to the breeding shed. Mare owners also may have to submit an information sheet for the mare, setting out the animal's health and breeding history, vaccination schedules, and other pertinent information.

Contracts generally give the stallion manager the right to refuse to breed any mare if the breeding would endanger the health or welfare of the stallion. This provision could include mares that are vicious or unmanageable, as well as mares that are sick.

Health of the Stallion

A wide variety of circumstances can arise that make it impossible for a stallion manager to fulfill his or her contractual obligations to mare owners. The stallion might die, be injured, or become too ill to breed; the stallion might be sold and moved out of the area; the horse might become infertile; or the size of his book might be reduced. Under these or similar circumstances, most breeding contracts become null and void, and neither the stallion manager nor the mare owner has any obligation to the other party. Some contracts give the mare owner access to another stallion, if feasible.

Substitution of Mares

So what happens if a mare is booked to a stallion, and then the mare gets sick or dies? Can another mare be substituted under those circumstances? Maybe, depending on the contract and the timing.

Many breeding contracts allow a mare owner to substitute one mare for another, if the mare originally booked to the stallion dies or becomes unfit for breeding *before* she is bred to the stallion for the first time in a season. Mare owners generally are prohibited from substituting one mare for another if the mare originally booked to the stallion already has been bred at least once to the horse. If the contract allows substitution of one mare for another, a veterinarian's certificate stating that the original mare cannot be bred is required.

Occasionally, particularly when a manager is trying to fill the book of a young stallion, a mare owner will be required to breed a substitute mare to the horse if the original mare cannot be bred for some reason.

Security Agreement

Nearly all breeding contracts include a security agreement that gives the stallion owner or manager a way to force payment of the stud fee if the mare owner welches on the obligation. Your signature on a contract with such a provision transfers a security interest in the mare, in the foal resulting from the breeding (both before and after birth), and in the foal's registration documents, to the stallion owner or manager. Many contracts also allow the stallion owner or manager to retain the breeding certificate until the stud fee is paid.

The implication of such security agreements is two-fold. First, by retaining a security interest in the mare and foal, and in the foal's registration papers, the stallion owner or manager can more easily repossess and sell the mare and foal if necessary to pay the bill. Second, without a breeding certificate, the owner of the mare may have difficulty registering the foal; depending on the rules of the particular breed registry, registration may be impossible. Both possibilities are powerful incentives for a mare owner to pay the agreed-upon stud fee.

Other Provisions

Mare owners also should expect to find the following provisions in a typical breeding contract:

• Complete identification of the stallion, mare, mare owner, and stallion owner or manager, and farm where the stallion stands;

• Addresses and emergency contact numbers for all the parties to the contract;

• A statement that the stallion owner or manager has a good and marketable title to the season being sold, and that there are no liens on the season;

CASE STUDIES

Beason v. Bemak N.V., d/b/a Ashford Stud, unpublished case, No. 2002-CA-002490-MR (Ky App, rendered April 9, 2004)

Attention should be paid to the terms of a contract because the document sometimes does not actually say what one, or both, of the parties intended. In this case "Beason and Ashford Stud were experienced horse breeders" who "had contracted for stallion service contracts before." Beason entered into an agreement to breed two of his mares to Thoroughbred stallions standing at Ashford near Versailles, Kentucky. The stud fee for one horse was $40,000, for the second $20,000. Both of the mares produced foals, which were sold at the Keeneland fall yearling sales for $3,000 and $2,000.

Relying on a provision in the stallion service contracts stating that the stud fees "shall be due and payable from … sales proceeds," Beason dutifully paid Ashford the $5,000 realized from the sale of the two yearlings but refused to pay the $55,000 difference owed. He argued that he "negotiated a contract with Ashford to pay the fees from a specific fund, that being the sales proceeds, and that he had no individual liability to pay any sum in excess of the sales proceeds." Beason argued that he was a small breeder who could not afford the stud fees of $40,000 and $20,000 and would not have entered into the contract if he had personal liability for the fees.

Ashford, understandably, interpreted the stallion service contracts differently. Relying on standard language used in all its stallion service contracts, Ashford argued that the clause was added at Beason's request and that it merely postponed the date upon which the full stud fees would be due. The trial court agreed and awarded Ashford $55,000 for the outstanding stud fee balance, plus applicable sales tax, interest, and attorney fees.

The Kentucky Court of Appeals agreed with the trial court and affirmed the judgment in Ashford's favor. The court found that taken as a whole the stallion service contract made "clear that the service fee is due and owing at the time a live foal is born. The additional clause in the contract at issue here merely provided additional time (through the date the foals were auctioned) before such payment was due. There is no basis in the contract or the record for the court to find that Ashford agreed to release Beason from the contractual sum due and owing should the foals sell for less than the service fee."

The Court of Appeals did not address the question of whether Beason tried to offer oral testimony to support his interpretation of the contract. Generally, oral testimony (called "parol evidence") of an earlier agreement cannot be used to vary or contradict the terms of a written contract unless there is evidence of fraud, duress, or mutual mistake by the parties.

Jewett, d/b/a Walnut Hall Limited v. Hertrich and Arno, unpublished case, No. 02-CI-03440 (Ky App, rendered July 2, 2004)

In early 2002 the defendants, Hertrich and Arno, entered into a stallion syndicate agreement with Walnut Hall Ltd., a Standardbred farm near Lexington, Kentucky. The subject of the agreement, Western Shooter, was a two-year-old at the time and was not scheduled to enter stud until after his three-year-old year. Hertrich and Arno bought one share each under the following terms: a $10,000 down payment followed by three annual payments of $10,000 plus interest. Their total investment would be $80,000 for two shares.

Before making the down payment, the defendants expressed concern that Western Shooter might not perform as well as expected on the track. They received a letter from Walnut Hall allowing them to "cancel your purchase of two shares in Western Shooter and receive a full refund of the $20,000 paid for the first installment." To be effective the cancellation had to take place on or before January 15, 2003. Satisfied that their interests were protected, Hertrich and Arno made the first payment.

A separate purchase agreement required all purchasers of a share in Western Shooter, including the defendants, to obtain mortality insurance on the horse in an amount that was at least equal to the unpaid balance for a share. The provision also stated that Walnut Hall was entitled to the unpaid balance if Western Shooter died.

In late March 2002 Western Shooter died, and Walnut Hall sent the defendants a letter demanding payment of the balance owed for their shares. Hertrich and Arno, who had not acquired mortality insurance, refused to pay the $60,000 and also demanded the initial down payment returned based on the letter allowing them to cancel their purchase prior to January 15, 2003. They argued that the letter released them from any liability or obligation to purchase mortality insurance for Western Shooter. Both sides filed suit, Walnut Hall asking for the $60,000 balance and Hertrich and Arno asking for the return of their $20,000 down payment.

The trial court determined that Hertrich and Arno won as a matter of law and ordered that their down payment be returned. On appeal, however, the Kentucky Court of Appeals reversed the lower court.

Three documents controlled the transaction: the cancellation letter, a syndicate agreement, and a purchase agreement. The defendants argued that the letter, the syndicate agreement, and the purchase agreement together constituted one document, and that the letter suspended the effectiveness of everything until January 15, 2003, the date for cancellation. The Court of Appeals disagreed, finding that the letter excused the defendants from the syndicate agreement but not from the purchase agreement. It was the latter agreement that included the requirement for mortality insurance.

The court explained:

> An agreement may have distinguishable parts that control distinct issues and that become effective at different times without being internally inconsistent or contradictory. We believe that the documents at issue were wholly separate, addressing discrete aspects of the transaction and containing separate sets of rights and obligations with respect to those varying interests. The Purchase Agreement governed the sale of the shares; the Syndicate Agreement governed the management of the syndicate. The provision in the letter that the Syndicate Agreement would be binding on Hertrich and Arno after January 15, 2003, is consistent with the fact that the syndicate was not to begin its management operation until the horse had finished racing-even though the actual purchase of the shares occurred a year in advance of his retirement. The Court ruled that the defendants incurred the obligation to purchase mortality insurance (or, in the alternative, to be liable for the balance of the purchase price) upon execution of the purchase agreement in early 2002. Their ability to cancel that purchase agreement at a later date did not eliminate their liability to Walnut Hall for the full purchase price.

The court also determined that the defendants' failure to purchase mortality insurance was a material breach of the contract and that they were not entitled to a refund of the $20,000 down payment.

• Waivers of liability for the stallion owner or manager and the owner of the farm where the stallion stands, in the event the mare is injured;

• The earliest and latest dates on which a mare can be bred;

• Estimated expenses for board, veterinary care, farrier service, and other costs if the mare will be boarded at the farm where the stallion stands; and,

• In states where it is required by laws limiting a farm owner's liability, a notice about inherent risks in equine activities.

Raising a foal can be a daunting job. Understanding a breeding contract before one is signed removes one level of uncertainty from the task.

Boarding, breeding, buying, selling, and leasing are typical business situations when a written contract should be used. While each situation is fact specific, there are basics of contract formation that will be common across the board. Your attorney can provide the best advice about your particular situation.

RESOURCES

Equine Law Forms Compendium, 2nd ed., University of Kentucky College of Law, Office of Continuing Legal Education, Suite 260 Law Building, Lexington, KY 40506. www.uky.edu/Law/cle.

The *Forms Compendium* is far and away the most comprehensive compilation of equine legal forms of all kinds. It is expensive ($315 for a bound volume and CD-ROM; $225 for a bound volume) but worth the price with almost 900 pages and some 150 sample forms.

6

LIENS AND SECURITY INTERESTS

Business transactions can be divided into two general categories —
those in which money is exchanged for goods or services at the time
of the transaction and those in which goods or services are provided in
anticipation of receiving payment at a later date. Paying cash for a bridle at
the local tack store and writing a check to the farrier when he or she comes
to the farm to trim the horses are examples of the former. Selling a horse
to a buyer who will make payments and providing boarding or training
services before a client is sent an invoice are examples of the latter.

The first group of transactions seldom results in payment problems, aside
from an occasional bad check. The second group of transactions, on the
other hand, presents a frequently realized potential for problems. People
fail to pay their bills for a variety of reasons, some legitimate, some not, but
the end result is the same — financial hardship for the business owner.

There is an obvious solution to unpaid bills for many service providers —
simply quit the job, cut your losses, and go home. This option generally is
not available to the person who boards or trains horses for others, however.
Unlike a barn painter, who can limit his loss by refusing to finish the job
when the client refuses to pay, a person who boards horses assumes a moral
(and often legal) responsibility for the continuing welfare of the animals.

Horses neither know nor care whether their board bills are being paid.
Blissfully unaware of their owners' financial problems, they continue to eat,
occupy a stall or pasture, and require regular veterinary care and farrier
services. A trainer may be able to suspend the conditioning of a client's
horse until the bill is paid, but there are both legal and humane reasons to
continue to provide for the basic needs of the horses boarding at your farm.

The result is a delinquent board bill that continues to grow while the profit margin shrinks.

Unpaid bills can be the ruin of any business. Whether you operate a large training stable, a modest boarding farm, or a lesson business, the way you deal with the inevitable client who cannot, or for some reason will not, pay the bills may determine whether the business ultimately succeeds or fails. Fortunately, the impact of unpaid bills often can be minimized through a little advance planning. This chapter addresses several ways to deal with delinquent bills: statutory liens, consensual security interests, agricultural liens under Article 9 of the Uniform Commercial Code, and lawsuits.

THE BASICS OF GETTING PAID

The best solution to delinquent bills and the hard feelings that inevitably result is to avoid them in the first place.

The first step should be an obvious one: Screen your clients. When a potential client whom you do not know approaches you, at the very least you should ask for references. Talking to the owner of a farm where the potential client boarded horses in the past can be an invaluable source of information, for example. If the transaction involves a high-priced horse bought on time, references from bankers and a credit check would be appropriate.

If you decide to ask for references, take the next step and check them. If the potential client refuses to provide references or if a boarder has kept his or her horse at several different farms in the past few months, those should be red flags that require more investigation.

It may be tempting to take on every customer who comes onto the farm, especially for a new business. Keep in mind, though, that a few reliable customers who pay their bills on time without grumbling are far better than a barn full of boarders who can't, or won't, pay.

Second, keep your record keeping up to date and bill regularly. Many small business owners — farm owners included — are caught between the proverbial rock and a hard place. They don't have the time for bookkeeping and may not be very good at the task anyway but at the same time cannot afford to hire an accountant. If you are in this position, bite the bullet, buy a small business bookkeeping software package and learn to use it.

Finally, identify overdue bills as soon as possible and make the client aware that there is a problem. Even if your initial contact with the client is by telephone, follow up with a letter. Certified mail with return receipt provides proof that the communication actually was received. Regular mail and e-mail lack that assurance. If you are forced into court, a thorough paper trail often will help you recover an overdue bill. Clients occasionally forget to pay a bill, of course, and checks really can be lost in the mail. The sooner you inform a client about a payment problem, the sooner the problem can be resolved.

Good communication runs in both directions. If you are a horse owner in financial difficulty, you should contact your creditors, explain the situation, and try to come up with a workable solution. A creditor is much more likely to work with a person who is upfront about a financial problem than with someone who doesn't return telephone calls and letters and is evasive about when a bill might get paid.

Sometimes, though, the best efforts are not good enough, and you find yourself with a growing stack of client bills that you know will not be paid. Depending on the circumstances there are several possible options.

AT A GLANCE

- Clients' unpaid bills are a frustrating part of running a business, but business owners do have recourse through liens, security interests, and lawsuits.
- A lien is an interest in property that secures payment of a debt.
- In theory, agister's liens can give boarding farm owners the right to sell a client's horse to satisfy unpaid bills.
- Buyers should insist on full disclosure of any liens against a horse before purchase.

AGISTER'S LIENS

An "agister," according to the mammoth *Oxford English Dictionary*, is a person who takes in and feeds livestock. In today's parlance, agister is an archaic term for the owner of a boarding farm. The word does not come up often anymore, generally appearing only in state statutes that give agisters a lien on the livestock they board for other people.

A lien is an interest in real or personal property that secures payment of a debt. In the case of an agister's lien the personal property is the horse or horses being boarded and the debt is the overdue board bill. The creditor is the farm owner and the debtor is the horse owner. One important aspect of statutory liens is they arise through the operation of law, without the necessity of an agreement between the parties.

A statutory lien comes into being when a horse is moved onto a boarding farm, without either party having to take any other action. A written contract is not required (although one is always advisable), which means that a statutory lien provides some protection for people who rely on oral boarding agreements.

Even if agister's lien is an unfamiliar term, chances are good that most everyone has had some experience with liens in the past. When a buyer borrows money to purchase a car or truck, for example, the lender probably retained an interest in the vehicle. That interest is a lien, and it protects the lender by creating the right to repossess the vehicle if the buyer does not keep up the monthly payments. A lien also gives the lender the right to recover his money in the event the vehicle is sold before the loan is satisfied.

In theory, at least, an agister's lien statute gives a farm owner the right to sell a client's horse and apply the proceeds of the sale to satisfy the delinquent board bill. In practice, however, things usually are not that simple. Most states have some form of agister's lien statutes on their books, but the terminology and requirements vary greatly among jurisdictions. With that caveat in mind, it is essential that a farm owner be aware of the nuances of his or her state's law before taking any action involving a client's horse.

In some states, for example, a person who boards horses on a farm that is leased rather than owned may not be a qualified lienholder. In such a circumstance, an attempt to sell a client's horse to cover a board bill could be conversion, a legal term for taking another person's property without the right to do so. Civil penalties for conversion can be levied against the seller, as well as possible criminal charges for theft or unlawful taking.

Agister's lien statutes vary regarding which charges can be recovered by a farm owner using the statutory procedures. Third-party charges for things such as vanning, some veterinary care, advertising, and sales preparation may be recoverable in some states but not in others. Some states have "possessory liens," which means that the lien is lost if the horses are removed from the property. "Non-possessory liens," on the other hand, remain in force even though the lienholder no longer has physical possession of the collateral property.

The statutory language in your state, as well as any applicable case law interpreting that language, should be reviewed to determine the scope of the law. Agister's lien statutes for many states are listed in the appendix to this book.

Many other questions must be answered based on your state's specific statutes. This chapter provides some general direction, but for answers directly related to the particular circumstances at your boarding farm, you should consult an attorney familiar with your state laws and with equine issues.

Who can take advantage of an agister's lien?

By definition, an agister's lien works for the benefit of the owner of a boarding farm. Whether your state's laws are expansive enough to include the bills of a trainer who keeps horses at the racetrack or third-party expenses depends on the language in the statutes and courts' interpretations of that language. Some states also may provide separate protection for veterinarians and others.

When does the lien take effect?

In some states the lien comes into existence at the time the board charges are incurred, without any further action on the part of the farm owner. Some other states' statutes require a farm owner to take subsequent action, often in court, to validate (the legal term is "perfect") the lien. The distinction is important.

If the statute requires some action by the farm owner to perfect the lien, such as posting public notices prior to the sale of the client's horse or filing an action in court, the farm owner has no right to sell or retain the client's horse until the required action is taken. In a state where a farm owner must perfect the lien in some manner, prior sale of the horse could amount to conversion, and the farm owner could wind up with legal bills far in excess of the delinquent board bill.

What happens if the horse is returned to the owner before the board bill is paid?

It should be obvious that a boarding farm owner is in a stronger position if he or she retains physical possession of the horse, both practically and legally. A farm owner cannot sell a horse that is in someone else's control, and there are instances in which relinquishing possession of the animal defeats the lien.

In some states the farm owner has a lien on a client's horse only so long as the horse remains in the lienholder's possession. This is the possessory lien discussed earlier. In those states a farm owner's lien will be defeated if the horse is returned to the client while the bill is still outstanding. The circumstances under which the client regains possession also may be important. A client who slips onto the farm under cover of night to take back his or her horse may not defeat the lien, and he or she may be guilty of trespassing as well.

The agister's lien statutes in some states explicitly allow the farm owner to retain the horses until the overdue bill is satisfied. Without such legal authority a farm owner may be on shaky ground by refusing to return the animal to its owner.

In other states the lien's validity does not depend on whether the farm owner has retained the horse or returned the animal to the client. These are non-possessory liens. In those states where the lien is not defeated by return of the horse to the client, the farm owner retains a secured interest in the horse even after the animal is returned to the client, and the lienholder should be able to demand satisfaction of the lien if the horse later is sold. Even if a lien is non-possessory, however, the duration of the lien may be limited. In Kentucky, for example, an agister's lien lasts only one year after a horse is removed from the boarding farm.

What are the consequences if the farm owner refuses to return the horse to the client upon demand?

Because of the potential problems that can arise if the horse is returned to the client, generally it is to the farm owner's advantage to retain possession of the horse if at all possible. A minority of state statutes give the farm owner the explicit right to retain the horse while other statutes do so only implicitly. If a farm owner has no legal right to retain the horse, refusal to return the animal to the owner upon demand could amount to conversion and might result in civil and/or legal penalties.

If your state's statutes authorize sale of the horse to satisfy the lien, how must the sale be conducted?

State statutes also differ in the requirements they impose for a valid sale to satisfy an agister's lien, and a farm owner must be familiar with the requirements in his or her locale. There may be, for example, time limits imposed by law that a farm owner must observe. A few statutes allow the lienholder to conduct the sale of the horse if there is proper notice, but in virtually all cases it is a safer course for the farm owner to enter the horse in a recognized public auction, if possible. Satisfying a lien by selling the horse at a recognized auction may generate a higher price and also will make it more difficult for the client to claim later that the horse was not sold for a fair price.

Selling the horse for a fair price is important for two related reasons. If the horse sells for more than the outstanding board bill and associated expenses, the owner of the horse will be entitled to the difference. But if the horse sells for less than the board bill, the horse owner generally will remain liable to the farm owner for the difference. It is to everyone's advantage to sell the horse for the highest possible price.

If a horse must be sold to satisfy a lien, how are the proceeds of the sale distributed?

This is not a problem if the only interests in a horse are the animal's owner and the owner of the boarding farm. However, in many situations, the farm owner may not be the only party with a security interest in a particular horse. A bank that has loaned money to a person to buy a horse probably has a secured interest in the animal (just as the bank retained a lien on a buyer's car), and there also may be other statutory liens in addition to the farm owner's lien. In Kentucky, for example, a statutory lien is created in favor of a veterinarian for work done. You may need the assistance of an attorney to help you sort things out if there are competing interests.

The priority of competing interests must be resolved before the proceeds of a sale can be distributed. In other words, even if you do everything required under your state's statutes, you still might wind up without the ability to recover the full amount of the overdue bills. There also will be situations in which the attorney fees and other costs associated with recovering an overdue bill are larger than the bill itself. You need to be prepared to cut your losses and give up if necessary.

In sum, agister's lien statutes create significant rights for a farm owner, but those statutes can be minefields for the unwary. The statutory requirements must be followed or your rights may not be protected. And some agister's lien statutes may allow you to recover only board charges and related expenses but not third-party charges such as payments you make to a farrier, veterinarian, or van service. It is better to know the fine points of your state's statutory lien scheme before you need to put the law into effect.

Some statutes also might be unconstitutional because they do not provide for sufficient due process of law — the debtor's right to notice and a hearing before his or her property is seized and sold. If courts in your state have questioned the constitutionality of local agister's lien statutes and possibly found them lacking, a safer course of action may be to sue in state court for the delinquent board bill and then proceed as a judgment creditor. You need the advice of an attorney here. In this way, judicial determination of the validity of the lien will help forestall subsequent questions from the delinquent client. Depending on the size of the bill, you may be able to proceed in small-claims court without an attorney.

AGRICULTURAL LIENS

The owner of a boarding farm also may be able to utilize an agricultural lien pursuant to Article 9 of the revised Uniform Commercial Code to recover an overdue board bill. The code generally defines an agricultural lien to include statutory liens for goods or services provided to a debtor for his or her farming operation. The goods or services must be provided in the ordinary course of the lienholder's business operation and the statutory lien must not depend on possession of the collateral. Filing with the state generally is required to perfect an agricultural lien unless the collateral is in the possession of the lienholder.

Whether an agricultural lien is available in any particular state is a very fact-intensive question. Considerations include the version of the Uniform Commercial Code adopted in your state, whether your state's agister's lien is possessory or non-possessory, and how your state laws define horses and farming operations. In some states, for example, horses might be classified as farm products even if the debtor's business does not classify as a "farming" operation. Other states may make a different distinction.

Availability of an agricultural lien and its enforcement are questions best answered by your attorney.

CONSENSUAL SECURITY INTERESTS

In the best of all possible worlds, all clients would pay their bills on time, without complaint. No one lives in that world, of course, and the inevitability of unpaid board bills should encourage you to include a security interest clause in your written boarding contracts. By doing so, you will facilitate the process if you are forced to sell a boarder's horse to satisfy a delinquent bill.

A consensual security interest represents an agreement between the parties, which can be both an advantage and a disadvantage. The owner of a horse clearly can give a farm owner permission to sell a horse to satisfy an overdue board bill, which greatly simplifies things for the farm owner. Some horse owners will be reluctant to give a farm owner a security interest in a horse, however, and the farm owner may have to choose between demanding a security interest and losing a client.

Language similar to the following should be included in a consensual security interest clause. This sample is provided for informational purposes only and is not intended to meet the particular needs of any individual situation.

> **SECURITY INTEREST: To secure full payment of all charges due under this boarding contract, including attorney fees and costs, the owner of the horse, or horses, identified in Paragraph _____ hereby grants to _____ (the farm owner) a security interest in said horses. In addition, the owner authorizes _____ (the farm owner) and/or his agents to act as attorney-in-fact for the owner of the horse for the purpose of executing any financing statements**

that the owner, in his sole discretion, shall deem necessary to perfect the security interest granted herein. This agreement may serve as a financing statement. Upon failure of the owner of the horse, or horses, identified in Paragraph ____, to make payment in full within thirty (30) days following receipt of any statement, _____ (the farm owner) may declare the owner of the horse, or horses, to be in default and may exercise all rights granted to a secured party under Article 9 of the Uniform Commercial Code and the laws of the state of _____.

The effect of a security interest clause is to give the farm owner all the rights associated with being a secured party under the Uniform Commercial Code, a comprehensive body of law that governs commercial transactions. The code has been adopted in some form in all states. A discussion of the code is well beyond the scope of this book. Your attorney can provide information about the code in your state and its application to your horse business. Relying solely on this book or any other generic reference is dangerous.

In general, a secured party under the Uniform Commercial Code may take possession of collateral (a boarder's horses) after default and may dispose of the collateral in a commercially reasonable manner. This is what a farm owner wants to do: sell the horse for the board bill without a lot of legal hassle. Before proceeding, however, the farm owner (or a potential buyer) should determine whether the breed registry involved will recognize the sale and transfer ownership without a court-ordered sale.

Secured creditors generally must give the horse owner notice of the pending sale. If the creditor sells the horse for a sum greater than the delinquent board bill and the costs associated with the sale, that excess amount usually must be returned to the owner. The owner of the horse may be liable for any deficit still existing after sale of the horse.

You may also have to file certain documents with the state to make your security interest valid (a process called "perfecting" the lien) or to establish priority in the event of multiple security interests. The general rule is that the first security interest or lien filed has priority in the distribution of any funds realized through sale of the collateral. Priority for agister's liens also may be determined by date of filing, unless state law provides a different method.

Whether you choose to include a security interest clause in your boarding contracts, plan to rely on your state's agister's lien statutes, or both, you always should require that the horse owner identify any outstanding liens on the animal. Otherwise, you might wind up as one of several creditors claiming proceeds from the sale of the horse in the event of a default. This situation can arise in several ways.

One of the most common involves a horse owner who has financed the purchase of the animal, either through a commercial lender or though a seller who has agreed to accept payments over time. Until the loan is satisfied the lender or seller almost certainly will have a lien on the horse and the purchase moneylender's lien, if filed earlier, will have priority over your interest.

PROCEEDING AS A JUDGMENT CREDITOR

Talk of liens and security interests and their associated legal complexities sometimes blinds a farm owner to the simple fact that a boarding contract is, foremost, a contract. Assuming that the farm owner has held up his or her end of the bargain and has provided the services set out in the agreement, a boarder who falls behind on a bill can be sued in civil court for breach of contract.

There are advantages and disadvantages to filing a lawsuit for an overdue bill. One advantage is that filing a lawsuit may be less time-consuming for the creditor. In some states only a farm owner can utilize an agister's lien, whereas breach of *any* valid contract can be the subject of a lawsuit. Even if you can utilize your state's agister's lien laws, a lawsuit may be quicker that proceeding according to the statute. This is especially true if the lien statute requires action in one court to establish the lien and action in another court to enforce the lien. In that case filing a lawsuit must happen anyway and jumping ahead may save time.

A court-ordered sale also eliminates some of the uncertainty of agister's lien statutes that do not provide sufficient notice and opportunity for a hearing to the horse owner. A court-ordered sale also may provide more

CASE STUDIES

Carney v. Wallen and Wallen Stables, 2003 Iowa App LEXIS 197, unreported decision (Iowa App 2003)

Although this case was not published by the appellate court in Iowa, which means that it did not establish a legal precedent, the Court's reasoning is illustrative of how agister's lien statutes are interpreted.

Evidence presented at trial showed that Judy Carney signed a written "board and training agreement" with the defendants for one horse in February 1998. Later that year the parties entered into an oral agreement to board and train a second animal, the show horse Lovely Looken. Initially, the Carneys received a single bill from Wallen Stables for both board and training for Lovely Looken. Later, James Wallen, son of the Wallen Stables owner, began sending a separate bill for training the horse. He eventually stopped billing for training. He indicated that the Carneys should continue paying for training at the "usual rate and that he would send separate bills for any additional expenses."

Joan Carney continued to pay the board bills for Lovely Looken, but she did not pay for any training during the time Wallen did not send out bills. Several months later Wallen sent the Carneys a training bill totaling $19,810. Joan Carney refused to pay and attempted to remove the horse from Wallen's care. He refused to give up possession of the horse and claimed a lien on the animal for the outstanding training bill. The Carneys subsequently filed a lawsuit asking that Wallen be ordered to return Lively Looken.

The Iowa agister's lien statute states, in part, that, "Livery and feed stable keepers, herders, feeders, or keepers of stock shall have a lien on all property coming into their hands ... for their charges and the expenses of keeping ..." Relying on a case decided more than a hundred years earlier, in 1895, the Iowa Court determined that the outstanding bill was limited to a fee for training Lovely Looken by James Wallen, and that a trainer did not fit within the statutory definition of an agister.

The Court explained:

> While we acknowledge some of the duties inherent in training a horse may overlap with the duties inherent in keeping a horse, we conclude the statute was not intended to cover trainers of horses who are not keepers, herders, or feeders.

There was no dispute that the board bills sent by Wallen Stables had been paid in full. Because the defendant did not satisfy the statutory definition of an agister, he could not take advantage of the statute to recover his training expenses. The trial court earlier had ordered that Lovely Looken be returned to the Carneys.

legitimacy than the sale of a horse conducted by a farm owner proceeding as a secured party.

One major disadvantage is that filing a lawsuit is expensive. The legal fees easily can exceed the amount recovered if the board bill is relatively small. It may be possible to include attorney fees in the award sought in the lawsuit, especially if your boarding contract has a provision allowing the recovery of such fees, but you shouldn't assume that your attorney fees can be recovered. The general rule in court, the so-called "American rule," is that each party pays his or her own legal fees, win or lose.

Some attorneys take cases on a contingency basis, which means that the attorney does not get paid until the lawsuit is won or settled. Although contingency cases most often are for personal injuries rather than breach of contract, you may be able to locate an attorney who will take your case without money up front. Contingency fee agreements generally give the attorney around one-third of the amount recovered and the client may or may not be expected to pay filing fees and other costs. In most states a contingency agreement must be in writing.

Even the simplest means of securing payment for a board bill in default is fraught with complications. It always will be to the farm owner's advantage to avoid overdue bills than to attempt to collect money after the fact.

BUYER BEWARE

Liens also are important to buyers of horses. If a lien travels with a horse when the animal is sold, the new owner may have difficulty obtaining a clear title. Problems with reselling the horse also may arise.

According to the Uniform Commercial Code a buyer of goods in the regular course of business acquires the goods free of any security interest created by the seller, unless the transaction involves the purchase of farm products such as horses from a person engaged in a farming operation. In that situation the buyer takes possession subject to any liens or security interests that might exist. A buyer obviously should insist on full disclosure of any liens or security interests before purchasing any horse.

The Uniform Commercial Code as adopted in Kentucky includes an important exception. Kentucky Revised Statute 355.9-320(6) provides that the buyer of a racehorse, or an interest in such a horse, at a public auction takes title to the animal free of any lien or security interest. The Kentucky version also insulates the sales company from liability to the lienholder. The lien or security interest does attach to the proceeds of the sale, however, which protects the creditor. Your attorney can identify any similar nuances in your own state's law.

RESOURCES

Selected state agister's lien statutes are listed in the Appendix to this book.

The text of the Uniform Commercial Code and links to the various state versions can be found at www.law.cornell.edu/ucc.

7

LIABILITY

Horses often seem to be accidents waiting to happen, and everyone who has owned horses for any significant period can recount at least one horror story that starts with: "You aren't going to believe this, but ..." Less apparent, but equally true, is the realization that horse businesses, by their very nature, can be "accident prone." Agricultural jobs traditionally are among the nation's most dangerous. Whether horses are your vocation or avocation, it is important to shield yourself from as much potential liability as possible. Failure to do so can be devastating, personally and professionally.

Liability is an extremely broad legal concept, encompassing everything from an obligation to repay a debt to the responsibility everyone has for the consequences of their actions. For someone in the horse business, liability lurks behind every stall door, in every paddock, on every trail, and in every business transaction. When you buy a load of hay on credit, for example, you are incurring a liability, in this case the obligation to pay for the hay at some future point. Such liability, voluntarily assumed, is part of the normal course of doing business and is not the type of liability this chapter will address.

More troublesome is the potential liability that results when your actions cause harm to a third party. Liability for personal injury can include financial responsibility for medical bills, lost wages, loss of consortium, and punitive damages. Liability for damage to another person's property generally is limited to the economic value of the property, but that amount can be substantial.

The sources of potential liability are endless:

- If you board horses for other owners, you might be responsible for damages if one of those horses becomes injured while in your care.

- If you give riding lessons, you might be liable for injuries suffered by one of your riders.

- If you open your land for trail rides, you might be liable if a horse or rider gets hurt on your property.

- If you sell a horse, you may have a duty to disclose certain physical conditions of the animal, and you might be liable for damages if you do not do so.

- If a horse escapes from your property and causes injury to a person, another animal, or someone's property, you might find yourself responsible.

- If you lease your horse to another person, you might be liable if the horse injures the lessee.

- If an employee becomes injured, you might be liable.

- If you agree to transport another person's horse in your trailer, you might be liable if the horse is injured.

- You may even incur liability by doing nothing more than keeping your own horses on your own property. This could happen if a court finds that the horses are an "attractive nuisance," and thus an unreasonable danger to trespassing children who are injured.

The list continues.

Adequate insurance (See Chapter 8.) is a necessity, and you should discuss your needs with a reputable insurance agent who is familiar with the horse business. It should be obvious, though, that the only way to insulate yourself from all potential liability is to abandon the horse business altogether. Few horse enthusiasts are willing to do that, however, and the next best thing is to identify potential problem areas and plan accordingly.

Accidents do happen, no matter how careful a person is, and there always is a risk you will find yourself on the wrong end of a lawsuit. Being blameless does not make you immune from a lawsuit, and being right does not guarantee you will win in court if you are sued. Even if you do win, you likely will be faced with thousands of dollars in legal bills. When dealing with potential liability, it always is better to be safe than sorry. Attorneys like having a client ask them, ahead of time: "This is what I plan to do. Are there any problems?" Attorneys dislike having a client tell them, after the fact: "This is what I did. Can you fix it?"

This chapter addresses several fundamental concepts related to liability and offers some suggestions about how to protect yourself and your business.

PRACTICE PREVENTIVE LEGAL MEDICINE

Many attorneys endorse the concept of a "legal audit," a review of your horse business with emphasis on potential problem areas and possible solutions. If you board horses and do not require written contracts with your boarders, for example, your attorney should be able to recognize the potential problem and draft a suitable document. If you do use a written contract, your attorney can suggest changes, if needed. After reviewing your plans and aspirations, your attorney can identify and thereby help you avoid many of the pitfalls on the path to your business goals.

Whatever your objectives in the horse business — from owning a safe and sound pleasure horse, to managing a band of productive broodmares, to competing successfully on the "A" show circuit — you probably already rely on the expertise of a team of professionals. A veterinarian and farrier are essential members of the team, no matter what the activity, and depending on your goals, you also may need a trainer for your horse and a coach to help hone your own riding skills.

Just as important is your business team. The members should be selected with care and should include an accountant, an attorney, and an insurance agent. All should be familiar with the horse industry. A good accountant can be the difference between a business that shows a profit and one that does not, by offering financial planning and bookkeeping services and

AT A GLANCE

- The sources of potential liability in your horse business are endless.
- A "legal audit" of your business by an attorney can help find potential liability issues and possible solutions.
- Equine activities are inherently dangerous; thus, someone who chooses to participate — in a trail ride, for example — assumes the risk of that activity.

by guiding clients though the maze of state and federal tax laws, payroll questions, and workers' compensation requirements.

Attorneys and insurance agents can help guard a business investment, the former by anticipating problems and drafting written agreements to protect the owner's interests and the latter by providing adequate insurance coverage. An attorney also can help a business owner operate in compliance with local or state laws, among the most important of which are those designed to limit potential liability in certain situations. There will be more about this later.

Locating professionals with experience in the horse business can be simple or difficult, depending on where you live. Personal referrals from other horse owners in your area are probably the best recommendations, and many states' bar associations offer lawyer referral services for attorneys. It is important that the team understands your business operation and your goals. You should have the team in place before you need its services. Prevention and risk management, not damage control, should be your goals.

ASSUMPTION OF THE RISK

A long-standing legal principle is the straightforward idea that an injured person should not be allowed to recover damages resulting from an activity that the person participated in voluntarily, while understanding the hazards. In other words, a person "assumes the risk" of injury if he or she knows that an activity is dangerous but decides to take part anyway.

Assumption of the risk is more than an interesting legal concept. Depending on the facts, it is a defense that may be raised in a personal injury lawsuit to shift responsibility for harm from the defendant to the plaintiff. To be successful, a defendant must prove that an injured plaintiff (1) knew of a dangerous condition, (2) appreciated the nature and extent of the danger, and (3) voluntarily exposed himself or herself to the danger despite knowing of the hazard.

Implicit in the notion of assumption of the risk, at least as it relates to the horse business, is the idea that equine activities are inherently dangerous. An inherent risk is a hazard that is a fundamental and foreseeable consequence of the activity. Being kicked or bitten by a horse is a good example. If a person knows that horses often kick or bite but chooses to participate in an equine activity anyway, it is reasonable to think that the individual assumes the risk of being kicked or bitten.

Assumption of the risk has become a less viable defense in recent years, largely due to the influence of aggressive personal injury attorneys whose television advertisements create the impression that being injured is akin to winning the lottery. The proliferation of personal injury lawsuits and large damage awards by juries led to a meteoric rise in insurance rates for the organizers of horse shows, trail rides, and other recreational activities. Faced with growing concerns over increased liability and decreased profits due to high insurance premiums, the owners of many horse operations were forced out of business.

The legislative response to the situation was passage, in nearly all the states, of legislation that provides some protection for horse businesses. Discussed more fully later in this chapter and in the case studies, these equine activity statutes limit the duty of equine-activity sponsors and insulate them from lawsuits in many circumstances.

NEGLIGENCE

Not every injury that results from participation in an equine activity is the product of an inherent risk, however. While falling off a horse that shies away from a rabbit might be an unfortunate but not unexpected risk of riding, falling off because a stable employee failed to tighten the girth properly or because the tack was faulty is another matter entirely. If injury actually is someone else's fault, an award of damages against the individual causing the harm is proper.

In a very small number of situations generally involving the sale of unreasonably dangerous consumer products, courts will impose liability without a showing of fault on the part of the defendant. This legal concept is called "strict liability," and it has little application to the horse business. Generally, though, some injuries truly are the result of unavoidable accidents, and there is no liability without fault. The fault most often alleged in a personal injury lawsuit is negligence.

In the broadest sense, negligence is the failure to act reasonably given the facts of a particular situation. A reasonable person would be certain that a girth was tight and secure before putting a rider up on a horse, for example, and the failure to do so almost certainly would be negligent. Nor would a reasonable person use tack that was in poor condition.

To succeed on a legal claim of negligence a plaintiff must prove four elements: duty, breach of that duty, harm, and proximate cause.

• *Duty* — A duty is a legal obligation either to take or not take some action. The law imposes a general duty of reasonable care or behavior under the circumstances of the situation, and there may be specific laws that impose additional duties as well. Animal welfare laws that require the owner of an animal to provide adequate food, water, shelter, and veterinary care are good examples of legal duties.

• *Breach of the duty* — If there is no breach of the duty, there is no fault and no negligence. Failure to act reasonably and to follow whatever laws are applicable is a necessary predicate to a claim of negligence.

There also is a distinction between a legal duty imposed by statute or common law and a moral duty resulting from the idea of "doing the right thing." Giving aid to an accident victim may be a legal duty for some first responders or medical professionals, but it is a moral duty only for most civilians. While a moral duty might be more pressing than a legal duty, breach of a moral duty generally does not give rise to a winnable negligence claim.

• *Harm* — This is the "no harm, no foul" rule familiar to everyone who has played pickup basketball. Breach of a duty, no matter how egregious, generally will not sustain a claim of negligence if there was no harm as a result because there is nothing that warrants compensation. A plaintiff who can prove breach of a duty but who suffered no harm has no damages. In a more practical sense, most personal injury attorneys take cases on a contingency basis, which means that the attorney gets paid a hefty percentage of the award (usually about one-third) *if* the lawsuit is successful. Attorneys are reluctant to take a case if there is no reasonable chance of a damages award, and a plaintiff who has suffered no injury will have difficulty finding representation.

• *Proximate cause* — The final element of actionable negligence is a direct relationship between the breach of the duty and the harm suffered. Just as it is possible for there to be a breach of a duty without any resulting harm, it is possible for there to be an injury not directly related to the breach of duty.

Consider the following example. A stable employee fails to tighten the girth for a client who is taking part in a trail ride in a mountainous area. The employee clearly has breached his duty of reasonable care, satisfying the first two elements of a negligence claim. If the saddle slips and the client is injured, the third and fourth elements are satisfied. But if the client is injured by a falling rock before the saddle slips, and the injury is unrelated to the loose girth, the necessary link between the breach of duty and the injury is broken.

A distinction also should be made between "ordinary negligence," the topic of this chapter thus far, and "gross negligence." The latter is more serious and amounts to intentional conduct on the part of the defendant that puts others at risk. The principle difference between the two is that ordinary negligence generally results from inattention or carelessness while gross negligence involves an actual or constructive intent to do harm to a person or property. The difference is especially important in the enforcement of liability waivers. While some courts are reluctant to enforce waivers for ordinary negligence, a waiver for gross negligence almost never will be enforced in court.

In some states, a related defense to a personal injury lawsuit is "contributory negligence," which recognizes the duty of *both* parties to a transaction to act reasonably. While it may be negligent for a stable owner to put a green rider on a green horse, it also may be negligent for the green rider to misrepresent his or her riding ability. Contributory negligence reduces but does not eliminate an award of damages.

Probably the most important thing anyone can do to forestall a lawsuit is to conduct the business in a "reasonable" manner, but you must know what this standard of reasonable care means in practice.

Separating the paddocks of two aggressive breeding stallions with a double row of four-board plank fencing almost certainly is reasonable conduct; separating those two stallions with a single strand of barbed wire probably is not. It is not sufficient that a farm owner did the best he or she could under the circumstances — perhaps a single strand of barbed wire is all the fencing the owner could afford — the standard of care is objective, that of a hypothetical "reasonable person," not subjective, relating to a specific individual. Nor is it always safe to do things the same as everyone else in your area. It is possible, although not likely, that everyone you know fails to meet the reasonable care standard.

On the other hand, reasonable care does not require a superhuman effort. Nor does it require you to always adopt the best option. The fencing examples above represent two extremes, and there may be a middle ground that also would constitute reasonable care under the circumstances. Usually, reasonable care will be simple common sense: Make certain that your fences are in good repair and that no dangerous holes are in the paddocks; inspect stall interiors for nails or other protruding objects; keep tack and other equipment in good repair; be aware of the physical condition of the horses in your care; hire competent help (often easier said than done); match the ability of your riders to your horses; and pay attention.

BAILMENT

Negligence becomes even more problematic if the law presumes that you did not exercise reasonable care, and you must prove that you did. Strange as that might sound, it happens frequently thanks to the law of "bailments," which flips the common notion of innocent until proved guilty on its head.

A bailment has nothing to do with money paid to get a friend out of jail. Instead, a bailment is created when one person (the "bailor") transfers possession of personal property to another individual (the "bailee") for safekeeping. A bailment is created, for example, when you send your horse to another person's farm for boarding or for any other purpose, or when you give your horse to a commercial van driver for transport, or if you leave your horse at a veterinary clinic for treatment.

Bailment does not involve a transfer of ownership of the property, only possession. The bailee has a legal duty to exercise reasonable care with respect to the property until it is returned. If the property cannot be returned to the bailor in the same condition as when it was transferred to the bailee, a rebuttable presumption that the bailee was negligent is created. In a lawsuit for seeking reimbursement for damages to the property, the bailee has the burden of rebutting the presumption of negligence.

A general word about presumptions might be in order here. A legal presumption is an assumption that a particular fact is true, based not on actual proof of the fact, but instead on the existence of another fact or other facts. In the case of bailments the fact that the property was not returned to the bailor in the same condition it was in when transferred to the bailee creates the assumption that the person who was taking care of the property, the bailee, was negligent.

In a lawsuit the plaintiff, the bailor, must initially prove only that the property was not returned in the same condition as it was when it was transferred to the bailee. At that point the burden of proof shifts to the bailee, who must try and prove that he or she was not negligent. This can be a daunting task, and if that burden cannot be met, the bailee loses. It should be clear that the general rule of bailments favors the owner of a horse being boarded rather than the owner of the boarding farm.

The general rule can be altered by contract if the parties agree that the transfer of possession of property does not constitute a bailment. Claim tickets for self-parking an automobile at an unattended lot frequently attempt to disclaim the creation of a bailment for the obvious reason that the owner of the parking lot does not want to shoulder the responsibility of reasonable care to keep the cars safe.

AT A GLANCE

- In negligence cases, a plaintiff must prove duty, breach of that duty, harm, and proximate cause.
- To exercise reasonable care, use common sense in operating your business.
- A bailment is created when one person transfers property, such as a horse, to another for safekeeping.
- Equine liability laws usually benefit horse business owners and equine activity sponsors by recognizing the inherent risks involved to participants.

Courts generally enforce such claims, particularly if the lot is unattended and the driver selects the parking space, locks the car, and keeps the keys. There is no reasonable parallel when the property in question is a horse rather than an automobile. A court is more likely to find a bailment when possession and control of the property is surrendered to another person such as a valet parking attendant or a farm owner.

The general rule of bailments also can be altered by law, such as a peculiar

CASE STUDIES

ASSUMPTION OF RISK
Taylor v. Howren, 606 SE2d 74 (Ga App 2004)

After assisting Howren in bandaging a wound on the leg on a horse, Taylor decided to ride another of Howren's horses. Howren recently had purchased the horse at an auction, where he reportedly was told that the horse was "green broke." Things did not go well, as the court reported:

> With the help of another person, Taylor placed a saddle on the unnamed horse and led it out into a pasture. Taylor then attempted to mount the horse, but, as he was doing so, the horse unexpectedly reared its head backward, striking Taylor in the left eye. The blow knocked Taylor unconscious, and, in the ensuing fall, he broke his neck, thereby rendering him paralyzed.

Not surprisingly, Taylor filed a lawsuit. Howren defended himself on two grounds, arguing that he was protected by Georgia's equine activity law and that Howren had assumed the risk of getting injured. The court did not accept either of Howren's arguments.

Taylor testified that Howren told him that the horse was "a good, rideable horse" despite knowing that the animal actually was green broke and never had been ridden. The court determined that the state's activity law did not apply because "it cannot be said that one who actively misrepresents the domesticity of a steed has taken prudent efforts to determine whether a proposed rider can safely manage the animal in question (a requirement of the equine activity law)."

The court also determined that Taylor could not have assumed the risk of being injured because "Taylor was misled regarding the nature of the horse, (and) he could not be expected to have full knowledge of the likely danger he faced in riding the horse." Necessary to assumption of a risk are knowledge of the risk and voluntary participation in the dangerous activity.

Kinara v. Jamaica Bay Riding Academy, 783 NYS2d 636 (NY App Div 2004)

Kinara, the plaintiff in this case, was injured when a horse kicked her during a trail ride conducted by Jamaica Bay Riding Academy, the defendant. Kinara filed a lawsuit and the riding stable defended itself by claiming that the plaintiff assumed an inherent risk of being injured when taking part in an equine activity. There was evidence that prior to the ride Kinara heard the trail guide comment that the horse was "wild" and that Kinara had observed the horse kicking before she was injured.

The court determined that there was no genuine issue of fact because of three factors: First, a horse kicking or acting in an unintended manner is an inherent risk of an equine activity; second, the plaintiff was aware of the fact that the horse who kicked her was "wild"; and third, the plaintiff was an experienced horsewoman who had ridden for fifteen years. Because the plaintiff had knowledge that the horse that kicked her was "wild" and nevertheless voluntarily assumed an inherent risk of riding, the court affirmed a grant of summary judgment in favor of the riding school. (Summary judgment means that the defendant won without a trial because there was no factual dispute to present to a jury.)

Burke v. McKay, 679 NW2d 418 (Neb 2004)

Burke had been competing in high school rodeo competitions for several years. Burke drew horse "No. 18" in a bareback event, and upon leaving the chute the horse "stood up on his back legs and threw himself to the rear in such a way that he fell over backwards, suddenly crushing (Burke) between his back and the ground." Burke and his family filed a lawsuit against the company that supplied livestock for the rodeo and the state high school rodeo association.

The Nebraska Supreme Court affirmed a grant of summary judgment in favor of the defendants on the basis of assumption of the risk. The court determined that a successful defense based on assumption of the risk has several elements: "(1) the person knew of and understood the specific danger, (2) the person voluntarily exposed himself or herself to the danger, and (3) the person's injury or death or harm to the property occurred as a result of his or her exposure to the danger."

The court initially determined that while a rider might expect to be thrown from a bucking horse in a rodeo, it was not reasonable to expect that a horse would flip over backwards. The plaintiff nevertheless had knowledge of that particular risk when riding "No. 18" because there was evidence that he and his father had seen the horse rear and fall over backward during a previous competition.

The court also concluded that Burke had voluntarily exposed himself to the specific danger because he had been given an opportunity to select another horse prior to the competition. There was evidence that Burke had discussed the matter with another competitor and had decided not to change horses because he thought the earlier incident had been a "one-time deal."

Because Burke knew of the specific risk and voluntarily exposed himself to the danger, there was no genuine factual issue to present to the jury.

ATTRACTIVE NUISANCE
North Hardin Developers v. Corkran, 839 SW2d 258 (Ky 1992)

The question for the court in this case was whether horses with no vicious tendencies kept on a farm in close proximity to two subdivisions were an attractive nuisance. The lawsuit arose from serious injuries suffered by a five-year-old child who was kicked by a horse. The child climbed the fence in response to a dare from her playmates, who challenged her to go into the field and touch one of the horses. She apparently approached one of the horses from the rear, and she was kicked in the head. She suffered a fractured skull.

Kentucky law, as is the case in most states, imposes very little duty to a trespasser unless the attractive nuisance doctrine applies. The court explained that:

> A possessor of land is subject to liability for physical harm to children trespassing thereon caused by an artificial condition upon the land if
> (a) the place where the condition exists is upon which the possessor knows or has reason to know that children are likely to trespass, and
> (b) the condition is one of which the possessor knows or has reason

to know and which he should realize will involve an unreasonable risk of death or serious bodily harm to such children, and

(c) the children because of their youth do not discover the condition or realize the risk involved in intermeddling with it or in coming within the area made dangerous by it, and

(d) the utility to the possessor of maintaining the condition and the burden of eliminating the danger are slight as compared with the risk to children involved, and

(e) the possessor fails to exercise reasonable care to eliminate the danger or otherwise to protect the children.

The trial court found in favor of the landowner, who knew that children were trespassing and who had taken measures to keep them out of his pastures. The Court of Appeals reversed and found the landowner liable for the child's injuries. The Supreme Court of Kentucky reversed that decision, finally concluding that the horses were not an attractive nuisance and that the child was a trespasser.

While acknowledging that horses might be an attractive nuisance in some circumstances, the court explained that "these horses were not kept in a residential yard, but on a twenty-seven-acre farm. The landowners had attempted, albeit unsuccessfully, to prevent trespassing by the children, and the cost of rendering the farm inaccessible to children would have been prohibitive." At least in Kentucky, horses and other domestic livestock without a history of dangerous propensities do not constitute a foreseeable risk of harm and are not attractive nuisances.

Some other states, Louisiana, for example, follow this reasoning. Other states do not, and no general conclusion is possible about whether horses constitute an attractive nuisance.

EQUINE ACTIVITY STATUTES
Steeg v. Baskin Family Camps, 124 SW3d 633 (Tex App 2003)

Texas has an equine activity law that protects the sponsors of such activities from liability for inherent risks but does not offer any protection for an injury resulting from negligence. Steeg, the plaintiff, was injured when he fell from a horse during a trail ride. Steeg suffered a ruptured spleen, which required surgery, then subsequently suffered a stroke that impaired his vision. The stroke was directly related to the surgery and the blood loss due to the injury.

Steeg fell from the horse after his saddle slipped during the trail ride. He filed a lawsuit but the trial court dismissed it based on the Texas Liability for Equine Activity Act. The lower court determined, among other things, that a saddle that slips is an inherent risk of riding and granted summary judgment in favor of the riding facility.

Steeg appealed the grant of summary judgment, and the Texas Court of Appeals reversed the trial court. The appellate court agreed that a slipping saddle *could be* an inherent risk of riding under some circumstances: "A saddle may slip for many reasons, several of which arise from inherent risks of equine activity-horses sweat, saddles stretch, saddle pads compress, riders sit off-center." The court also found that there were other potential reasons for the problem, however, such as a negligent failure to tighten the girth properly in the first place. The Texas equine activity act would insulate the riding facility from inherent risks but not from negligence.

Summary judgment is appropriate only when there is no genuine issue of fact for the jury. Here the appellate court found that there were facts supporting both sides of the question. The court sent the case back to the lower court for further proceedings to resolve the factual dispute.

McGraw v. R and R Investments, Ltd., 877 So2d 886 (Fla App 2004)

The plaintiff, an experienced horse trainer, was injured when she was thrown from a horse owned by the defendant. The trial court granted summary judgment in favor of the defendant based on the state equine activity law that insulates an activity sponsor from liability for injuries resulting from "inherent risks." There was no dispute about several significant facts: The defendant was an "equine sponsor" and the plaintiff was a "participant" under the statutory definitions, and the plaintiff's injuries were the result of an "inherent risk."

The Florida law, like those in many other states, requires the sponsor of an equine activity to post warning signs informing participants about the inherent risks of equine activities. The law does not, however, explain the consequences of a failure to post the required warning signs. The defendant did not post the required signs and the appellate court determined that this omission disqualified the defendant from the protection of the statute. The grant of summary judgment was reversed, and the case was sent back to the trial court for further proceedings.

While this seems to be a sensible conclusion, failure to post required warning signs does not have such dire results in all states with equine activity statutes. Close examination of the statutes and court interpretations in your state are necessary to evaluate your obligations and responsibilities properly.

LIABILITY WAIVERS
Saccente v. LaFlamme, 2003 Conn Super LEXIS 1913 (Conn Super 2003)

The plaintiff, a minor, was injured when she fell from a horse during a lesson at the defendant's riding school. The allegation was that a water hose negligently left in the riding arena by an employee spooked the horse. Both the minor and a parent signed written documents that purported to release the riding establishment from liability and provide for an assumption of the risk. The father argued that he had read the releases, but that it was not his intent to waive the defendant's liability for injuries to his daughter.

In an earlier decision the trial court ruled that the releases were enforceable against the father and that the documents were applicable to injuries resulting from negligence. The court explained that, "the general rule is that where a person of mature years and who can read and write, signs or accepts a formal written contract affecting his pecuniary interests, it is [that person's] duty to read it and notice of its contents will be imputed to [that person] if [that person] negligently fails to do so."

In this decision the court expanded that initial ruling to conclude that a release signed by a minor and a parent or legal guardian serves to waive any claims the minor might have in his or her own right:

> The decision here by her father to let the minor plaintiff waive her
> claims against the defendants in exchange for horseback riding

lessons at their farm is consistent with the rights and responsibilities regarding a child possessed by a parent and recognized by the legislature and cannot be said to be against public policy. The plaintiff's father made a conscious decision on the behalf of his child to go to the defendants' farm for the purpose of obtaining horseback riding lessons for her. This was obviously an independent decision made upon what he viewed as her best interests ... Since [the releases] provide that the plaintiff releases and holds harmless the defendants from all suits, and any and all claims, demands, and liabilities whatsoever, both in law and equity, which she has against them, the plaintiff cannot pursue her claims against the defendants.

Owners and operators of any horse business that offers services to minors should insist that a parent or legal guardian sign a written liability waiver.

McDermott v. Carrie, 124 P3d 168 (Mont 2005)

Although a court may be reluctant to enforce a liability waiver, having clients sign a release may be valuable anyway. In this case a rider at a dude ranch in Montana suffered an injury to her hand when a horse she was holding spooked. The rider sued the dude ranch owner for negligence, despite having signed a liability waiver. Under Montana law a prospective liability waiver (one that anticipates an injury in the future) is not enforceable. The trial court allowed the document to be used as evidence in the trial, however, but with the liability waiver language removed. The owner of the ranch used the release, without the waiver language, to show that the rider assumed the risks of participating in the equine activity, and a verdict was entered in favor of the owner. The outcome was affirmed on appeal.

Kentucky statute that in very limited circumstances negates the usual presumption of negligence on the part of the bailee. Kentucky Revised Statute 422.280 provides that the owner of a horse being boarded remains responsible for damage to or loss of the animal unless the harm is due to the negligence of the farm owner. That's normal and expected.

Then the law adds a twist that appears to be unique to Kentucky: "Evidence that the (bailor) delivered horses to the (bailee) and that the horses were damaged or lost while in the care and custody of the (bailee) shall not be sufficient to create a presumption of negligence on the part of the (bailee) ..." In other words, the horse owner still can collect if the animal was harmed while in the farm owner's care, but only if the horse owner can prove negligence. The law shifts the burden of proof from the farm owner (who as a bailee ordinarily would have to prove that he or she was not negligent) to the horse owner (who must prove that the farm owner was negligent).

Several years ago, following a devastating fire at a prominent American Saddlebred farm in Central Kentucky, the owner of two horses that were killed in the fire sued the farm owner. At the close of a trial in federal district court, the jury was instructed that the burden of proof was on the horse owner to show that the farm owner had been negligent and had failed to exercise the reasonable care expected of an ordinary prudent trainer of American Saddlebreds. The owner of the horses failed to do so and lost the lawsuit.

It is speculative to suggest that the verdict was unique to Kentucky and would have been different in a state where the general rule of bailments would have applied. But there is no doubt that the owner of the farm would have had the burden of proof elsewhere.

DUTY TO OTHERS

Landowners have a duty to persons on the property. The extent of that duty depends on the legal relationship between the parties.

A landowner has the highest duty of care to an "invitee," a person who is on the property for the mutual economic benefit of both individuals. Typical examples are customers shopping in a store or clients visiting a farm. The property owner has a duty to protect an invitee from harm, either from risks the owner is aware of or from risks that the owner could discover with reasonable care. An obviously icy sidewalk outside a store is an example of the former; rickety but not obviously dangerous chairs in an area adjacent to a show ring are examples of the latter. In either case the property owner generally has a duty to make the land safe for the customers.

A "licensee" is an individual who has permission to be on another person's property, but who is there without providing any economic benefit to the owner. Foxhunters who cross a farmer's land with the owner's permission, for example, are licensees. So are social guests. The property owner owes a licensee a duty of reasonable care but not an affirmative duty to make the grounds safe.

"Trespassers" are individuals who go onto another person's property without permission to do so and under that circumstance the landowner's duty of care is very limited. Landowners generally are not liable for injuries suffered by a trespasser unless those injuries are intentionally inflicted. The same is true for animals trespassing onto another person's land.

This does not mean that a landowner cannot defend himself or his property from an intruder if threatened. It does mean that a property owner cannot install booby traps designed to harm trespassers and that being on another person's property illegally, standing alone, seldom warrants an attack on the offender. The use of deadly force against another person almost never is appropriate to protect property, even if that property is a horse that's treated as a member of the family. A horse owner probably would be justified in shooting a pack of dogs attacking a foal, however.

SO WHAT'S ATTRACTIVE ABOUT A NUISANCE?

The situation changes dramatically if the trespasser is a child, and state laws impose a higher duty of care on a landowner under a legal principle called "attractive nuisance." A landowner generally is liable for injuries suffered by trespassing children if:

(1) the property owner knows, or has reason to know, that children trespass on the property;

(2) the property owner knows, or has reason to know, that a condition on the property poses an unreasonable risk of harm to children;

(3) the trespassing children, because of their youth, are unlikely to recognize the danger posed by the dangerous condition;

(4) the property owner fails to exercise reasonable care to protect the children;

(5) the condition can be corrected rather easily.

A backyard swimming pool is the classic example of an attractive nuisance and anyone owning a pool is well advised to fence it in to keep roaming children out. Horses grazing in a pasture, like swimming pools, are magnets for curious children, and a property owner may be liable if a trespassing child is injured by a horse.

Liability will depend on whether your state considers horses in a pasture to be an attractive nuisance. Not all states do and you should consult an attorney familiar with the law and with court interpretations of that law in your area. In Kentucky and Louisiana, for example, horses grazing in a field generally are not considered an attractive nuisance.

WHAT'S A PERSON TO DO?

Potential liability lurks in every horse accepted for boarding, in every riding lesson, in every trail ride, and the economic repercussions of losing a personal injury lawsuit can be devastating to your business. "Always act reasonably is good advice," but there are other things you can do, and should do, to protect your business.

Ownership Choices

A comprehensive discussion of the various forms of ownership appeared in Chapter 3. In summary, a horse business can be operated in several modes, including a sole proprietorship, a partnership (either general or limited), a corporation (either a "C" corporation or an "S" corporation), or a limited liability company.

The way you own and operate your business may affect your future personal liability in case of a lawsuit against you and your business. Choosing to incorporate or to operate as a limited liability company, for example, may prevent a successful litigant from reaching your personal assets. You should weigh that potential advantage against the increased administrative responsibilities and possibly unfavorable tax treatment before making a final decision.

Contract Options

The horse business traditionally has operated on a handshake and a promise. This approach worked, more or less, for years, and many people still conduct their businesses this way. Many, but not all, oral agreements can be enforced in court, provided that the plaintiff is able to prove that a contract actually existed and if so, what the terms were. The potential difficulties of enforcing oral contracts make it prudent to obtain a written agreement for every significant business transaction. (Contracts are discussed more fully in Chapter 5.)

At a boarding establishment, for example, each horse owner should be required to sign a boarding contract that explains the responsibilities of the parties. If the business is riding lessons, the students (and their parents if the student is a minor) should sign contracts. If a farm owner offers trail riding or makes land available for trail riding, the participants should sign a liability release. If you think this is too much trouble, think again.

Every contract should include an exculpatory clause, or waiver of liability, that excuses the party performing the service — the owner of a boarding farm or the provider of horses for trail rides, for example — from liability in the performance of the contract. The effect of such a clause is to limit the farm owner's liability in the event that something goes wrong.

Whether a liability waiver will be enforced is a matter of state law. Courts in some states, such as Montana, refuse to enforce prospective liability waivers (waivers that anticipate future events) as a matter of public policy. Even if you can protect yourself and your business from some claims, many courts will not enforce a waiver that attempts to excuse ordinary negligence on the theory that such protection eliminates the incentive to be careful. In almost no situation will a waiver eliminate liability for gross negligence, no matter how well written the contract. This emphasizes the need to act reasonably at all times.

Even if there is no clear authority in your state for the enforceability of an exculpatory clause, and this varies from state to state, it always is better practice to include such a waiver of liability in all contracts. Some liability insurance policies require such language, and an injured person might be less likely to initiate a lawsuit if he or she has signed a waiver.

The value of a written contract depends entirely on how well the document is drafted, and you should consult your attorney for guidance. It is tempting to buy one of several available books of fill-in-the-blank legal forms and run off a few copies at the local print shop. While this might make economic sense in the short run, it will be pure happenstance if one of those fill-in-the-blank contracts matches all — or any — of the requirements of your particular situation in your state. One-size-fits-all legal forms can be a good starting point, but you and your attorney should review the document carefully and adapt it to your needs. It will be money well spent if a problem arises.

STATE LIABILITY LAWS

An old joke asks: "What are the nine most frightening words in the English language." The answer: "I'm from the government, and I'm here to help."

Negative perceptions aside, the government sometimes manages to do something that actually makes a horse business easier and more economical to run. One of the best examples in recent years is the passage, in nearly all states, of laws that limit the liability of farm owners, horse owners, and sponsors of equine activities. As of this writing (fall 2006), a total of forty-six states have some type of equine liability law on their books. The only holdouts are California, Maryland, Nevada, and New York.

Texts of the laws in your particular state can be found in statute books at college or local libraries, from your local legislators, on the Internet, or from an attorney. The last-named is the best source for advice on these laws. A list of selected statutory references is included in the appendix to this book.

Because the equine liability laws vary greatly from state to state, a comprehensive, jurisdiction-specific discussion is beyond the scope of this book. Generally, though, the laws recognize that any equine activity has certain built-in or inherent risks, and that a farm owner or equine activity sponsor has a responsibility to warn participants of those risks. The laws generally do not impose on the owner or sponsor a duty to eliminate the inherent risks, however. In other words, the equine liability laws require participants in an equine activity to assume many of the risks associated with that activity.

Kentucky's equine liability law, found at Kentucky Revised Statutes 247.401–247.4029, is similar to laws in many other states and is illustrative of what these laws can, and cannot, do for a farm owner. Keep in mind, though, that the law in Kentucky is not the law in any other state, and you should get professional advice in interpreting and implementing the equine liability law in your jurisdiction. By the same token, you should not rely solely on the cursory treatment in this book as your only authority on Kentucky liability law. Your best guide is an attorney familiar with the topic.

Kentucky's equine liability law is applicable to most, but not all, equine activities. The law covers horse shows and other competitions, training, boarding, trail rides, and farrier and veterinary services. Most horse racing activities, questions arising from fencing problems, and liability of landowners to trespassers are not covered. The inherent risks of working with horses, such as the simple fact they are big, powerful animals that can hurt you, their general unpredictability, and the fact that other participants might act negligently, are covered.

Negligent acts by the equine professional or sponsor, such as providing faulty tack or a dangerous horse, or the failure to post warning signs regarding known dangerous conditions on the land, are not covered. While the law does not protect a farm owner against his or her own negligence, it does establish non-negligent conduct as "adherence … to the standards of care within the profession." In other words, you are not negligent if you act like a reasonable horse person would in similar circumstances.

Equine liability laws are "get out of jail free" cards for farm owners and other equine professionals in Kentucky, provided they are not negligent and provided they follow the statute's guidelines regarding proper notice to participants. To receive the benefits of the Kentucky law, a farm owner or other equine activity sponsor must post a warning notice, or notices, in a conspicuous place. The sign must contain the following language:

WARNING

Under Kentucky law, a farm activity sponsor, farm animal professional, or other person does not have the duty to eliminate all risks of injury of participation in farm animal activities. There are inherent risks of injury that you voluntarily accept if you participate in farm animal activities.

In the few states where the matter has been the subject of a lawsuit, courts are divided about whether failure to post a required warning sign destroys the protection of the statute. Any doubt on that issue can be resolved by simply following the guidelines and requirements in your state's law.

A similar notice must be included in all written contracts for professional equine services, including instruction and the rental of horses and/or tack for trail riding and other activities. If such a notice is not part of the contract, the farm owner will not be able to rely on the favorable (to him or her) statutory provisions in the event of a lawsuit.

Consultation with an attorney familiar with equine law can tell you whether your state has an equine liability law (the odds are good that it does), how the law operates, and what the law requires that you do. You should consider equine liability laws as sound advice about how to stay out of trouble. You ignore that advice at your own peril.

INSURANCE

The final piece of the liability protection puzzle is adequate insurance. The amount and type of coverage necessary for a particular situation should be discussed with your agent. (Insurance is discussed more fully in Chapter 8.) When considering liability insurance, it is important to understand the limits of your policy and what is, and is not, covered. A typical liability policy covers acts of ordinary negligence and is a valuable addition to reliance on state equine activity laws (which generally exclude negligence) and liability waivers (which may or may not offer protection for negligence).

RESOURCES

References to state equine liability statutes are included in the appendix to this book.

INSURANCE

I nsurance and a spare tire are among the few things consumers purchase hoping never to use. They also can be among the most important purchases a consumer can make if disaster strikes, a flat tire on a deserted highway, for example, or an automobile accident or the death of a valuable animal. The former might be merely inconvenient; the latter can be financially and emotionally devastating.

This chapter addresses the various types of insurance in two contexts: first, the liability of a farm owner or service provider for injury to man or beast, and, second, protection for a horse owner in the event an animal is injured or dies. The chapter also offers some suggestions to help you decide what coverage might be applicable to your horse enterprise.

SETTING THE ODDS

Purchasing an insurance policy is a lot like placing a bet at a Las Vegas casino. The bettor/insured is gambling that a particular event will happen and that he or she will be protected if it does; the insurance company, the "house"/insurer, is gambling that a particular event will not happen.

The game is insurance, and the anticipated event can be nearly anything, at least anything that has a bad result — a lightning strike that destroys a barn, an accident that seriously injures a boarder, a potential stallion that turns up infertile, the unexpected death of a valuable horse. And unlike a bet at a casino or at a racetrack, buying insurance is a gamble the bettor hopes to lose. You "win" the insurance game when nothing bad happens and you *don't* collect.

Gamble at a casino long enough and you will wind up a loser because the odds for each and every game are skewed in the house's favor. Stay in the horse business long enough and you or one of your horses, one of your employees or boarders, or a horse in your care will have an accident. Although good management practices can tilt the scales somewhat in your favor, for nearly everyone the ultimate question is not *if* an accident will happen but *when* it will happen. Insurance does not replace good management, but a well-thought-out insurance plan can protect you when, despite your best efforts, something goes wrong.

The insurance carrier calculates its premiums based on probability. The more likely a covered event is to occur, and the greater the potential payout by the company, the higher the premium. Conversely, the less likely it is that a covered event will occur, the lower the premium. Insurance coverage generally can be tailored to offer as much, or as little, protection as the purchaser desires.

If there is a trick to winning the insurance game, it is being aware of your insurance needs and buying enough insurance — but no more — than is required to protect your interests. Under-insuring, or having no insurance at all, will not protect you in the event of a catastrophe; over-insuring, on the other hand, is a waste of money and benefits only the agent or insurance carrier. A good insurance agent can design a plan to fit your specific circumstances and can be a valuable ally both before and after you submit a claim.

You should choose an insurance agent with the same care you would use in picking any other professional. Personal references may be the best indicator, and if you have friends in the horse business, find out who handles their insurance. Ask questions: Was the agent helpful and knowledgeable, both about insurance matters in general and about the horse business in particular? Were claims handled promptly and fairly? Did they feel that they got value for their insurance dollars?

LEARNING THE LANGUAGE

Discovery by archaeologists of the Rosetta stone in 1799, with its parallel inscriptions in Greek, Egyptian, and demotic characters, allowed scientists for the first time to translate ancient Egyptian picture writing. While many insurance policies may seem as incomprehensible as Egyptian hieroglyphics, at least at first glance, you can learn the basics of your coverage with just a little work.

A typical equine mortality policy, for example, may contain the following sections:

1. *Definitions* — Basic terms are defined in this section of the policy, including "you" and "your" for the insured and "we," "us," and "our" for the insurance company. Other necessary terms, such as the insurance company's definition of "fair market value," may be found here as well. Many terms have common usage throughout the insurance industry, but it is imperative to understand the terms used in your particular policy. If you have questions, ask the agent. If he or she cannot, or will not, answer your questions, find another agent.

2. *Insuring Agreement* — This portion of the policy represents the company's agreement to provide the insurance coverage set out in the policy so long as the insured pays the required premiums and complies with the other terms of the policy. This agreement by the company to provide insurance, if you perform certain obligations, is the heart of the contract and allows for enforcement in court — if you have done everything required in the agreement. Always keep in mind that an insurance policy is a contract between you and the insurance carrier. There are obligations imposed on both sides, and a breach of the agreement on your part may void the coverage.

AT A GLANCE

- Be aware of your insurance needs and buy enough — but no more — than is required.
- Liability insurance provides coverage for ordinary negligence by you or your employees.
- A care, custody, and control policy can help protect a boarding farm owner from liability arising from a client's horse being injured.
- Equine mortality insurance can help protect an owner's investment in his or her horse.

3. *Coverage* — Here can be found the types of situations in which the insurance company will pay. With a full mortality policy, for example, the carrier is insuring the specified horse, or horses, against death that is the direct or indirect result of accident, illness, or disease. For a limited mortality policy, the company insures the specified animal or animals

against death resulting from specific, stated causes, which may vary from policy to policy. A careful reading of this portion of the policy is necessary to understand what your insurance does and does not cover. Few situations are more unfortunate than finding out after an accident that coverage you thought you had does not exist.

4. *Payment of Loss* — Here the company sets out in detail the method of valuation of the insured animal. Whether the policy provides "agreed value" or "fair market value" coverage, for example, will be stated in this section of the policy. Knowing how the company will determine the value of your animal and thus the amount that will be paid if the horse dies will help prevent misunderstandings.

5. *Exclusions* — One of the most important parts of the policy, this section explains the situations that specifically preclude recovery. Typical exclusions include death resulting from intentional or willful acts or omissions by the horse's owner, war, intentional slaughter, some surgical procedures, and administration of drugs under certain circumstances.

6. *Conditions* — This is generally the lengthiest section of the policy, addressing a variety of situations that may affect the coverage. Conditions often include a requirement that you must disclose pre-existing illnesses or injuries suffered by the horse prior to the application for insurance, responsibilities and obligations of the horse owner (including a duty to notify the insurance company in the event of accident or illness), an agreement to submit disputes to arbitration, conditions under which the policy may be canceled by either party, and modifications and extensions of the coverage. The policy also may require a veterinary certificate prior to issuing the coverage and a necropsy to determine cause of an animal's death. Anything less than strict adherence to these conditions may void coverage and defeat the goal of buying insurance in the first place.

7. *Limitations* — Insurance policies nearly always include limitations on the amount the carrier is obligated to pay. These limitations generally are either a "per occurrence" limit or an "aggregate" limit. A per occurrence limit sets a ceiling on the amount the carrier will pay for an individual claim. An aggregate limit sets a cap on the total amount the carrier is obligated to pay during one term period of the policy, subject to the per occurrence limit. For example, a policy with a $250,000/occurrence, $750,000 aggregate limit

will pay a maximum of $250,000 for an individual claim and no more than a total of $750,000 during the term of the policy.

Interpreting an insurance policy can appear daunting at first, but with a little homework you can understand both the nature and the limits of your coverage.

AN INSURANCE PRIMER — LIABILITY

As set out in the previous chapter, written liability waivers, reliance on your state's equine activity statutes, and adequate insurance coverage are essential to protecting your business and personal assets. Liability insurance may be the most important because it provides coverage for the ordinary negligence of you and your employees. Waivers and state equine activity statutes may not protect you in the event of an injury caused by negligence.

Most everyone is familiar with basic automobile and home owner's insurance, and it is tempting to assume that the standard home owner's policy you probably already have will adequately protect a modest horse business as well. You make this assumption at your own peril.

Home owner's policies are not business liability insurance and generally *do not* cover liability resulting from business activities. Your insurance carrier almost certainly will adopt a very broad interpretation of "business" when asked to pay a claim relating to your horse operation. It also is possible that a general farm owner's liability policy may include livestock generally but may specifically exclude horses. A reputable insurance agent should be able to review your current insurance coverage and recommend additional policies to fill in any gaps.

Your agent also may recommend an "umbrella" policy to increase the coverage limits of your liability policy. Although the name suggests additional coverage for occurrences not addressed in the original liability policy, this is not the situation. An umbrella policy only increases the maximum amount the insurance carrier might be obligated to pay (from $500,000 to $1,000,000, for example), but does not provide coverage for different types of claims beyond the terms of the original policy. Purchased as a supplement to a standard farm owner's commercial liability policy, an umbrella policy usually can be purchased with relatively little additional expense.

Even if your general farm owner's policy does cover business activities and does not exclude horses from its coverage, most such insurance policies specifically exclude coverage for horses, equipment, and other property not owned by the insured but that are in the insured's care. In other words, if you are conducting a boarding business or any other type of operation in which you assume the responsibility for a horse belonging to someone else, you should discuss with your agent "care, custody, or control" coverage.

A care, custody, or control policy generally protects a farm owner who boards horses for others against liability arising from an injury to or the death of a horse quartered at the farm. Typical policies also cover the legal expenses incurred as a result of the farm owner's defense of a lawsuit brought as a result of a boarded horse's injury or death. Considering the litigious nature of our society and the often-astronomical legal fees that can result from even the successful defense of a lawsuit, such protection should be considered a necessity for any farm owner who accepts responsibility for horses owned by others.

Care, custody, or control coverage also imposes, either directly or implicitly, a duty on the owner of a boarding farm to employ a standard of care at least as good as the standard employed at similar boarding farms. There is no hard and fast definition of an adequate standard of care, and acceptable management practices may vary from state to state. The standard of care on a Thoroughbred boarding farm in Central Kentucky, for example, might be excessive when compared to a Midwestern boarding stable for pleasure horses.

A generally acceptable standard of care likely will include some level of regular security and supervision of the horses; safely constructed and adequately maintained barns, run-in sheds, fences, and other structures; and provisions for adequate food, water, and veterinary care. An additional consideration is whether the farm owner transports boarded horses, a common scenario at farms that board broodmares that must be shipped to other farms for breeding, or show horses that must be vanned to competitions. If you fail to provide the understood and agreed-upon standard of care either at the farm or in transit, your insurance carrier may refuse to pay in the event of a mishap.

Separate coverage may be required for the owners or operators of a commercial riding stable. A commercial stable policy can be written to cover liability arising during the operation of a business that provides riding lessons or riding clinics, private lessons, or that conducts horse shows on the premises. Such policies typically protect a stable owner who is found to be legally liable for either bodily injury or property damage resulting from the stable operation.

It is important to discuss your insurance needs fully with your agent *before* an accident happens. Most insurance applications are quite detailed, but if the agent does not know the specific nature of your equine business at the start, you may wind up with unnecessary coverage for activities that do not apply to your business. Even worse, the coverage you get may not be comprehensive enough.

If you tell your agent that you board horses for others, for example, he or she logically might recommend a care, custody, or control policy. But if you neglect to mention that you also give riding lessons to some of the people who board horses at your farm and the agent doesn't ask, you might leave the office without separate stable owner's coverage. This won't be a problem until one of your lesson horses stumbles and tosses the rider, breaking the student's arm, and you find out that you aren't covered for such injuries. You have a right to rely on your insurance agent, but you also have an obligation to provide complete information to the agent. You also have an obligation to become familiar with your policies to verify that the coverage you get is the coverage you want and need.

Some owners of boarding farms or riding stables attempt to insulate themselves from liability and save money at the same time by foregoing adequate insurance coverage and relying instead on written waivers of liability from their clients. A liability waiver protects the farm or stable owner, at least in theory, by requiring the client to state in writing that he or she both understands the risks inherent in the activity and accepts them. This is the by-now familiar concept of "assumption of the risk."

In practice, however, the effectiveness of a liability waiver depends on several factors. The language used can determine whether the waiver will be enforceable as a defense to a lawsuit, and it is a safer practice to have an attorney experienced in equine matters draft the document rather than use a fill-in-the-blanks form from a book, magazine, or the Internet.

The laws of your particular state also may affect the enforceability of the waiver, and it is important to keep in mind that many courts frequently will not allow a farm or stable owner to use a contract to eliminate liability for his or her own negligence or for that of the employees. This is an important consideration because many liability insurance policies can be written to cover all but intentional or malicious acts and thus provide an additional layer of protection.

Most states also have statutes that limit the liability of a farm owner or equine activity sponsor, and you should become familiar with the laws in your particular state. (Equine liability laws for selected states are identified in the appendix to this book.) Equine liability laws generally recognize that horse-related activities have a certain amount of built-in risk and restrict the right of a person to sue a farm or stable owner for injuries suffered as a result of participation in the activity.

Most liability laws impose a notice requirement on the farm or stable owner. In many states a farm or stable owner must post a conspicuous notice warning clients and others that there are inherent risks associated with equine activities and that anyone taking part in the activity assumes the risk. Without the notice, which also must be included in written contracts and liability waivers, a farm owner or activity sponsor may not gain the benefit of the law.

You should include properly drafted liability waivers in your contracts, and you should understand and follow the requirements of your state equine liability laws. Neither, however, should be relied upon as a substitute for adequate liability insurance. Instead, waivers and state liability laws should be seen as the front-line defenses against a finding of liability, with your insurance coverage serving as the ultimate protection for your business and personal assets.

Also keep in mind that a history of claims against you and your business will result in higher premiums because the insurance carrier will assign a higher risk of loss to your operation. In extreme situations it may be impossible to obtain liability coverage.

AN INSURANCE PRIMER — MORTALITY

Unlike liability insurance, the purpose of which is to protect an individual against liability for bodily injury to others or for the loss of their animals or property, equine mortality insurance provides a mechanism for an owner to recoup at least some of his or her investments of time and money when a horse dies. There may be a tendency to think of equine mortality insurance as the equivalent of life insurance for humans, but the comparison is incorrect.

Life insurance is purchased to protect the insured's dependents by providing money that could have been earned had the insured lived. The protection is forward-looking and anticipatory. Equine mortality insurance, by comparison, is purchased to protect a horse owner's financial investment, reflected by either an agreed value or the animal's fair market value at the time of death. Equine mortality insurance is not designed to replace the anticipated earnings of a horse if the animal had lived to compete or breed.

The most common form of equine insurance, mortality insurance can be purchased as either "full mortality" or "limited mortality"/"limited risk." Full mortality insurance, which covers death of a horse either directly or indirectly from accident, illness, or disease, is the more comprehensive of the two and thus more expensive. Limited mortality insurance, on the other hand, provides coverage for a limited range of situations and consequently is much less expensive. Remember the basic rule of insurance: the greater the risk, the higher the premium.

A peculiarity of most equine mortality policies, one that has led to numerous misunderstandings, bad feelings, and a substantial amount of litigation, involves the determination of the insured animal's value at death. Most equine insurance underwriters initially insure a horse for a value determined by the owner, with the insurance premiums set accordingly — the higher the stated value, the higher the premium. If the horse dies due to a cause covered by an "agreed value" policy, and a proper claim is submitted, the full amount is paid.

The situation becomes more problematic if the policy covers the "actual cash value" or "fair market value" of the horse because those amounts can change dramatically and quickly during an animal's life. If fair market value insurance coverage is not changed periodically to reflect fluctuations in the animal's value, an owner who legitimately insured a national champion show horse for $100,000 at the height of the gelding's success and paid premiums on that basis may receive substantially less than the anticipated $100,000 when the horse dies several years into his retirement. Understandably, and probably unnecessarily, the owner will feel cheated.

The logic of the practice is inescapable, at least from the insurance company's point of view — a retired gelding with no breeding or resale value is worth substantially less than a successful show horse, regardless of the premiums paid. The practice of limiting recovery to fair market value also discourages unscrupulous owners from over-insuring a horse and then killing the animal to collect the insurance, schemes that have made national headlines in recent years.

Again, it is important for you to maintain a continuing dialogue with the insurance agent, both to determine the type and amount of coverage you need initially and to evaluate whether your insurance needs have changed. Assume for a moment that you purchased a fair market value policy for your show horse in the amount of $100,000, with premiums based on that valuation.

If the horse is entered in a public auction with a $100,000 reserve (the minimum amount you will take for the animal), and the bidding fails to reach the reserve figure, the insurance carrier may take the highest legitimate bid ($60,000, for example) as the animal's current fair market value. If the animal dies the next day, the insurance probably will pay only $60,000, regardless of the higher estimation of value when the insurance was purchased.

The same thing will happen if an insured Thoroughbred is entered in a claiming race, where anyone willing to pay the claiming price set for horses in the race can buy the animal. No matter what the owner estimated the horse's value to be when the fair market value mortality policy was purchased, in the insurance company's eyes the animal's fair market value will be his claiming price in his most recent race.

This does not mean, by the way, that an owner can insure a horse for $10,000, then enter him in a race for $50,000 claimers and collect the higher amount if he dies. All mortality policies set the maximum amount to be paid by the company as the insured value stated in the policy. The company may pay less but never more than the agreed-upon insured value of your horse. If the value of the horse increases significantly, a new policy should be negotiated to reflect the increase in value.

An insurance agent may be able to help determine the proper value to place on a horse, but a horse owner should not rely exclusively on the agent's advice. A potential conflict of interest exists when an insurance agent, whose commission is based on the premiums charged, is asked to determine the value of the horse to be insured, a figure that will establish the premium amount. Also, if there is a question about the value of your horse, you may be required to prove that the valuation was reasonable.

The purchase price at public auction is a good indicator of a horse's fair market value, at least at the time of the sale. Establishing a value is more problematic if the horse was purchased privately and even more difficult if the horse is a homebred. An appraisal by a reputable bloodstock agent, comparison with auction prices for horses with similar bloodlines and performance records, and advice from other breeders may help you strike a balance between having too much or not enough mortality insurance.

Another way to establish a horse's value is through a professional appraisal. The mechanics of an appraisal should be familiar to anyone who has seen an episode of *The Antiques Roadshow* on public television. The owner of a dresser, or a piece of jewelry, or a supposed Tiffany vase with an indeterminate value presents the item to an expert. Combining his or her general knowledge of the field with experience selling similar items at auction or privately, the expert comes up with an estimate of the item's value. The expert, in other words, is making an educated guess about the item's fair market value. Just how reliable that estimate actually is depends on the expertise of the person making the guess.

An appraisal of a horse works the same way. An expert reviews pertinent information about the horse, then makes his or her best estimate about the animal's monetary value. One of the most common ways to do this is to research public and private sales of horses with similar pedigrees and performance or produce records. If an owner is lucky enough to negotiate a private sale of a stakes-winning, stakes-producing mare in foal to Storm Cat, or a Quarter Horse mare carrying a foal by a leading reining horse, prior auction sales of similar mares should give a good estimate of the fair market value.

Anyone seeking an appraisal should expect to provide the appraiser with at least the following:

• Information positively identifying the horse being appraised. This is necessary to avoid fraud. It does not mean that the appraiser thinks that you are dishonest. It does mean that there are unscrupulous persons who might try to inflate the appraised value of a cheap horse in an attempt to cheat a buyer or an insurance company.

• The horse's pedigree; the more detailed the better.

• The horse's performance and produce records, if any.

• The purpose of the appraisal (pending sale or purchase, valuation for insurance or litigation, for example).

• Contact information for the owner.

• Any other relevant information, including necessary deadlines.

The appraiser might also want to see a veterinarian's health certificate for the horse, especially if the appraiser is not going to examine the animal physically. An appraisal does not take the place of an examination by a veterinarian, and unless qualified in some way an appraisal generally assumes the animal is sound and in good health.

A horse owner should expect from an appraiser the following:

• Credentials establishing his or her expertise. The American Society of Equine Appraisers offers training, continuing education, and certification for appraisers, and members of that organization agree to follow a code of ethics in their work. A non-certified appraiser might be able to do a competent job, but certification provides an added measure of confidence in the appraiser. Certification takes on a more important role if the appraiser must be qualified as an expert witness in court.

An appraiser should have experience in the horse business in general and specifically with your horse's breed. You might want to look for membership in relevant breed organizations. An appraiser who has experience only with Quarter Horses, for example, might not understand the significance of a placing in a class at the Arabian Nationals.

If the appraisal is being done for litigation, the appraiser should have experience testifying in court as an expert witness. Rules of evidence generally allow an expert to offer an opinion if it would assist the jury in making a decision. Parties to a lawsuit want an appraiser who uses fundamentally sound and defensible methods for estimating a horse's value and who can make those methods understandable to a jury.

• The fee to be charged for the appraisal. Depending on the purpose of the appraisal, the expected fees could include the appraisal itself, communication with an insurance company, pre-trial depositions, and court appearances.

• Full disclosure of any financial or other interest the appraiser might have in the horse being appraised.

Always keep two things in mind about an appraisal:

1) An appraisal, even one done by the most knowledgeable expert in the business, is a well-informed estimate of value but not a guarantee of anything. An appraisal that estimates the fair market value of a horse for $10,000 does not mean that the horse actually would bring $10,000 if offered for sale at auction or that there are any willing buyers at that price. Nor does an appraisal mean that the appraiser is offering to buy the horse for the estimated value. Finally, if the appraisal is being done for litigation, an ethical appraiser will not make any promises about a successful conclusion to the lawsuit.

2) An appraisal is an estimate of your horse's value at the time the appraisal is done. The value of a horse can change over time and usually does. Your horse can appreciate in value if you are lucky or depreciate if you are not. The latter situation can mean disappointment at sale time or an unexpected shock if it becomes necessary to collect on an insurance policy.

A COMMON GROUND

One of the most heart-wrenching decisions that a horse owner must make is whether an animal's condition warrants euthanasia. Although the ultimate choice obviously involves both the horse owner and the veterinarian, the insurance carrier also has an interest if there is mortality insurance on the horse. A mortality policy almost certainly includes a requirement that the carrier be notified immediately if the horse suffers an injury or illness.

This notice requirement may not be practical in all situations, such as a catastrophic breakdown in a race that results in an injury that cannot be treated. Generally, though, a failure to notify the insurance carrier before a horse is euthanized is likely to void the policy.

CASE STUDIES

Hiscox Dedicated Corporate Member Ltd. v. Ralph C. Wilson Jr., 246 FSupp2d 684 (EDKY 2003)

The defendant, Ralph Wilson, was "an experienced entrepreneur with diverse business holdings, including highway construction, radio stations, trucking, the thoroughbred horse business, ownership of the Buffalo Bills, and previous ownership of an insurance brokerage firm." Wilson purchased a son of Unbridled at the 2000 Keeneland September yearling sale and subsequently insured the colt for an agreed value of $875,000.

In January 2001 the colt fractured a right hock, which required surgery. The manager of the farm where the colt was being boarded provided written notice of the injury and the proposed surgery to the insurance carrier, which acknowledged receipt of the notice. Several days after surgery the colt developed a serious bacterial infection in the injured hock joint. He was treated at a local equine veterinary hospital and at the farm for almost two months, but the treatment was not successful.

In late March it became necessary to euthanize the colt for humane reasons. The insurance carrier was notified and approved the decision. It was undisputed by the parties that there were no communications between the farm and the insurance carrier during the period from January 10 and March 30.

Before paying Wilson's claim for the death of the colt, the insurance carrier initiated an investigation into the circumstances of the injury and subsequent treatment. The carrier ultimately refused to pay the claim on the grounds that failure to provide notice of the post-surgery infection and treatment violated a condition precedent to the policy. Specifically, the policy required that "in the event of any illness, disease, lameness, injury, accident or physical disability whatsoever of or to the HORSE, ... the INSURED shall immediately give notice" to the insurance carrier or the carrier's agent.

The court agreed with the insurance carrier and found that failure to give immediate notice of the post-surgery infection and treatment violated a condition precedent of the policy and that coverage was "null and void." The court also ruled that a lack of personal knowledge about the colt's condition on Wilson's part did not excuse the failure to give notice because the individuals who actually had "care, custody, or control of the horse," the farm owners, knew of the infection.

It also didn't help that Wilson's attorney, who handled equine insurance matters for five years, had provided notice to an insurance carrier of a non-fatal injury *and subsequent complications* suffered by a horse two years earlier.

Ellis v. Hartford Livestock Insurance Co., 170 SW2d 51 (Ky 1943)

In this old Kentucky case the plaintiff purchased insurance on a Thoroughbred racehorse in the amount of $2,500. The policy included an endorsement providing that the insured value would decrease if the horse was entered in a claiming race. The colt died of disease and the insurance paid only $1,200 because the horse had been entered in a claiming race and could have been purchased for that amount. The carrier also refunded a portion of the premium.

The plaintiff argued that the value of the policy was fixed at $2,500 despite the claiming endorsement, but that argument was unsuccessful. The court determined that the policy actually fixed two values for the horse, $2,500 initially and a value to be determined later only if the horse was entered in a claiming race for less than $2,500. The court found that the claiming endorsement was a valid portion of the insurance contract, and the plaintiff had no further recourse.

It is important to keep in mind that the claiming endorsement only worked to lower the horse's insured value. If the horse had been entered in a race for $5,000 claimers, the insured value would not have automatically increased beyond the $2,500 figure stated in the policy. Any increase in coverage requires a renegotiation of the policy and almost certainly an increased premium.

United States v. Lindemann Jr., 85 F3d 1232 (7th Cir 1996)

Litigation regarding insurance claims usually is civil in nature and involves the question of whether a company has an obligation to pay on a claim. Notable exceptions were the criminal investigation and subsequent trials surrounding a multi-state conspiracy to kill horses and defraud insurance carriers that came to light in the late 1980s and early 1990s. In this case the Court of Appeals for the Seventh Circuit affirmed the conviction of prominent show horse owner George Lindemann Jr.

The court described the facts of the case as follows:

Charisma, a show horse, died in its stall on the night of December 15, 1990. The insurance company that had issued a policy on Charisma's life concluded that the death was the result of natural causes and paid the $250,000 value of the policy. Subsequently, the Federal Bureau of Investigation uncovered an alleged conspiracy between Tommy Burns and Barney Ward to kill horses for pay, allowing the horses' owners to collect insurance proceeds. Burns gave the FBI information indicating that George Lindemann Jr., a partial owner of Charisma, had arranged the horse's death in order to gain the proceeds of its life insurance policy. Lindemann was tried and convicted of three counts of wire fraud ...

On appeal the Court of Appeals for the Seventh Circuit affirmed Lindemann's conviction on all counts. During the trial Burns testified that he had been involved in the killings of more than a dozen horses and that the schemes involved some thirty people. Trainer Barney Ward, a well-known trainer and exhibitor of show jumpers, entered a guilty plea in a separate proceeding. He was banned from attending recognized competitions by the American Horse Shows Association (now the United States Equestrian Federation), an administrative ruling upheld in court and reviewed in Chapter 2 of this book.

A strict reading of most notice provisions requires the owner to notify the insurance company of *every* accident or illness, no matter how minor. An owner certainly should notify the carrier of a condition so serious that it may necessitate euthanasia, and failure to notify the company of all injuries or illness may give the company grounds to refuse to pay. The purpose of insurance is to eliminate risk; failure to follow a requirement of the mortality policy simply creates an additional risk of loss and is not a sound management practice.

This notice requirement also makes it essential to inform the owner of a farm where a horse is boarded that the animal is insured. In the event the horse is injured, the farm owner cannot notify the insurance company directly without current contact information.

It is possible but unlikely that a disagreement will develop between your veterinarian and the veterinarian acting on behalf of the insurer about whether a horse's condition warrants immediate euthanasia or whether time should be allowed for a possible recovery. To assist veterinarians facing such a situation, the American Association of Equine Practitioners several years ago adopted guidelines and justifications for euthanasia.

When deciding whether a horse should be put down, a veterinarian should consider the following:

1. Whether the condition is chronic and incurable;

2. Whether the horse has a hopeless prognosis for life as a result of the immediate condition;

3. Whether the horse is a hazard to himself or to his handlers;

4. Whether the horse will require continuous medication to relieve pain for the remainder of his life.

The American Association of Equine Practitioners also recommends that "justification for euthanasia of a horse for humane reasons should be based on medical and not economic considerations; and, further the same criteria should be applied to all horses regardless of age, sex or potential value."

The American Association of Equine Practitioners' guidelines and justification for euthanasia do not address specific situations. They do make it possible for both your veterinarian and the insurance carrier's veterinarian to evaluate the condition of your horse from the same frame of reference and to reach a decision based on the animal's best interests.

AN INSURANCE PRIMER — OTHER OPTIONS

Many other types of insurance can be purchased and should be considered based on your individual circumstances and budget. Insurance plans are limited only by the agent's imagination and the budget of the insured.

Various kinds of fertility insurance are available, including coverage for new stallions that pays if a certain proportion of mares bred to the stallion during his first year of stud duty do not get in foal. Mare owners can insure their broodmares against either failing to conceive or losing the foal, coverage that gains importance if the mare is being bred to a pricey stallion on a "no guarantee" basis.

Health insurance that covers veterinary charges for illness or accident, surgical insurance that covers emergency surgery and postoperative care, and coverage for tack and equipment also are available. Like policies for people, major medical and surgical policies usually have a deductible that must be paid by the insured.

Loss of use coverage and theft insurance are other options. Similar to disability insurance for people, loss of use insurance pays when a horse becomes incapacitated and permanently unable to perform. Theft coverage pays if an insured animal is stolen. Most policies require evidence of a forced entry, a report to the authorities, and a waiting period. A "mysterious disappearance," with no evidence of theft, may be excluded. When a carrier pays a theft insurance claim, the company takes title to the horse in the event it is eventually recovered.

RESOURCES

The number of companies offering equine insurance has decreased in recent years, due in part to a number of high-profile and very expensive payouts. Savvy insurance buyers will look for a reputable agent and a well-established company. The A.M. Best Company rates insurance companies, and their ratings can be obtained online at www.ambest.com.

Information about equine appraisals is available from the American Society of Equine Appraisers, P.O. Box 186, Twin Falls, ID 83303-0186, (800) 704-7020, www.equineappraiser.com.

9

SALES

How does the sale of a horse differ from a lease? How does the purchase of a share in a syndicated stallion differ from the purchase of a breeding season?

Simple questions, they demonstrate the most fundamental aspect of a sale — transfer of title, commonly known as ownership. When a horse is sold, the seller transfers both physical possession of the horse and its title to the buyer. A lessor also transfers physical possession of a horse to a lessee, who has the right to use the animal, but there is no title transfer. In other words, a lessee has the right to use the horse, but the lessor retains ownership.

Similarly, the purchaser of a share in a syndicated stallion is getting an ownership interest in the horse, although probably not actual physical possession of the animal. The buyer of a breeding season, on the other hand, gets the right to breed a mare to the stallion, but there is no transfer of title. The owner, or owners, of the stallion retain ownership of the horse.

This chapter examines the differences between public auctions and private sales, express and implied warranties, and sales and use taxes. The following chapter discusses the law of agency in general and the role of bloodstock agents in particular.

PRIVATE SALES

A private sale is exactly what the term implies, a transaction between a buyer and seller, and possibly a bloodstock agent or trainer, outside the structure and confines of a public auction setting. A private sale represents one of the cornerstones of capitalism and free enterprise, the idea that parties should be free to contract without interference for what they want.

Unless a contract is for an illegal purpose, there are few restrictions on the bargaining between the parties.

When the object of the contract is the sale of a horse, everything is open for negotiation — the identity of the horse, the purchase price, the terms of the sale, warranties, time and method of delivery, and the passing of the risk of loss.

Cash or Credit?

Cash sales are common and quite simple — the parties agree on a price, then money and the horse change hands. The seller and buyer should execute a written bill of sale and/or a purchase agreement every time a horse is sold. There is no standard form for either document, but, at a minimum, the bill of sale and purchase agreement for a cash transaction should include:

1. Identity of the parties, contact information, and a complete description of the horse.

2. Demand from the seller that the horse undergo a complete and thorough physical inspection, including a pre-purchase examination by a veterinarian of the buyer's choosing and acknowledgment by the buyer that an opportunity for such inspection was offered. A seller cannot force a buyer to have a horse examined by a veterinarian prior to purchase. If the opportunity for such an examination was offered and refused, however, the buyer assumes responsibility for any conditions that would have been discovered by a pre-purchase checkup. If a pre-purchase veterinary examination was done, the results of the examination might be included as well.

3. Language similar to the following, in conspicuous type and location, unless the seller intends to offer a warranty of some kind. (It may be difficult or impossible to disclaim some warranties, although sellers often try to do so. Whether this or similar language works to disclaim all warranties will be a question of state law for the courts in each jurisdiction to resolve.)

SELLER MAKES NO WARRANTIES OR REPRESENTATIONS
WHATSOEVER, EXPRESS OR IMPLIED, WITH RESPECT
TO THE HORSE, INCLUDING WARRANTIES CONCERNING

THE PHYSICAL CONDITION, HEALTH, OR SOUNDNESS OF THE HORSE, OR WARRANTIES OR REPRESENTATIONS WITH RESPECT TO THE MERCHANTABILITY OR FITNESS OF THE HORSE FOR ANY PARTICULAR PURPOSE, ALL OF WHICH WARRANTIES ARE HEREBY EXCLUDED. THE PARTIES TO THIS AGREEMENT ACKNOWLEDGE THAT THE HORSE IS SOLD "AS IS" AND "WITH ALL FAULTS." BUYER ACKNOWLEDGES THAT HE HAS CONDUCTED SUCH INVESTIGATIONS AND INSPECTIONS, INCLUDING THE USE OF A QUALIFIED VETERINARIAN, AND IS SATISFIED WITH THE HORSE'S CONDITION.

4. The purchase price and the terms for payment. Will the purchase price be paid in one lump sum, for example, or will the seller accept a down payment with the balance due on delivery? Is a personal check acceptable to the seller or is cash or a cashier's check required?

5. Warranty by the seller of clear and marketable title. If there are liens on the horse, they should be identified. Even if no liens or security interests are identified by the seller, a prudent buyer will check the accuracy of that information. Depending on the jurisdiction, liens and security interests can and should be registered with either a state or local agency. In many jurisdictions, registration is made through the secretary of state. Those records should be checked.

6. A statement setting a date on which the risk of loss passes from the seller to the buyer.

7. A statement outlining when, where, and how the horse will be delivered by the seller to the buyer.

8. The date upon which the buyer becomes responsible for boarding expenses and third-party charges if the buyer does not take immediate delivery of the horse.

9. An agreement between the parties as to the governing law, and where any disputes will be litigated if non-judicial resolution is not possible. A requirement that disputes be submitted to binding arbitration may be appropriate.

10. Statement of liability for sales tax. The sale of a horse may be subject

to state sales tax. This is a question for your local attorney. If sales tax is due on the transaction, the seller usually will be required to collect the tax from the buyer, then forward the tax to the state treasury. A failure to collect the applicable sales tax from the buyer does not eliminate the seller's liability to the state for the tax, and an unexpected tax bill can reduce the profits from a sale. The sales agreement should state clearly that the buyer is responsible for any applicable sales tax, and the seller should follow through and actually collect the tax due.

11. Prohibition against assignment by the buyer of any interest in the sale agreement without consent of the seller. For example, a buyer might negotiate the purchase of a horse with a seller, then assign (or transfer) any rights he or she might have as a buyer to a third party. Assignment can be a problem for a seller, who might not want to do business with the third party for some reason.

12. Signatures of the parties and the effective date of the agreement.

The majority of horse sales, just like most other transactions in the horse business, proceed from inception to conclusion without problems, despite a generally high level of informality. As a result, it is easy to assume that there will not be problems in *any* of your business dealings.

This is not a realistic way to do business, however. Instead, hope for the best, but prepare for the worst. Plan business transactions with an eye toward preventing problems by making sure that the parties to a sale understand their rights and obligations before money changes hands. A well-drafted bill of sale should recognize the competing interests of the buyer and the seller, and it should protect *both* parties.

Another option, especially for expensive animals, is an installment purchase, similar to buying an automobile and financing it for a number of months or years. Bank financing may be available, particularly in parts of the country where the horse business represents an important part of the economy, but many commercial lenders will be reluctant to loan money with a horse as collateral. More often the seller simply agrees to accept installment payments for the horse, in effect loaning the buyer the purchase money. Interest always will be a part of a commercial loan and may or may not be added if the seller provides the financing.

Installment sales present more opportunity for problems because the transaction is stretched over a sometimes-lengthy period. The process is complex and fraught with danger for the unwary, and installment sellers and installment buyers should take all possible steps to protect themselves. One simple step is for the seller to ask for financial references from a potential buyer and then to check them. A credit check also might be in order, especially for a high-priced horse. The advice of an attorney is highly recommended, either to draft the installment sales agreement or to review an agreement you are asked to sign if buying on time.

Most important, and this should not come as a surprise, is that the installment purchase agreement should be in writing. In addition to

AT A GLANCE

- A buyer and seller should have a written bill of sale and/or purchase agreement every time a horse is sold.
- If a buyer refused the offer to have a pre-purchase exam conducted on a horse he or she is buying, the buyer assumes responsibility for any conditions the exam might have found.
- Any liens or security interests on the horse for sale should be identified for the buyer.

the elements of a cash sales agreement or bill of sale already identified, an installment agreement or bill of sale should address, at a minimum, the following:

1. The seller should retain a security interest in the horse until the purchase price is paid in full. Loans generally require collateral to secure payment of the debt, and here the collateral is the horse. Discussed more fully in Chapter 6, a security interest in a horse allows the seller to keep his or her hand, legally if not physically, on the animal until the price is paid in full. It also is advisable for the seller to require the buyer to execute a separate promissory note for the purchase price. By doing so, the seller has additional legal options and protection if the buyer defaults. The seller should take whatever steps are required by state law to register the security interest.

2. The payment terms, including interest, and any penalty due if the buyer is late making one or more payments should be part of the agreement. The agreement also should set out in detail the circumstances that will constitute default on the part of the buyer.

3. There should also be a requirement that, until the purchase price is paid in full, the buyer provide adequate veterinary and farrier care, food, water, and shelter for the horse.

4. A requirement should be included that until the purchase price is paid in full, the buyer will maintain adequate insurance on the horse. (Although desirable protection for the seller, requiring insurance may not be economically feasible for some buyers. If this is the case, it might be possible for the parties to share the insurance premiums.)

5. The agreement should include authorization to recover attorney fees if one party defaults and legal action is necessary to enforce the contract. This provision can be important considering the ever-growing cost of litigation.

WARRANTIES, EXPRESS AND IMPLIED

Caveat emptor, let the buyer beware, is a principle that should be familiar to buyers and sellers alike. It means, simply, that buyers have a responsibility to examine carefully any item before purchase, and that failure to do so generally leaves the buyer without legal recourse in the event of a problem. Some people also interpret the maxim to mean that sellers bear no responsibility for the integrity of a sale, but that simplistic approach fails to take into account various warranties that may apply to a transaction.

The Uniform Commercial Code is a body of law that governs a wide variety of commercial transactions, including most sales of goods. Some version of the code has been adopted by all fifty states, and buyers and sellers should be aware that the code comes into play every time a horse is bought or sold. The code governs the sale of "goods"; horses, foals *in utero*, and most shares in stallions and other horses fall under that definition.

The Uniform Commercial Code serves as a general guide to how sales should operate. If a dispute arises, a court also may use the code to fill in specific missing terms in a sales contract. State versions of the code are similar in most respects, but there may be nuances in your jurisdiction's law. Your attorney is the best source of information about local law.

Sellers want to encourage a potential client to buy their horses, but they generally do not want to make specific promises about the horse's ability or guarantees about future success in the show ring, on the racetrack, or even as a pleasure horse. Buyers, on the other hand, have specific ideas about what they want in a horse and may expect assurances from the seller that the horse fits the bill.

Neither approach is totally realistic, and Article 2 of the Uniform Commercial Code attempts to set a middle ground between the concerns of the seller and the desires of the buyer when it comes to warranties. Usually associated with automobiles, large appliances, and electronics, a warranty is nothing more than a promise or guarantee from the seller that the article being sold will perform in a certain way. Sales of horses may encompass a wide range of warranties, and a breach of warranty may be grounds for the buyer to cancel or rescind the sale and demand return of the purchase money.

Warranties fall into two general categories: express or implied. An express warranty requires some affirmative action on the part of the seller while an implied warranty arises as an operation of law and does not depend on the seller's actions.

An express warranty is created when the seller makes any affirmation of fact or promise about the goods being sold, in this case a horse, so long as the affirmation becomes a material part of the transaction. A statement is material to the sale if the buyer relies on it in deciding whether to buy the horse. If a seller manages to make an affirmative statement about the horse that is *not* material to the sale, courts generally apply the "no harm, no foul" rule if breach of warranty is claimed by the buyer.

A statement from a seller to a buyer that "this filly is eligible to compete in the yearling futurity at the American Saddlebred World Championship" creates an express warranty, assuming that the buyer relies on that fact when deciding whether to buy the animal. This is true even if the seller was just chatting with the buyer and did not intend to create a warranty. If it turns out the horse had not been entered for the futurity, there has been a breach of warranty, and the buyer can cancel the sale.

An express warranty also can arise from a description of the horse by a seller. A buyer who purchases a horse advertised as a three-year-old can cancel the sale for breach of warranty if the animal actually is some other age, for example. Or a parent looking for a show pony can cancel the sale if the height of the advertised "pony" turns out to be 15 hands, two inches too tall to compete in pony classes recognized by the United States Equestrian Federation.

Less obvious is an advertisement for a horse described as a "stallion." While the seller might intend to communicate only the fact the horse is not a gelding, use of the word "stallion" in the description also could be a warranty that the horse is fertile and sound for breeding.

Finally, an express warranty can be created by a sample or model. This type of express warranty is most applicable to sales of large lots of similar consumer goods and protects a buyer by warranting that all the goods in the lot will be identical to the sample or model. A hardware store buying one hundred snow shovels, for example, is entitled to rely on the appearance of a salesman's sample of the shovel in deciding whether to make the purchase.

A possible application to the horse business might be the widespread use of photographs and videotapes in advertising. Some breed organizations register horses based on a particular color or color pattern. A photograph of an Appaloosa, for example, might create an express warranty that the horse actually looks like it does in the photograph and can be registered because it fits the breed's color standard. Likewise, a mare owner searching for a stallion should be entitled to rely on a photograph of the horse in an advertisement. Use of a retouched photograph that hides a conformation defect or a color pattern that would prevent registration could be a breach of warranty.

A seller can create an express warranty without intending to do so. The only requirement is that a seller makes a statement about some fact material to the sale. This does not mean that *every* statement by a seller creates a warranty, however. Some statements by a seller do not relate to a material fact. Others, called "puffing" or "puffery," are either opinions about general quality or are simply outrageous or unbelievable. Puffing does not form the basis of an express warranty because a reasonable buyer would not rely on the statements in deciding whether to buy the horse in question.

Advertising stating that a farm's sale yearlings are "superior" to the horses in every other consignment is too general to constitute an express warranty. Likewise, telling a potential buyer that the horse under consideration is the fastest, prettiest, or smartest filly on the planet are examples of puffing. They are statements no reasonable buyer would accept as true and will not form the basis for legal action if the horse turns out not to be the fastest, prettiest, or smartest.

In addition to any express warranties a seller might make, either on purpose or inadvertently, the law may impose certain implied warranties on the horse being sold.

One of the most important is the warranty of title, which means when a seller offers a horse for sale, the law implies a promise there is a good and marketable title to the animal. This also means there are no liens or other security interests about which the buyer is unaware. In other words, when a horse is offered for sale, the buyer is entitled to believe the seller is the owner and has the legal right to transfer full title. A fundamental rule of property law is you cannot sell what you do not own.

A second type of implied warranty is the warranty of merchantability, which applies to sellers who hold themselves out as having some particular knowledge or expertise about horses. Most professionals in the horse business would satisfy this standard. If the seller thus qualifies as a "merchant" under the Uniform Commercial Code, the horse being sold must satisfy the contract description and must be suitable to the general purposes for which it is being sold.

Merchantability is a somewhat amorphous guarantee and simply means that a horse being sold as a dressage prospect, for example, has no condition that would prevent it from being trained for dressage. Nothing beyond general suitability is promised.

A third type of implied warranty, the warranty of fitness for a particular purpose, may arise if before the sale is complete, the seller becomes aware of any particular purpose the buyer has in mind for the horse and learns the buyer is relying on the seller to provide such an animal. In this situation, the buyer is entitled to rely on the seller's implied promise the horse will suit the intended purpose. Fitness for a particular purpose is more specific than the general warranty of merchantability.

Consider the following transaction, which is common in the horse business. A buyer goes to a trainer and says he is looking for a dressage horse capable of winning at third- and fourth-level competitions. He also says he is relying on the trainer to find such a horse. The trainer's knowledge that the buyer is looking for a particular kind of horse and is relying on the seller's expertise and advice means any horse sold probably comes with an implied warranty that the animal is ready to compete successfully at third and fourth level.

A seller can, under some circumstances, disclaim the implied warranties of merchantability and fitness for a particular purpose. Such disclaimers should be, and in the case of a disclaimer of fitness for a particular purpose generally must be, in writing.

A seller can disclaim most implied warranties by using the Uniform Commercial Code magic words "as is" or "with all faults and defects," although the market for such a horse may be extremely limited. Disclaimers of implied warranties must be in writing if there is a written sales contract, in which case the disclaimer must be conspicuous. Oral disclaimers are only effective to the extent they can be proven, which can be difficult or impossible without having them in writing.

Whether an "as is" sale effectively disclaims express warranties made by the seller is more problematic. Courts may refuse to enforce such disclaimers on the public policy theory that a seller should not be allowed to make express promises and then negate them on a technicality.

A seller should request that a buyer examine the horse completely before finalizing the sale, and a buyer should consider a pre-purchase veterinary examination a necessity. If the buyer either has the horse examined or declines to do so, there no longer are any implied warranties covering conditions that could have been discovered during the examination.

Prospective buyers should understand what a pre-purchase veterinary examination can, and cannot, accomplish. The American Association of Equine Practitioners has issued "Guidelines for Reporting Purchase Examinations," which outline the requirements of a pre-purchase exam.

In brief, the examining veterinarian should give the buyer a report in writing identifying the horse and indicating the date and place of the examination. The report should include "all abnormal or undesirable findings," and the veterinarian should "give his or her qualified opinion as to the functional effect of these findings." The veterinarian should not state an opinion about the suitability of the horse to a particular purpose, however, and a buyer should not demand one.

The position of the American Association of Equine Practitioners is that suitability for a particular purpose is a business decision that should be made by the buyer based on a variety of factors, only one of which is the purchase examination. If you are new to the horse business, you should consider having your trainer or some other more experienced person accompany you to examine the horse.

The situation may require the buyer to employ the veterinarian who also is the animal's regular treating veterinarian. If this undesirable scenario is necessary, buyers should be aware that confidentiality concerns will prevent the veterinarian from disclosing anything about the horse's condition not resulting from the pre-purchase examination.

Finally, if a buyer discovers a problem after completing the sale but before "accepting" the horse, the animal can be rejected and returned to the seller. Under the Uniform Commercial Code, a buyer still can reject the horse within a reasonable time after taking physical possession of the animal. In other words, acceptance of the horse and taking physical possession are not the same under the code. If the problem goes undiscovered for a significant period of time, however, the code does not authorize returning the animal to the seller. Instead, the buyer must file a lawsuit for damages based on the seller's breach of either an express or implied warranty. At this point the parties might consider some form of non-judicial alternative dispute resolution, which is discussed in Chapter 2.

Intentional misrepresentation by a seller almost certainly will give rise to various breach of warranty claims. More important, such conduct may constitute fraud, which can be a separate cause of action if a lawsuit is filed. Although state laws vary, the general requirements necessary to prove a claim of fraud regarding a sale are:

1) A material misrepresentation by the seller that the seller knew was false;

2) The seller's intent that the buyer rely on the misrepresentation;

AT A GLANCE

- Warranties fall under two main categories: express and implied.
- Intentional misrepresentation of a horse by a seller can result in breach of warranty claims and could constitute fraud.
- At public auctions, risk of loss — financial responsibility for damage to property — passes from seller to buyer at the fall of the hammer.

3) Actual reliance on the misrepresentation by the buyer;

4) Some harm suffered by the buyer as a result of the reliance on the misrepresentation.

RISK OF LOSS

Buyers and sellers have different and often opposing interests in a horse sale, and the ultimate goal of pre-sale negotiations is to accommodate those differing interests as much as possible. One way this can be accomplished is through the allocation of risk of loss.

Risk of loss is a legal term for the financial responsibility for damage to property when transferred from the seller to the buyer. In other words, the party bearing the risk of loss in a horse sale is the party who will suffer a financial loss if the animal is injured or dies. Risk of loss always starts with the seller and transfers to the buyer at some point during the transaction.

At public auctions the risk of loss generally passes from seller to buyer at the fall of the auctioneer's hammer. In private sales, on the other hand, transfer of the risk of loss can be negotiated between the parties. A seller will want the risk of loss quickly transferred to the buyer. A buyer, on the other hand, wants the risk of loss retained by the seller for as long as possible.

Consider, for example, the sale of a show jumper from a seller in New York to a buyer in California, with the horse to be shipped by van from the East Coast to the West Coast. The seller would like the risk of loss to be passed to the buyer before the horse steps onto the van, so that the buyer bears the financial risk of the horse being injured in transit. The buyer, of course, would prefer the risk of loss to stay with the seller until the horse arrives safely in California. When the risk of loss actually passes from seller to buyer can be a bargaining chip for either party, with agreement between the parties the only requirement in a private sale.

PUBLIC AUCTIONS

Some sellers relish the give-and-take bargaining inherent in a private sale; other sellers do not. For the latter, a public auction may be a more attractive alternative to selling horses privately. The principal differences between the two are a more structured environment offered by a public auction and the presence of a third party, the sales company. A sales company functions as a middleman of sorts to expedite the transfer of horses and dollars from sellers to buyers.

For those unfamiliar with horse auctions, the process works something like this: After locating a suitable auction, the seller enters into a written contract with the sales company. Depending on the auction, the seller also may have to pay an entry or consignment fee for the horse.

The consignment contract authorizes the sales company to auction the horse for the seller and will set out the general rights and responsibilities of the seller and the auction company. Among other things, the contract should establish that the consignor has clear title and the authority to sell the horse, the commission that the sales company will receive if the horse is sold or fails to meet its reserve price, circumstances under which the company can refuse to accept the horse, and procedures to be followed if a buyer fails to make payment.

The contract also probably will include a waiver of liability holding the sales company harmless for loss or damage and an explicit agreement to be bound by the company's conditions of sale. The contract may seem complicated in its own right, but the conditions of sale will be far more comprehensive. This was not always the case.

A hundred years ago, when life was simpler, the catalog for Fasig-Tipton Company's annual sale of Thoroughbreds in Lexington, Kentucky, listed just five conditions of sale:

First — The highest bidder to be the buyer; and if any dispute arises between two or more bidders, the lot so disputed shall be immediately put up again and re-sold.

Second — The purchasers to give in their names and places of abode (if required), and to pay down 25 per cent of the purchase money (if required), as earnest and in part payment, in default of which, the lot so purchased may be immediately put up again and re-sold, if the Auctioneer shall think fit.

Third — The lots to be at the buyer's risk and expense upon the fall of the hammer, and the remainder of the purchase money to be absolutely paid at the conclusion of the sale.

Fourth — Upon failure of complying with the above conditions, the money deposited in part of payment shall be forfeited to the owner of the lot, he paying thereout all just expenses; and the lot shall be re-sold by public or private sale, and the deficiency (if any) shall be immediately made good by the defaulter at this sale.

Fifth — If any person shall purchase a lot and not pay for it within the time limited by the Third Condition, nothing contained in the Fourth Condition shall prevent the Auctioneer or the owner of the lot from compelling the purchaser to pay for it, if the Auctioneer or seller shall think fit.

Some things have not changed in a century. The risk of loss still generally passes from the seller to the buyer at the fall of the auctioneer's hammer and a buyer's failure to pay for a horse is a concern to everyone involved.

Other things have changed significantly. The catalog for a recent auction conducted by Keeneland in Lexington, Kentucky, listed twenty-four conditions of sale comprising almost twenty-five pages of small, tightly packed type. Modern auction companies spend a substantial amount of time informing potential buyers that they are purchasing horses "as is, with all faults and defects" and that all warranties other than the few specifically stated in the conditions are disclaimed. As noted in the case studies following this chapter, courts generally enforce these disclaimers.

The conditions also explain the resolution of bidding disputes, terms of payment, default by successful bidders, physical conditions that are warranted (including cribbers, wobblers, ridglings, and horses that have vision problems or that have undergone wind or abdominal surgery), responsibility for accuracy of catalog information (usually the consignor), that time is of the essence (a legal term meaning that deadlines in the conditions must be strictly followed), and the responsibility of buyers to fully inspect the horses offered for sale before bidding.

Also common in many conditions of sale is a requirement that disputes over warranty issues must be resolved by binding arbitration rather than through legal action. Giving up the right to file a lawsuit can be an unpleasant surprise for a buyer who has not read the conditions of sale.

Consider, for example, a racing prospect with an undiagnosed wind problem covered by a warranty in the conditions of sale. If the wind problem is discovered in a post-sale veterinary examination and the sales company is notified within the specified time (buyers take note: this usually is a very short period), the dispute will be sent to a panel of impartial veterinarians. Serving as arbitrators, the members of the panel will examine the horse and decide whether there was a breach of warranty. If there was a breach, the sale is cancelled and the purchase price refunded. If the panel finds no breach of warranty, however, the buyer cannot cancel the sale. There is no further recourse.

After making a successful final bid on a horse, the buyer signs an "acknowledgment of purchase" form identifying the purchaser and indicating the sales price and other pertinent information. The agreement also provides that the buyer will be bound by the conditions of sale printed in the catalog. After settling the bill with the auction company, the buyer is allowed to remove the animal from the grounds. The sales company then pays the purchase price, less the commission set out in the consignment contract, to the seller.

An auction company's "conditions of sale" and "acknowledgment of purchase" are binding contracts that establish the rights and responsibilities of the sales company, the seller, and the buyer. Like any other contract, they should be scrutinized carefully, preferably with the advice of your attorney, before signing. Ideally this would happen before the sale. Failure to read or understand a document almost never is a viable excuse for a breach of the contract, and sales documents are no exceptions to the general rule.

THE REPOSITORY

The usual requirement that buyers examine potential purchases before bidding certainly makes sense on its face — let the buyer beware, but it creates a problem for both buyers and sellers. Buyers might complain about the time involved and about the cost of having the examinations done, especially if they are looking at a large number of horses prior to a sale. Consignors of horses attracting many potential buyers might not want to subject their animals to the stress of a long succession of radiographs and endoscopic examinations. Both arguments are reasonable.

One response has been the establishment by some sales companies of a "repository," a central location where consignors at their expense can provide one set of radiographs, records of endoscopic examinations, and explanatory statements and veterinary certificates. The collected veterinary information then is made available to the buyers and their veterinarians. Buyers always retain the option of additional veterinary examinations, but the repository eliminates the need in many instances.

If a sales company chooses to offer a repository service, buyers have a duty to examine the information contained therein. Keeneland's conditions of sale, for example, include the requirement that "purchasers shall inspect fully each horse that they may purchase," and the definition of full inspection "shall include a review of all repository information for each horse." Buyers should be aware that inclusion of veterinary information in a repository could eliminate the sales company's obligation to announce certain physical conditions.

Provision of a repository service does not mean that the sales company is vouching for the accuracy of the veterinary information in a horse's file. Instead, the sales company is merely providing a place for storage of records and an opportunity for sellers and buyers to exchange information.

A buyer will have difficulty asserting a claim based on a defect in a horse that could have been detected through a review of repository records, if the records were not examined prior to the purchase. Some sales companies limit access to the repository to veterinarians. Even if this is not the situation, buyers who lack specialized veterinary knowledge should retain a veterinarian to interpret the information contained in the repository records. This will increase the overall cost of buying a horse but can prevent a much more costly mistake.

Although examination of repository information is required as part of a buyer's full inspection of a horse, consignors are not required to use the service. If you are selling a horse at a sale where a repository service is offered, you may not have to participate as a requirement for selling at the auction. Consignors should make inquiries of the sales company to determine if there is a repository and if participation is optional or mandatory.

Consignors who do participate must bear the additional expense of radiographs and endoscopic examinations, but for many sellers that is a fair trade-off for sparing horses the stress of repeated examinations by prospective bidders. Sellers also should be aware that they may be inadvertently warranting some aspect of a horse's condition by providing records for the repository.

Although apparently never an issue, at least so far, it is not unreasonable for a buyer to argue that a radiograph in a repository constitutes a "model" and thus creates an express warranty of the horse's physical condition. For the repository to work, it is important that sellers provide complete and up-to-date information, that buyers use the service, and that both parties recognize the limitations of the system.

Private sales and public auctions have the same ultimate goal, money to the sellers and horses to the buyers, but the two are poles apart regarding how that goal is realized. The decision whether to buy or sell a horse privately or at public auction is both a personal and a business decision. The advantages of a public auction, such as a larger pool of potential buyers, a professional atmosphere, and the fact that there is a middleman to help collect the purchase price, may be offset by the sales commission that reduces your profit, the feeling that your horse is a small fish in a big pond, and the potential for less direct contact with the buyers.

SALES AND USE TAXES

Sales taxes and use taxes are different incarnations of the same creature, a tax paid by the purchaser of specified property. The difference depends on the locations of the buyer and seller. If you purchase property from a seller who is doing business in your own state, you may be required to pay a percentage of the retail price to the seller, who acts as a surrogate tax collector for the state. This is a sales tax, and the concept should be familiar unless you happen to live in one of the few states with no sales tax.

If, on the other hand, buyers who purchase property from a seller in another state where sales tax is not collected may nevertheless be required to pay a use tax in their own state based on a percentage of the retail price. This is a less-familiar concept, one that can result in an unpleasant surprise for out-of-state buyers who purchase a horse in another jurisdiction and bring it back home. Without proper planning, buyers may wind up facing a hefty use-tax liability.

Sales and use taxes are strictly matters of state law, and buyers should consult with a qualified attorney or tax professional in their jurisdiction for comprehensive planning advice.

Some states exempt the sales of all horses from sales/use tax. Other states, such as Kentucky, exempt from taxes the sale or use of *some* horses. In Kentucky, sales of horses (or interests or shares in horses) used exclusively for breeding are exempt from sales or use taxes. Other states with similar provisions for breeding stock include Arkansas, Colorado, Florida, Georgia, Hawaii, Idaho, Illinois, Kansas, Louisiana, Maryland, Missouri, New Jersey, New Mexico, New York, North Carolina, Utah, Wisconsin, and West Virginia.

Kentucky law also exempts from sales or use taxes stallion services and horses under two years of age at the time of sale. The latter exemption is available when the sale is made to a nonresident of Kentucky and the horse is transported out of state immediately after the sale or immediately after training within Kentucky so long as the horse's post-sale stay in the state is temporary and for training purposes only. A stable owner from New York, for example, does not pay Kentucky sales tax on a yearling purchased at Keeneland, provided that the yearling is either shipped immediately out of Kentucky or is shipped out of state following a temporary training period.

Creative tax planning generally is associated with efforts to reduce federal income tax liability, but state sales and use tax statutes also can be a fertile ground for legitimate tax avoidance. A horse purchased outside Kentucky then brought into the state within ninety days of the sale generally will be considered as purchased for use within the state and a 6 percent use tax will be imposed. However, use tax generally will not be imposed on the same horse if it was imported into Kentucky more than ninety days after the purchase. Also, buyers who do pay a sales tax in the state of purchase generally are not required to pay a use tax in their home state. Advance planning can save money, and, as always, buyers should consult an attorney or tax professional for specific advice.

A close reading of individual state statutes also may be necessary to learn if purchases of feed, hay, and farm equipment are subject to state sales and use taxes. In Kentucky, for example, feed for livestock and farm machinery used exclusively in the production of livestock are exempt from the state's 6 percent sales tax.

Anyone who reaches the obvious conclusion that this is a clear-cut benefit for horse owners should think again. Kentucky law limits the statutory definition of "livestock" to animals produced for food, and one Kentucky court noted that, "Happily, the legendary esteem in which Kentuckians have always held horseflesh has never extended to the dinner table." Feed for cattle is exempt from the sales tax; feed for horses is not, at least in Kentucky, where horses, by statutory definition, are not "livestock."

Although sales and use taxes might seem insignificant, at least when compared to income taxes, buyers should not ignore the possibilities these taxes offer for tax planning and possible savings.

LEASING — A VIABLE ALTERNATIVE?

Sometimes, for a variety of reasons, someone may want the use of a horse without actually owning the animal. This is often the case when a rider wants to compete with a horse for a show season or two or when a breeder wants to raise a foal without owning the broodmare. In those situations a lease may be the answer.

The owner of the animal (the lessor) allows you (the lessee) to use the horse for a specified purpose, for a specified period, and you agree to pay for that use. You also agree to accept responsibility for providing adequate food, shelter, and care during the time the horse is in your possession.

A proper lease agreement should identify the parties and the horse, the term of the lease, and the amount of money to be paid by the "lessee" to the "lessor." The lease also should set out in detail the schedule of lease payments, recourse of the horse owner if the lease payments are not made on time, and the fact that the owner can recover attorney's fees if the lease is broken by the lessee.

The document should state the purpose of the lease (whether the horse will be shown or bred, for example) and any warranty the owner wishes to make about the suitability of the horse to the stated purpose. Whenever possible, the owner should insist that the lessee provide insurance, either mortality or loss of use, or both, on the horse. This can be prohibitively expensive for many lessees, however.

Finally, many lease agreements include an option to purchase the horse at some future time. The terms of the future sale (date, price, whether the sale will be cash or installment, and whether the lease payments will be applied to the purchase price) should be included.

CASE STUDIES

Cohen v. North Ridge Farms, Inc., 712 FSupp 1265 (EDKY)

The plaintiff, Israel Cohen, purchased a son of In Reality—Lady B. Gay at the 1988 Keeneland summer yearling sale for $575,000. There was no pre-purchase veterinary examination. The day after the sale three veterinarians examined the colt and unanimously diagnosed a flaccid epiglottis, a condition of the throat that might, or might not, have affected the colt's training and racing. Based on the veterinary opinion, Cohen attempted to cancel the sale for a variety of reasons, including mistake; lack of consideration; violation of Kentucky's Consumer Protection Act; misrepresentation and fraud on the part of the colt's consignor, North Ridge Farm; and breach of fiduciary duty on the part of Keeneland.

The court decided in favor of the defendants (North Ridge Farm and Keeneland) on all counts, relying in large part on the disclaimer of all warranties contained in the conditions of sale. The court noted that Cohen was represented at the sale by a team of experts, including a trainer and veterinarian; that the veterinarian assisting Cohen recommended that every yearling on the "short list" of possible purchases be examined endoscopically prior to bidding; that no one representing Cohen ever asked permission to examine the In Reality colt; and that there was sufficient time for such an examination if one had been requested.

The plaintiff argued that no examination had been requested because of an understanding that North Ridge did not permit them. The court dismissed that argument, noting that "whether North Ridge would or would not have allowed a pre-sale endoscopic examination of this yearling is irrelevant because plaintiff's agents did not request same ..."

Based on the facts set out above, the court concluded:

> Therefore, these uncontroverted facts show that plaintiff assumed the risk of loss in two ways: (1) the conditions of sale expressly disclaimed all warranties and guarantees as to soundness and wind, and (2) plaintiff acted with "conscious ignorance" in electing to purchase this yearling in that he made the decision to purchase without even requesting a pre-sale endoscopic examination of this yearling, even though there was ample time to do so.

Because there were no genuine issues of fact to put to a jury, the court granted summary judgment in favor North Ridge Farm and Keeneland.

Several lessons can be learned from *Cohen*. First, the conditions of sale constitute a legal contract binding the buyer and seller to its terms. Second, a disclaimer of all warranties in a sales company's conditions of sale generally will be enforced, and buyers should be aware that they are buying horses "as is." Third, a buyer who fails to have a pre-purchase veterinary examination performed does so at his or her own risk and cannot later complain about a physical condition that could have been discovered by such an exam. The court also affirmed that Keeneland's duty to buyers was limited to using "ordinary care to ensure that information contained in the catalog is 'as accurate and comprehensive as possible.' This is where Keeneland's duty begins and ends."

Cohen was decided in 1988, before Keeneland instituted a repository for veterinary information. Under the current conditions of sale, examination of material in the repository would be included in the definition of a full examination.

Chernick v. Fasig-Tipton Kentucky, Inc., 703 SW2d 885 (Ky 1985)

This dispute involved the sale of the broodmare Fiddler's Colleen for $85,000 at the 1982 fall breeding stock sale conducted by Fasig-Tipton Kentucky. Earlier in the year, the mare had spontaneously aborted ("slipped") twin foals, and she did not conceive when bred to Match the Hatch. The mare subsequently got in foal when bred to a different stallion, London Company, but the mare also lost that foal prior to the sale in question.

The court described problems when the mare was entered in the sale:

> Completing the standard consignment contract and entry forms supplied by Fasig-Tipton, Caroline Chernick [the consignor] only just complied with the requirements by supplying information relevant to "this year's produce" and "last year's produce." Fasig-Tipton was to obtain information as to prior years from Pedigree Associates, Inc., by means of access to the Jockey Club Statistical Information. (It is to be noted that these statistics may be delinquent by as many as two years; however, in this instance the delinquency covered a four-year period.) Mrs. Chernick entered "Colt by Dantan" and "slipped" in the appropriate blanks, leaving much unstated. The Chernicks failed, in fact, to say that the mare had slipped twins which they were aware would reduce her value and probably greatly reduce her breeding potential. Ten days prior to sale the contract mandated the completion of a veterinarian's certificate provided by Fasig-Tipton indicating a mare's pregnancy status. The standard form forwarded by Caroline Chernick provided for five options relating to the mare's status: 1) in foal; 2) barren and free from infection; 3) maiden, free from infection; 4) barren and not in sound breeding condition; and 5) maiden and not in sound breeding condition. In compliance, [the Chernick's veterinarian] checked the second option and returned the form, which was subsequently lost. Realizing the high degree of reliance placed by a purchaser upon Fasig-Tipton's sale catalog which listed the mare as "believed in foal," the sale announcers made three references to the fact, while the mare was in the ring, that Fiddler's Colleen was "not in foal," that "she is barren." There was no reference made to her recent slip.

Cloverfield Farm purchased the mare for $85,000. Shortly thereafter the mare was examined by several veterinarians. Two found her unsound for breeding, one found her sound for breeding but noted that she would require suturing before she could carry a foal, and a fourth expressed no opinion. The buyer's attempts to return the mare to Fasig-Tipton and cancel the sale failed, as did the attempt to get the Chernicks to take the mare back. A flurry of lawsuits resulted.

After a trial, the judge determined that the Chernicks committed fraud and misrepresentation and ruled that Fasig-Tipton had been negligent in failing to use ordinary care to obtain accurate information concerning the mare's breeding history. Cloverfield was awarded $85,000 (the purchase price), plus interest; $40,000 in punitive damages from the Chernicks; and compensatory damages from both the Chernicks and Fasig-Tipton.

The Kentucky Court of Appeals affirmed the verdict against the Chernicks, explaining that the mare's "condition was deliberately and consciously suppressed. The Chernicks' attempt to unload this horse on an unsuspecting buyer amounts to 'conscious wrongdoing.' " The appellate court reversed the ruling against Fasig-Tipton, however, because the buyer had not made a specific claim for damages against the sales company.

The court did not accept Fasig-Tipton's argument that it served only as a "stakeholder" in the transaction, however, explaining that,

> [A]lthough under the terms of the consignment contract the Chernicks were responsible for the accuracy of all information contained within the catalog of sale, Fasig-Tipton had a fiduciary duty to the purchaser and to the Commonwealth's most prestigious and valued industry to use ordinary care to ensure that its catalog and/or announcements were as accurate as possible.

The court cited Fasig-Tipton's admitted knowledge that information from The Jockey Club might not be current as "notice that its sales catalog was incomplete and that it was under a duty to report such ensuing inaccuracies or to correct them. Fasig-Tipton failed to do so, breaching its duty, and thereby exhibited negligent behavior toward the purchasers who justifiably relied upon the information contained in the catalog of sale."

Morningstar v. Hallett, 858 A2d 125 (Pa 2004)

Morningstar placed the following as in a local newspaper:
SALE OR LEASE
Retired eventer. Lovely 11 year old thoroughbred mare. Flashy bay, 16+ hands, extension jumping & dressage, superb mover, perfect horse for any level rider. Reasonable offer considered to right home. Call [seller's telephone number].

Hallett, the purchaser and defendant, examined the horse twice, and despite noting that the mare was lame at the trot purchased her for $2,950. Hallett signed a sales agreement that stated, in part, that the mare was eleven years old and that the purchaser was buying the horse "as is." Hallett subsequently stopped payment on the check and tried to return the horse to Morningstar on the grounds that the mare actually was sixteen years old and had vision problems and a heart murmur. The parties filed lawsuits against each other, with Morningstar winning the first round when a trial court granted summary judgment in her favor.

The Pennsylvania Superior Court eventually ruled for Hallett and sent the case back to the trial court. The court explained that the "as is" language in the advertisement and sales contract served to disclaim any implied warranties, but that the language was insufficient to disclaim express warranties. The court said that the advertisement and sales contract language stating that the mare was eleven years old created an express warranty relating to the horse's age.

Sheffield v. Darby, 535 SE2d 776 (Ga App 2000)

The court set out the facts of this case of puffing as follows:

After watching a male horse owned by Terry and Manita Darby [the defendants] perform at a horse show, Ashley Sheffield [the plaintiff] contacted the Darbys about buying him. The Darbys assured her that the horse had no problems and would make a good show horse for use in competition. In the presence of and in consultation with her father (who raised horses for a business), Sheffield rode the horse and decided to purchase him for $8,500. Within three weeks, Sheffield and her trainer discerned that the horse was lame. Sheffield sued the Darbys for fraud and for breach of express and implied warranties ...

The trial court entered summary judgment in favor of the Darbys and the Georgia Court of Appeals affirmed. The court explained that, "a party may not justifiably rely on and assume to be true representations consisting of mere expressions of opinion, hope, expectation, puffing, and the like; rather, the party must inquire into and examine such representations to ascertain the truth." The court said statements made by the Darbys that the horse had no problems and would make a good show horse were merely opinions that constituted puffing and that the buyer's failure to have a pre-purchase veterinary examination done precluded a claim of reliance on those statements. Finally, the court stated that, "a statement purporting to be merely the seller's opinion or commendation of the goods does not create a warranty."

Bonvie Stables v. Irving, 796 A2d 899 (NJ App 2002)

Both the plaintiff and the defendant were professionals in the Standardbred business. Richard and Pat Bonvie bought a horse at auction for $35,000 and signed an acknowledgment of purchase in which they agreed to be bound by the auction company's conditions of sale. Those conditions included several statements that horses were sold "as is" and that there were no express or implied warranties.

There was conflicting testimony about conversations between the seller and buyer prior to the sale, the buyers claiming that Irving had told them that the horse had never received any injections, had no problems, and was "one hundred percent." Irving stated in a deposition that he told the plaintiffs that the horse "hadn't been injected from ear to asshole all summer," and that the horse "might have had one" injection. Irving contended that the plaintiffs never asked about any prior surgeries the horse might have undergone.

The horse became lame shortly after the sale, a condition that was treated with a series of injections. The plaintiffs later learned the horse had undergone surgery to remove calcium deposits and had received numerous pre-race and post-race injections. They also obtained medical records showing a variety of injections of other medications. The plaintiffs demanded a refund of the purchase price, which Irving apparently ignored, and then they filed a lawsuit.

The trial court ruled that the "as is" language in the conditions of sale precluded any complaints by the buyers. An appellate court disagreed. The court determined that the "as is" and no warranty language in the conditions of sale applied only to transactions between the buyers and the sales company but did not apply to transactions between consignors and the buyers. Even if the "as is" language did apply to the seller, the court stated that "those clauses were not intended to insulate defendants against their misrepresentations or their concealment of information they were required to disclose." The defendant failed to comply with a requirement to disclose any latent defect such as a broken bone or any surgery.

The appellate court also determined that statements by the seller to the buyer were not puffing. The court explained:

> Although we agree that mere opinion by an owner about the quality of a horse or speculation concerning the horse's future performance is "sales talk" or "puffing," we distinguish such non-actionable statements of opinion from specific knowingly false statements of fact upon which reliance is placed. Here, Irving's statement that no injections had previously been given was patently false ...

Calumet Farm, Inc. v. Revenue Cabinet, Commonwealth of Kentucky, 793 SW2d 830 (Ky App 1990)

In Kentucky, sales tax is applicable to "fees paid for breeding a stallion to a mare" but not to the sale of "horses, or interests or shares in horses, provided the purchase or use is made for breeding purposes only." When major winner Alydar was retired to stud at Calumet Farm in Lexington, Kentucky, Calumet took the unusual step of not syndicating the horse. Instead, Calumet sold a number of "lifetime breeding rights," giving each purchaser the right to breed one mare a year to Alydar each year and a second mare in alternating years, throughout Alydar's life. The purchasers of lifetime breeding rights acquired no interest in Alydar, only an interest in the breeding rights to the stallion.

Calumet considered a lifetime breeding right as functionally equivalent to a share in the horse and did not collect sales tax on the transactions. The Kentucky Revenue Cabinet took exception to this interpretation and sought to recover the delinquent sales tax.

The Kentucky Court of Appeals distinguished the lifetime breeding rights sold by Calumet from a share in a syndicated stallion on the ground that the former did not convey a share or an interest in the horse, while the latter did. The court explained that, "a lifetime breeding right is, in its simplest form, a fee paid, albeit substantial, for breeding a stallion, Alydar, to a mare in this state for the lifetime of the stallion, and thus, falls squarely within the confines of the taxing statute."

Everyone in the horse business eventually will buy, sell, or lease a horse. The familiarity of the transaction should not make you complacent, however, and you should be certain of your rights and insist on their recognition in a written agreement.

RESOURCES

Sellers and buyers interested in participating in public auctions should review the conditions of sale prior to either consigning or purchasing a horse. *The*

Blood-Horse Source, a comprehensive directory of Thoroughbred owners, breeders, and service and product providers includes a listing of contact information for Thoroughbred sales companies. *The Horse Source*, an all-breed directory, has similar information for other disciplines. Both are available from Blood-Horse Publications, (800) 582-5604.

Dual agency (discussed more fully in Chapter 10) is one of the issues addressed by the Sales Integrity Task Force (SITF), a group of Thoroughbred owners, breeders, buyers, and consignors organized under the auspices of the Thoroughbred Owners and Breeders Association. This task force produced a code of ethics that stressed the "fraudulent nature of dual agency without disclosure and pre-sale price manipulation," included a sample agreement for use by buyers and bloodstock agents; required disclosure of surgical procedures that permanently altered a horse's conformation; banned surgical procedures that temporarily altered conformation; required veterinarians to disclose their interest, if any, in horses they examine for potential buyers; encouraged full disclosure of ownership of horses; and established a procedure to educate new buyers. More information about the Sales Integrity Task Force, including the full text of the code of ethics and sample forms, can be found at www. salesintegrity.org.

Recommendations regarding disclosure of medications given to horses were developed by the American Association of Equine Practitioners' task force on medication at public auctions and approved by the organization's board of directors in 2005. The recommendations can be found at www.aaep.org.

10

AGENCY

It often seems as if everyone in the horse business either *uses* a bloodstock agent, *is* a bloodstock agent, or *wants to be* a bloodstock agent. While that statement may paint with too broad a stroke, the importance to the horse business of bloodstock agents cannot be overemphasized. While "bloodstock agent" is a term typically associated with the Thoroughbred industry, the use of third-party agents to facilitate the buying and selling of horses is common for all breeds. An Arabian trainer who locates a show horse for a client and negotiates the sale, for example, is working as a bloodstock agent, even if neither the trainer nor the buyer nor the seller uses that particular term.

Agency can be a consideration outside the bloodstock agent context, however. Employees are considered the agents of their employers, for example, and general partners can be agents of the partnership. This chapter addresses the general law of agency and the situations in which an agency relationship might occur, plus the potential problems that can arise from dual agency, a situation in which a single agent represents both the buyer and seller in a transaction.

THE LAW OF AGENCY

Agency is the general term that defines the legal relationship among three individuals: the agent, the principal, and a third party. It works like this: One person (the agent) has the express or implied authority to act on behalf of a second person (the principal). In the process the agent creates an enforceable obligation to do something on the part of the principal, for the benefit of a third party.

A simple and common example occurs when an employer sends an employee to the feed store to buy grain. Because employees are agents of their employers, the employee in this example can purchase grain for the employer's account and thus obligate the employer to pay the bill. If the employer does not pay the bill, the third party, the feed dealer, has a legal cause of action against the principal for payment. In this situation the agent incurs no liability for the purchase.

This example assumes two important things: that an agency relationship actually exists between the employer and employee and that the feed-store owner knows about the agency relationship. An employer-employee relationship is an example of actual agency, the agency arising as a direct result of the fact that the employee works for the employer.

Other examples of actual agency include situations in which a principal has given a non-employee the express authority to act on the principal's behalf. An agreement between a horse owner and a public trainer likely includes the express understanding that the trainer can act for the owner to enter the horse in shows or races, hire a van service, or secure veterinary care. (A private trainer, who works for one owner exclusively, is an agent of the owner by virtue of the employer-employee relationship.)

Some public trainers take a different approach and pay third-party expenses out of their own pockets, then bill the owners. Many van company owners, veterinarians, farriers, and other vendors prefer to be paid directly by the trainer rather than send bills to an owner, but either solution works.

Actual agency relationships show up throughout the horse business. Sales companies act as the agents of the consignors prior to the sale of a horse and probably as agents for both the seller and buyer after the sale, at least until the proceeds are distributed; bloodstock agents act on behalf of buyers or sellers; jockey agents represent riders; the managers of syndicated stallions act on behalf of the owners of the horses. The list goes on.

Agency relationships are effective only because a third party knows that one individual has the authority to act as the agent of another. Otherwise, the third party would have no reason to allow the agent to bind the principal to an obligation of any kind. The knowledge of a third party also may give rise to a different kind of agency, called an implied agency.

Implied agency arises when two parties have no express understanding that an agency relationship exists, but together they act as if one does. This is not as complicated as it might sound. Consider, for example, a successful show jumper that has been imported and syndicated by its owner. The former owner, now the syndicate manager, selects a trainer for the horse, who sends bills to the syndicate manager. The training bills then are paid by the syndicate manager on behalf of the share owners, who reimburse the manager.

Even without an express authorization by the syndicate share owners for the manager to act as their agent, their actions make it reasonable for the trainer to assume that an agency relationship exists and to expect payment from the syndicate share owners if the syndicate manager fails to pay the bills. The implied agency is as effective as an actual agency relationship to obligate the syndicate share owners to pay the training bills. Again, the syndicate manager incurs no liability.

Although agents generally incur no liability for transactions on behalf of a principal, that is not always the situation. The non-liability of an agent to a third party may change if there is fraud on the part of the agent or if the identity of the principal is not disclosed.

FIDUCIARY DUTY

What can a principal reasonably expect of an agent?

An agent is expected to act in the best interests of the principal, even if that means the agent's personal interest must take a back seat to the principal's interests. This is because the agent-principal relationship imposes a fiduciary duty on the agent. In a non-equine case, *Steelvest, Inc. v. Scansteel Service Center*, the Supreme Court of Kentucky defined fiduciary duty as follows:

> [A]s a general rule, we can conclude that such a relationship is one founded on trust or confidence reposed by one person in the integrity and fidelity of another and which also necessarily involves an undertaking in which a duty is created in one person to act primarily for another's benefit in matters connected with the undertaking.

This means that an agent, bloodstock or otherwise, owes an unwavering duty of loyalty to the principal. While the parameters of an agency relationship are fluid and are defined by the agreement between the parties, the nature of a fiduciary duty suggests some basic guidelines. An agent obviously should not represent a competing interest at the principal's expense, should not take personal advantage of the relationship to the exclusion of the principal, should not compete directly against the principal, and should not accept bribes or other kickbacks related to the transaction about which he or she is acting as agent.

In all of those examples, the agent has put his or her personal interests (almost always financial) ahead of the interests of the principal. This does not mean that an agent cannot ever represent competing interests, however. Although it seems difficult to imagine a situation in which an agent could represent both the seller (who is looking for the highest price possible) and the buyer (who is looking for the best deal, usually the lowest possible price) at the same time without breaching the fiduciary duty owed to one principal or the other, such a transaction generally is allowed if there is full pre-sale disclosure and if both parties consent.

The requirement for full disclosure and consent prior to an agent representing both parties in a sale has been the rule of law in general commercial transactions for years. A similar rule is applicable to agency relationships in the horse business, although only a handful of states (including Kentucky and California) have laws specifically addressing equine sales. The full text of Kentucky Revised Statute 230.357, enacted in 2006, is included in the Case Studies section in this chapter.

The statute requires, in part, that all sales of horses in the state must be memorialized with a written bill of sale setting out the purchase price and signed by the seller and buyer; that dual agency is prohibited without prior written consent of both parties to the sale; that an agent cannot accept "compensation, fees, a gratuity, or any other item of value in excess of five hundred dollars ($500) and related directly or indirectly" to the sale without disclosure and written consent of both parties; and that anyone harmed by a breach of the statute may recover triple damages, costs, and attorney fees.

A curious exception exempts sales of show horses for less than $10,000 from any of the requirements of the revised statute. This begs the question of whether the legislature considers conduct harmful only if a certain amount of money is involved.

Fiduciary duties also arise in other contexts, including partnerships and corporations. Courts traditionally have imposed fiduciary duties on partners, both to each other and to the partnership, and this should remain the case in most situations. *Marsh v. Gentry*, discussed in the chapter on ownership, for example, addressed a violation of a partner's fiduciary duty. Some states that have adopted a version of the Revised Uniform Partnership Act (see Chapter 3) have altered the traditional fiduciary duty concept, and the usual caveat applies: Check with an attorney familiar with the law in your jurisdiction to determine what duties are applicable to partners.

Generally, though, partners should

AT A GLANCE

- The use of third-party agents to facilitate the buying and selling of horses is common.
- An agent should act in the best interests of the principal, even at the expense of the agent's personal interests.
- Full disclosure to and consent of both parties is required for an agent to legally represent both the buyer and seller in a sale.

expect of each other the same loyalty a principal should expect of an agent: good faith, fair dealings, and disclosure of relevant information about business opportunities. Nor should a partner co-opt business opportunities offered to the partnership for his or her own personal gain.

The directors and officers of a corporation also owe a fiduciary duty to the shareholders to act in their best interests, and shareholders are entitled to expect fair dealing and good faith. Recent corporate scandals suggest this expectation is not always realized.

THE JESS JACKSON LAWSUIT

Unresolved at this writing is litigation instituted by Jess Jackson, a successful businessman and Thoroughbred owner against several bloodstock agents. Filed in 2005 in California, the lawsuit alleges that several bloodstock agents defrauded Jackson on numerous occasions. Jackson, who entered the Thoroughbred business after amassing a fortune as a wine

CASE STUDIES

Beasley v. Trontz, 677 SW2d 891 (Ky App 1984)

The issue of dual agency arose in Kentucky two decades before Jess Jackson's California lawsuit. In this case the Kentucky Court of Appeals considered the following dispute.

Beasley (the appellant) and a relative, owners of a mare named Black Eyed Lucy and her unnamed Inverness Drive foal, wanted to sell the mare and foal as a package. They contacted bloodstock agent Art Baumohl (not a party to the lawsuit) to locate a buyer. Coincidentally, at the same time, one of Baumohl's established clients and two partners were looking for a well-bred mare to breed to Alydar.

At this point the facts became convoluted, as the Court of Appeals explained:

> On September 30, 1982, Baumohl and Trontz [an appellee] viewed the mare and foal for the first time at the farm of Nancy Penn Morgan where the horses were boarded. After viewing the package, Baumohl sent a letter to Beasley [the plaintiff] at his home in Hartsville, Tennessee, setting forth the terms of the agency contract as follows:

>> In our discussion over the phone the other day, we agreed to sell this package, the mare and foal, for not less than $175,000, such price to include a 5% commission, if we are fortunate enough to sell them. After I have a vet examine them in the next couple of days for a clean bill of health, I will price them on the market at $200,000. I feel fairly certain that we can get an offer of somewhere around the $175,000 range. In any event, I will not come below that figure.

>> I believe I would probably try to get a contract with some earnest money placed in escrow with the balance due in middle of January.

>> I don't plan on pushing this package until the vet has had time to look at them for me.

> Beasley signed this agreement and returned it to Baumohl.

> On October 4, 1982, Trontz informed Janice Heinz, another appellee, that he had negotiated the purchase of the mare and foal for $175,000, and offered her a one-quarter interest in the deal. She accepted. Trontz also submitted BLACK EYED LUCY's pedigree to J.T. Lundy, president of Calumet Farm, home of ALYDAR, who on October 4, 1982, caused his acting secretary, the appellee, Heinz, to write to Trontz's banker that Trontz had a confirmed 1983 season with the famous stallion. This letter further stated that BLACK EYED LUCY was currently residing at Lundy Farm in Lexington, Kentucky. Trontz, Heinz, and Lundy all admitted in their depositions that BLACK EYED LUCY had never resided at the Lundy Farm and that the Lundy Farm was not located in Lexington or Fayette County. Lundy explained these minor liberties with the truth were indulged in "on account of the bankers."

On October 7, 1982, Baumohl contacted Dr. Baker, a veterinarian, to examine the mare and to perform a uterine biopsy. Dr. Baker conducted his examination on October 20, 1982, and sent specimens to the lab at the University of Kentucky for analysis. While the appellees all agree a deal was secured much earlier in the month, Trontz testified he delivered to Baumohl a written contract for the purchase of the package and a personal check for $20,000 as a deposit made payable to Baumohl, on the 20th. Baumohl never deposited this check into an escrow account, nor is there any explanation in the record for his failure to present the check for payment. Trontz's bank statements for this period from September 1, 1982 to December 1, 1982, show that his largest balance was $8,252.42. Nevertheless, he testified that he was not aware that Baumohl had not presented the check for payment until after this action was commenced in mid-November.

Trontz's banker testified that he would have called Trontz before dishonoring the check had it been presented for payment.

Baumohl testified that he first communicated the purchase contract to Beasley on October 25, 1982. Baumohl refused to reveal the buyer's identity to Beasley and testified that he didn't mention the $20,000 deposit. On or about October 29th, Beasley decided that the price of $175,000 was too low and informed Baumohl he would not sell the package for that amount. On October 30, 1982, an offspring of BLACK EYED LUCY, ROVING BOY, won a stakes race in California, which increased her value as a brood mare. On November 1, the appellant sent Baumohl a letter rescinding that portion of the agency contract concerning the price of the package. On November 2, 1982, Dr. Baker notified Baumohl that he had approved the mare on the pre-purchase examination, a condition precedent to the purchase agreement, and the appellees demanded delivery of the mare and foal. Beasley refused to relinquish the horses and the appellees commenced this action on the 8th of November, seeking specific performance, compensatory and punitive damages. Beasley filed a counterclaim, alleging there to have been collusion between his agent, Baumohl, and the buyer, Trontz.

The trial court granted the appellee's motion for summary judgment and ordered Beasley to deliver the mare and foal to Trontz and his partners. The Kentucky Court of Appeals reversed that decision on the ground that there were questions about Baumohl's role in the transaction that should have been submitted to a jury.

Specifically, the court stated that,

[I]t is a well established rule of agency law, however, that one cannot act as the agent of both the buyer and seller in a transaction unless both parties are aware of, and consent to, the dual representation ... That Baumohl was to receive no consideration from Trontz, or even that no bad faith was exercised, does not make the contract valid in the absence of Beasley's knowledge that Baumohl was acting in a dual role.

Kentucky Revised Statute 230.357

Twenty years later the Kentucky legislature codified into law the long-standing principle set out in *Beasley v. Trontz* by passage of Kentucky Revised Statute 230.357. The law, which took effect in July 2006, states:

(1) Any sale, purchase, or transfer of an equine used for racing or showing, including prospective racehorses, breeding prospects, stallions, stallion seasons, broodmares, or weanlings, or any interest therein, shall be:

(a) Accompanied by a written bill of sale or acknowledgment of purchase and security agreement setting forth the purchase price; and

(b) Signed by both the purchaser and the seller or their duly authorized agent or, in a transaction solely relating to a season or fractional interest in the stallion, signed by the syndicate manager or stallion manager.

(2) In circumstances where a transaction described in subsection (1) is accomplished through a public auction, the bill of sale requirement described in subsection (1) may be satisfied by the issuance of an auction receipt, generated by the auction house, and signed by the purchaser or the purchaser's duly authorized agent. An agent who signs an auction receipt on behalf of his or her principal shall do so only if authorized in writing. When presented with such authorization, all other parties to the transaction may presume that an agent signing on behalf of his or her principal is duly authorized to act for the principal.

(3) It shall be unlawful for any person to act as an agent for both the purchaser and the seller, which is hereby defined as a dual agent, in a transaction involving the sale, purchase, or transfer of an interest in an equine used for racing or showing, including prospective racehorses, breeding prospects, stallions, stallion seasons, broodmares, or weanlings, or any interest therein, without:

(a) The prior knowledge of both the purchaser and the seller; and

(b) Written consent of both the purchaser and the seller.

(4) It shall be unlawful for a person acting as an agent for either a purchaser or a seller or acting as a dual agent in a transaction involving the sale, purchase, or transfer of an equine used for racing or showing, including prospective racehorses, breeding prospects, stallions, stallion seasons, broodmares, or weanlings, or any interest therein, to receive compensation, fees, a gratuity, or any other item of value in excess of five hundred dollars ($500) and related directly or indirectly to such transaction from an individual or entity, including any consigner involved in the transaction, other than an agent's principal, unless:

(a) The agent receiving and the person or entity making the payment disclose in writing the payment to both the purchaser and seller; and

(b) Each principal for whom the agent is acting consents in writing to the payment.

(5) Any person acting as an agent for a purchaser or seller or acting as a dual agent in a transaction involving the sale, purchase, or transfer of an equine used for racing or showing, including prospective racehorses, breeding prospects, stallions, stallion seasons, broodmares, or weanlings, or any interest therein, shall, upon request by his or her principal or principals, furnish copies of all financial records and financial documents in the possession or control of the agent pertaining to the transaction to the principal or principals. However,

disclosure of compensation arrangements described in subsection (7) of this section shall not be required. For purposes of this subsection, financial records shall not include the agent's or owner's work product used to internally evaluate the equine.

(6) Any person injured by a violation of this section shall recover treble damages from persons or entities violating this section, and the prevailing party in any litigation under this section shall be entitled to an award of costs of the suit, reasonable litigation expenses, and attorney's fees. As used in this section, treble damages shall equal three (3) times the sum of:

(a) The difference, if any, between the price paid for the equine and the actual value of the equine at the time of sale; and

(b) Any payment made in violation of subsection (4) of this section.

(7) Nothing in this section shall require disclosure of compensation arrangements between a principal and an agent where no dual agency exists, where the agent is acting solely for the benefit of his or her principal, and where the agent is being compensated solely by his or her principal.

(8) Notwithstanding any provision of the Kentucky Revised Statutes to the contrary, for transactions contemplated by this section that are accomplished through a public auction, this section shall not require disclosure of the reserves, the identity of the principals, or the auctioneer's commissions. Auction companies shall not be deemed to be dual agents for all purposes under this section.

(9) The provisions of this section shall not apply to the sale, purchase, or transfer of an equine used for showing if the sale, purchase, or transfer does not exceed ten thousand dollars ($10,000).

(10) No person shall be held liable under this section unless that person has actual knowledge of the conduct constituting a violation of this section.

maker, retained several individuals to advise him on the purchase of horses. Section 19525 of the California Business and Professional Code prohibits an agent from accepting "a commission, fee, gratuity, or another form of compensation in connection with the sale or purchase of a racehorse, prospective racehorse, stallion, or broodmare, unless the purchaser or seller have agreed in writing to the payment of the commission, fee, gratuity, or other compensation."

The complaint (which presents only Jackson's side of the dispute) alleges that Jackson's advisers "artificially inflated the purchase prices of horses bought by Jackson both at auction or privately and failed to communicate the vendor's actual sale prices for the purpose of receiving undisclosed commissions or payments." Jackson identified several specific transactions, including the private purchases of a colt named Rhythm Mad and the broodmare Maggy Hawk, dam of 2005 Preakness and Belmont stakes winner Afleet Alex.

Jackson alleged that one of his agents told him the purchase price for

Rhythm Mad was $850,000, but that the owner of the colt received only $675,000 from the agent, who allegedly pocketed the difference. In like manner, Jackson alleged that he paid $750,000 for Maggy Hawk, when the actual purchase price negotiated by a bloodstock agent representing Jackson was only $600,000. In those and other instances, Jackson claimed that his advisers refused to provide written bills of sale or to disclose the actual purchase prices for a number of horses.

Jackson's complaint also alleged that his agents received secret kickbacks or commissions from consignors to various auctions in return for directing Jackson to purchase particular horses for inflated prices. The complaint alleges damages totaling several million dollars.

A year later, in September 2006, prominent Thoroughbred owner James McIngvale filed a federal lawsuit alleging similar problems with his advisers and agents. Resolution of these lawsuits will shape the way bloodstock agents do business in the future. Jackson also was a vocal supporter of KRS 230.357, and he indicated he will continue his fight for the licensing of bloodstock agents.

RESOURCES

Dual agency is one of the issues addressed by the Sales Integrity Task Force, a group of Thoroughbred owners, breeders, buyers, and consignors organized under the auspices of the Thoroughbred Owners and Breeders Association. The task force produced a code of ethics that stressed the "fraudulent nature of dual agency without disclosure and pre-sale price manipulation," included a sample agreement for use by buyers and bloodstock agents; required disclosure of surgical procedures that permanently altered a horse's conformation; banned surgical procedures that temporarily altered conformation; required veterinarians to disclose their interest, if any, in horses they examine for potential buyers; encouraged full disclosure of ownership of horses; and established a procedure to educate new buyers. More information about the Sales Integrity Task Force, including the full text of the code of ethics and sample forms, can be found at www.salesintegrity.org.

TAXES

The federal tax code, comprising Title 26 of the U.S. Code, runs to some 3.5 million words. That is the equivalent of thirty-five to forty popular novels, a stack of books roughly six feet tall. It is impossible to review the entire tax code in a chapter, a single book, or a series of books. Instead, this chapter will focus on four areas of particular interest to taxpayers in the horse business: whether your horse activity is a business or a hobby; whether you have material participation in your horse activity; depreciation and capitalization of assets; and capital gains. The discussion will be limited to federal income tax issues, and no attempt will be made to decipher the myriad state tax schemes in place around the country. Also, nothing in this chapter is specific to any particular horse activity, and consultation with a tax professional is absolutely necessary to avoid costly mistakes.

THE BASICS

The basic business model is familiar to anyone who ever set up a lemonade stand on a hot summer day. Money comes in from customers, money goes out for sugar, lemons, and other supplies, and at the end of the day the lemonade stand shows a profit or a loss, depending on whether the income is greater than the expenses (good) or the expenses exceed the income (bad).

The IRS formalized this simple model in sections 61 and 162 of the tax code. Section 61 simply defines "gross income" as "all income from whatever source derived." Gross income includes compensation for services provided (such as training horses, giving riding lessons, or providing farrier services), money generated by a business (through the sale of horses or the operation of a boarding farm, for example), and gains derived from the sale or lease of real or personal property.

Surprisingly, gross income also includes profits from illegal activities and the failure to declare such income on a tax return is a violation of federal law. The U.S. Supreme Court reached this conclusion in *United States v. Sullivan*, a case decided in the late 1920s. Then in 1930, when no other criminal charges seemed likely, notorious gangster Al Capone was indicted for tax evasion. Capone was incredulous. At one point he reportedly said, "the income tax law is a lot of bunk. The government can't collect legal taxes from illegal money."

He was wrong. The architect of much of the violence that marked Chicago during Prohibition, Capone was found guilty of failing to file income tax returns and failing to pay taxes on his illegal income from 1925 through 1929. He was sentenced to eleven years in prison.

Section 162 of the tax code allows taxpayers to reduce their gross income by allowing the deduction of all "ordinary and necessary" expenses incurred in "carrying on" a business. Identifying the expenses that are "ordinary and necessary" depends to some extent on the nature of the horse activity.

Such expenses might include wages paid to employees or independent contractors; repairs and maintenance; interest on business loans; federal, state, and local taxes; insurance premiums; health insurance if the taxpayer is self-employed; rent; dues to trade associations; business-related books and periodicals; feed; stud fees; training fees and related expenses; vanning charges; travel; losses from theft or death of an animal; business vehicle expenses; utilities; legal and accounting fees; expenses for a home office (this deduction often is a red flag for IRS auditors); self-employment taxes; advertising; and depreciation and capitalization of assets.

The IRS then applies the following formula:

(Gross Income) – (Allowable Deductions) = Taxable Income

The federal income tax due is based on the amount of taxable income for the tax year and the taxpayer's tax bracket — the higher the taxable income, the higher the tax bracket. For example, as of this writing (late 2006), Section 1 of the tax code establishes the tax for married individuals filing joint returns as follows (see chart):

If taxable income is over—	But not over—	The tax is:
$0	$15,100	10% of the amount over $0
$15,100	$61,300	$1,510.00 plus 15% of the amount over $15,100
$61,300	$123,700	$8,440.00 plus 25% of the amount over $61,300
$123,700	$188,450	$24,040.00 plus 28% of the amount over $123,700
$188,450	$336,550	$42,170.00 plus 33% of the amount over $188,450
$336,550	no limit	$91,043.00 plus 35% of the amount over $336,550

There is federal income tax due only if there is taxable income for the year. If a taxpayer's allowed deductions exceed the gross income, on the other hand, the activity shows a loss for the year. If the activity is the taxpayer's only source of income, he or she is in trouble and probably won't stay in business much longer. If the taxpayer has other sources of income, however, he or she *may* be able to use the loss generated by the horse activity to reduce taxable income from other sources. This is a classic tax shelter, using a loss from one activity to reduce or sometimes eliminate taxable income from another activity.

Whether a taxpayer can take advantage of a loss depends on several factors. They include whether the activity is a business or a hobby and whether the taxpayer had material participation in the activity during the tax year.

After a tax return is prepared and filed, one of two things will happen. Either the IRS will accept the return or there will be questions and an audit of the taxpayer will be scheduled. The possibility of a tax audit should emphasize the importance of good record keeping discussed in Chapter 4. It will be difficult, if not impossible, for a taxpayer to survive an audit without adequate records. A shoebox crammed to the top with personal and business receipts won't do the job.

Audits generally start when an individual agent meets with the taxpayer and reviews the return. The taxpayer can and should be accompanied by a professional tax preparer. If the ruling is against the taxpayer at the initial stage, there are several possibilities for appeal, to the agent's supervisor, to an IRS appeal hearing (where many disputes are resolved), and finally to Tax Court. If the taxpayer loses, he or she will be required to pay delinquent taxes and may face interest and penalties as well.

The good news is that the IRS only audits a small fraction of tax returns. That fact is small consolation if your tax return is audited, and it is better to hope for the best but plan for the worst when it comes to tax preparation.

THE HOBBY HORSE DILEMMA

For some people, owning horses is a pleasurable hobby with no expectation of profit. Many others run profit-motivated horse businesses, but often the expectation of profit exceeds the realization at the end of the tax year. Ideally, such horse-business losses can be deducted against income from other sources, reducing the horse owner's overall tax burden, but in reality this often is not the case.

Wary of people who might characterize their expensive recreational horse activities as businesses in an attempt to gain a tax advantage, the IRS in 1969 enacted Section 183 of the tax code. Better known as the "hobby loss provision," Section 183 has confounded horse people for decades. Simple in theory but difficult in practice, Section 183 says that losses from any activity (not just horse activities) can be used to reduce income from other profitable business ventures only if the activity generating the losses is "engaged in for profit."

Technically, an activity that lacks a profit motive is a hobby rather than a business, and a taxpayer may deduct losses generated by a hobby only to the extent of the hobby's income. In other words, a business can show a taxable loss but a hobby cannot, at least for tax purposes.

Consider, for example, a hypothetical taxpayer engaged in two different activities: a restaurant that last year produced $100,000 in taxable income and a small stable of show horses that during the same period generated losses of $25,000. According to Section 183, the taxpayer can use the $25,000 loss from the show stable to reduce the $100,000 taxable income from the restaurant business for income tax purposes *only if* the taxpayer's horse activity was engaged in for profit. Clearly, it is to the taxpayer's advantage to have his show stable be considered an activity "engaged in for profit" because such a determination will result in a lower overall tax bill for the year. If, on the other hand, a determination is made that the show stable is not an activity "engaged in for profit," a "hobby" in other words, the taxpayer will not be able to deduct the stable's losses against his restaurant business income. But how does a horse activity qualify as a "business" in the eyes of the IRS? The easiest and most certain way is to show a profit, at least occasionally. Section 183 provides that any activity with a major emphasis on breeding, training, showing, or racing horses will be presumed to be an activity engaged in for profit if the activity really does show a profit for two of the seven consecutive taxable years ending with the year under consideration. (This provision represents one of the few positive things in the current tax code for horse enthusiasts. Non-horse farm activities must show a profit in three out of five years, a tougher test to satisfy.)

For an on-going activity, the "profit presumption" applies to the second year in which there is a profit, with the seven-year "safe" period starting with the first profitable year.

An established show stable with the following balance sheet thus will be presumed to satisfy the requirements of Section 183, unless the IRS can prove to the contrary, for the seven-year period running from 2000 (the first profit year) through 2006.

2006	loss
2005	loss
2004	loss
2003	profit
2002	loss
2001	loss
2000	profit
1999	loss

Although the seven-year presumption period started to run in 2000, only the second profit year and three years *after* the second profit year are protected by the presumption. A profit motive is not presumed for the years *before* the second profit year.

(A different and generally more favorable presumption applies to a new business during the first seven years of operation, but a taxpayer must elect to use this presumption. When or whether a taxpayer should make such an election and the varied factors that should be considered are well beyond the scope of this chapter. Specific questions should be addressed to a qualified tax adviser.)

Despite satisfying the Section 183 presumption, two profitable years out of seven do not guarantee that the IRS will not attempt to show that your horse activity has no profit motive, especially if two years of negligible profits are balanced against five years of very large losses. On the other hand, there is not a negative presumption — that the activity is *not* engaged in for profit — against a taxpayer who does not show a profit in at least two of seven years. In that situation the taxpayer must rely on several factors to establish that the horse activity satisfies Section 183.

THE QUACK TEST

An old saying holds that if something looks like a duck, walks like a duck, and quacks like a duck, it probably is a duck. The IRS uses a similar test to determine whether a horse activity satisfies the Section 183 threshold when the two-profitable-years-out-of-seven presumption cannot be met. If a horse activity is conducted in a businesslike manner, it will be easier to convince the IRS of a profit motive.

IRS regulations spell out nine factors that must be considered when making the business/hobby determination. The regulations specify that no single factor is determinative, and that all facts and circumstances of the individual activity must be taken into account. The list of nine factors also is not exclusive, which means that other factors can be considered. Generally, though, auditors and judges rely on the following nine enumerated factors:

1. *The manner in which the taxpayer carries on the activity.* Conducting your activity in a businesslike way, with complete and accurate books and records and separate business accounts and credit cards, can indicate a profit motive. At a bare minimum, you should have a business plan (preferably written), maintain separate financial and business records and checking accounts, and employ a professional accountant with experience in the horse business, if possible. An IRS agent may want to visit the farm and also may compare your operating methods with those of other similar businesses that are profitable. Again, the necessity for accurate and thorough record keeping cannot be overemphasized. Even a cursory review of tax court decisions shows that this factor often is the most important in determining whether a horse activity is a business or a hobby.

Another important consideration is how the taxpayer responds to an activity that is not making a profit. It is very difficult to show a profit motive if a taxpayer fails to make changes in the operation in the face of several loss years. On the other hand, a profit motive is easier to establish if a taxpayer makes changes to the operation in light of strategies that have not worked in the past.

2. *The expertise of the taxpayer or his advisers.* Although it should go without saying, you either need to be an expert in your horse activity, become an expert, or employ someone else who is for advice. It will be very difficult to convince the IRS that you expect to show a profit with your sport horse breeding operation if you have not done your homework or if you do not hire someone who is an expert in the sport horse business. You will face a similar problem if you have the necessary expertise or hire someone who gives you good advice and then fail to conduct the activity in a way you or your advisers recognize is likely to be profitable. Getting competent advice is only part of the process; following that advice in an attempt to make a profit is the other part.

3. *The time and effort expended by the taxpayer in carrying on the activity.* The IRS expects you either to devote a substantial amount of time to your horse activity or to hire knowledgeable and competent persons to do the work for you. If you fail to do either, proving a profit motive to the IRS will be difficult. Failure to document substantial participation in the horse activity also may create problems if the IRS determines that the activity is "passive," a situation that limits the use of otherwise legitimate losses to reduce taxable income from other sources. Passive loss is discussed later in this chapter.

4. *Expectation that assets used in the activity may appreciate in value.* Purchasing land that you expect to appreciate in value for your horse activity may indicate an expectation of profit, but specific IRS regulations may limit the applicability of this approach. If the IRS considers the land and the horse activity to be a single activity, the appreciation in land value may easily offset losses by the horse activity.

"Single activity" characterization is less likely in some situations, however. If the land was purchased for your future retirement, for example, it may be difficult to argue that appreciation in land value should be used to offset losses from the horse activity. Horses also are assets, and you may be able to point to the appreciation in value of a successful racehorse or show horse that is being syndicated for a high price as an indicator of profit motive.

The question of whether land appreciation should be included to a taxpayer's benefit appears to confound some auditors and courts.

5. *The success of the taxpayer in carrying on other similar or dissimilar*

activities. A proven track record in other horse pursuits may help you convince the IRS that your current activity has a profit motive, even if it is unprofitable at the present time.

6. *The taxpayer's history of income or losses with respect to the activity.* The IRS notes, helpfully, that if you show a profit in a "series of years," it is a good indication that you have a profit motive for your horse activity.

7. *The amount of occasional profits, if any, that are earned.* In general, a substantial profit every now and then is better than a series of modest profits, especially if the occasional profits are small in comparison to the losses or to your investment in the activity. The obvious way to generate profits for a horse activity is through sales of horses, and it may be advantageous to concentrate your sales in one tax year as much as possible to create a profit year. Again, though, your tax professional should be consulted to help plan a comprehensive sales strategy.

8. *The financial status of the taxpayer.* The IRS is more likely to attribute a profit motive to a horse activity that is the taxpayer's sole source of income. On the other hand, a taxpayer with several other profitable businesses along with a horse activity that bleeds money year after year will have a harder sell, especially if, as the IRS puts it, "there are personal or recreational elements involved."

9. *Elements of personal pleasure or recreation.* This factor may be the most troublesome because it seems to suggest that there cannot be a profit motive in an activity you also happen to enjoy. This makes sense from the IRS perspective because a "hobby loss" is precisely what Section 183 is supposed to curtail. On the other hand, the mere fact you enjoy your horse activity does not automatically mean there is no profit motive.

Application of IRS rules and regulations baffles tax experts and novices alike. The best way to understand Section 183 and the "hobby loss" regulations is to see them in action in the following examples. Both are actual cases decided by the U.S. Tax Court in September 2000. Other examples are summarized in this chapter's Case Studies.

WINNERS ...

The taxpayers began breeding, showing, and selling Quarter Horses in 1993 and expanded to open a boarding operation in 1995. They also leased some of their horses to others. From 1993 through 1996, their horse business produced gross income of $16,296 and generated total losses during the same period of $89,678. The taxpayers used the losses to reduce their taxable income from other sources. After an initial determination that the activity was not operated for profit, the IRS assessed additional taxes of $13,398 for 1995 and $10,687 for 1996. The taxpayers eventually would up in the U.S. Tax Court.

Because the horse activity did not ever show a profit, the two-out-of-seven presumption did not apply. Instead, the Tax Court applied the nine factors mentioned earlier in this chapter as follows:

1. The court found that the taxpayers conducted their business in a "serious and organized manner." The court noted the taxpayers had lifelong experience with horses and they used that expertise in establishing and operating the business. The taxpayers kept accurate records of both the activity's finances and their horses, continually expanded and improved the facilities at their farm, and expanded into boarding and leasing their horses to others while starting to acquire quality broodmares.

The taxpayers did much of the work on the farm themselves to help reduce expenses. The taxpayers did not have a separate business checking account during their first years of operation, but the court said their computerized records allowed them to generate reports of horse-related income and expenses. The court also noted the taxpayers consulted experts, including an accountant to help set up their bookkeeping system and an attorney to draft boarding and leasing contracts. The first factor favored the taxpayers.

2. Citing the experience of the taxpayers, the court also noted that they "read books and periodicals, viewed videotapes, attended seminars, and consulted with experts." The court determined the taxpayers had sufficient expertise to conduct a profitable business. The second factor favored the taxpayers.

3. The court found the taxpayers devoted a significant amount of time to their horse business. The third factor favored the taxpayers.

4. Although the taxpayers testified they expected the value of their horses to appreciate enough to cover the business losses, the court found the evidence inconclusive. The fourth factor was neutral and favored neither

the taxpayers nor the IRS.

5. The court noted that although the taxpayers had been successful in other business ventures, none were sufficiently similar to their horse activity to enable the court to reach a conclusion. The fifth factor was neutral and favored neither the taxpayers nor the IRS.

6. Because the taxpayers' business was relatively young, the court was unable to reach any conclusions regarding their history of income or loss. The sixth factor was neutral and favored neither the taxpayers nor the IRS.

7. Although the taxpayers' business had not shown a profit, the court found this to be reasonable during the startup years of the activity. The court also noted the fact that one of the taxpayers' broodmares and her foal had died in 1994, reducing by one-fourth the taxpayers' broodmare band. The seventh factor was neutral and favored neither the taxpayers nor the IRS.

8. The IRS argued that the taxpayers' substantial non-farm income indicated they did not have a profit motive for their horse activity. The court did not agree, noting an almost 40 percent drop in the taxpayers' non-farm income from 1995 to 1996 and the facts that one of the taxpayers retired in 1993 and that another expected to retire in 1998, indicating no long-term need to shelter income. The eighth factor favored neither the taxpayers nor the IRS.

9. The court found that although the taxpayers enjoyed breeding and showing their horses, their decisions to board and lease horses to others were not motivated by personal pleasure. The ninth factor also was neutral and favored neither the taxpayers nor the IRS.

With three of the nine factors favoring the taxpayers, and the other six favoring neither the taxpayers nor the IRS, the court ruled there was a legitimate profit motive during the years in question.

The taxpayers in this example did some things wrong, such as mingling their personal and business funds in the same checking account, but they did many more things right. They evaluated the market and predicted a growing interest in Quarter Horses in their area; they maintained complete and accurate business records; they worked to keep expenses low; they changed their business plan in logical ways in attempts to make money; they studied to expand their own expertise and also sought and relied upon the advice of knowledgeable persons in the Quarter Horse business; and they retained experts, such as an accountant and an attorney, for assistance.

By operating their Quarter Horse operation like a business, the taxpayers were successful in countering IRS arguments that the activity was merely a hobby.

... AND LOSERS

The taxpayers were husband and wife, both of whom had full-time non-farm employment. The wife had been involved with horses her entire life and had a degree in microbiology, with an emphasis in pre-med for veterinarians.

They started breeding Paso Fino horses in 1987. Although they had general knowledge and experience with horses, they had no specialized knowledge about Paso Finos. They never took any classes or attended seminars regarding either the financial or business aspects of raising horses. Also, unlike the taxpayers in the first example, this couple did not research the marketability of Paso Finos nor did they have any sort of business plan to guide them. They did not seek any expert assistance before buying their first Paso Finos. Instead, the taxpayers chose Paso Finos because they liked the horses' appearance and smooth gait and because they thought the horses would be good for people with back problems.

The taxpayers did secure the assistance of a bloodstock agent, but his advice was questionable. For example, while encouraging veterinary pre-purchase examinations for horses he recommended the taxpayers buy from others, he discouraged such examinations for horses he sold them. The taxpayers did not sell any horses for seven years, and when they did start selling horses, the sales frequently were to cull less-desirable animals. Generally poor record keeping made it impossible to allocate expenses to each horse sold and impossible to determine whether some, or any, of the sales were actually profitable.

The taxpayers kept their horses on a "modest and functional" California farm, where they did much of the maintenance and improvements. The court noted that although the taxpayers kept voluminous records, the record-keeping activities were aimed at recording deductible expenses and were not directed toward generating financial reports that could have been used to track the success, or lack thereof, of the activity or to predict future profitability.

Finally, the taxpayers also had operated two other businesses, a dog breeding operation and an antiques store, neither of which generally was profitable.

From 1987 through 1997, the taxpayers' Paso Fino operation never approached profitability. For those years, a total loss of $542,751 was reported. Following an audit for the years 1991, 1992, and 1993, the IRS made an initial determination that the taxpayers were not operating their Paso Fino farm for profit.

Because there were no profitable years, the taxpayers were not entitled to rely on the presumption of a profit motive discussed earlier. The Tax Court relied, instead, on an evaluation of the nine relevant factors.

1. The court determined that the taxpayers' record-keeping system was insufficient because no evidence was presented to show the records "were used to implement cost-saving measures or to improve profitability" and that the taxpayers did not "prepare any financial statements, profit and loss projections, budgets, breakdown analyses, or marketing surveys." While giving the taxpayers credit with attempting to breed their mares every year, sometimes to well-bred, established stallions, the court characterized their marketing efforts as "unfocused and anemic." The court also noted that despite a lack of success selling their horses, the taxpayers never changed their marketing strategy.

Finding the "trappings of a business" to be absent, the court concluded the taxpayers did not operate their farm in a businesslike fashion. The first factor favored the IRS.

2. Although the taxpayers did consult with other breeders from time to time, nothing indicated they had sought advice before deciding to raise Paso Fino horses. The court found that the taxpayers "did not prepare for the economic aspects of the activity by study or consultation with experts" and that before starting their business they had no "concept of what their ultimate costs might be, how they might achieve any degree of cost efficiency, the amount of revenue they could expect, or what risks might impair the production of such revenue." The second factor favored the IRS.

3. Despite holding down full-time jobs, the taxpayers also managed their

Paso Fino farm during the years at issue. They hired someone to clean stalls, but they did the rest of the work themselves, including feeding, grooming, training, bookkeeping, and paying bills. The court explained that while it was clear the taxpayers loved their horses and enjoyed some of the farm work, there were many tasks, such as feeding, washing, and worming the animals, that had no recreational value. The third factor favored the taxpayers.

4. The court determined the taxpayers expected assets acquired during the course of the business to appreciate in value. These assets included the farm, which was purchased for $316,000 in 1991 and which had an appraised value of $409,000 seven years later, and some of the horses, which had increased in value some 18 percent from their purchase price. The fourth factor favored the taxpayers.

5. In evaluating the taxpayers' past success in other businesses, the court weighed the objective facts regarding net losses in a dog breeding business and antiques store, with the taxpayers' statements that they were "entrepreneurial" and that they closed the other businesses because they were not profitable. The court found other reasons for closing the businesses and said the mixed results of the taxpayers' other business ventures did not indicate a profit motive. The fifth factor favored the IRS.

6. The court compared the losses recorded during eleven consecutive non-profitable years ($542,751) with the income reported during the same period ($56,010). The court was not persuaded by the taxpayers' explanations for the losses that included a depressed market for Paso Fino horses, the loss of some horses to medical problems, and reliance on a questionable expert. The sixth factor favored the IRS.

7. The taxpayers claimed they were focusing on producing a national champion Paso Fino, which might have a value of $250,000 or more, and that their eleven consecutive losing years reflect that intent. The court explained such a belief could indicate a profit motive but determined that under the facts of the case, such a belief on the part of the taxpayers was too speculative. The court noted that during the years in question the taxpayers did not have breeding stock of sufficient quality to produce a national champion and that they never had shown any of their horses at national shows. The court also noted the taxpayers' advertising was directed at a local rather than national market. The seventh factor favored the IRS.

8. By using the losses from their Paso Fino operation to reduce their non-farm income, the taxpayers lowered their taxable income by approximately $60,000 a year during the period at issue. The IRS argued that the tax savings, plus the recreational value of the activity, showed a lack of profit motive; the taxpayers countered with the argument that the level of money spent, in comparison to their overall income, was more than anyone would spend on a hobby. The court found merit in both arguments. The eighth factor was neutral and favored neither the taxpayers nor the IRS.

9. The IRS argued that the taxpayers loved their horses, which they did not deny, and that they chose Paso Finos because they provided a social outlet for the taxpayers. The IRS also argued that the taxpayers chose Paso Finos, in part, because the husband could ride them despite his bad back and pointed to the taxpayers' e-mail address (Pasolove) as proof of their emotional involvement in the activity. The court apparently agreed, stating that the taxpayers' attachment to their animals "may explain why [the taxpayers] devoted so little effort to culling their herd, improving the quality of their horses, and reducing their operating expenses prior to 1994." The ninth factor favored the IRS.

With six of the nine relevant factors favoring the IRS, two favoring the taxpayers, and one favoring neither, the Tax Court ruled against the taxpayers, holding that their Paso Fino operation was not engaged in for profit. The court said that despite some conflicting evidence, their overall conclusion was that the taxpayers "enjoyed breeding and showing their horses and, therefore, were willing to sustain continuing losses, despite the improbability of profit."

This example, like the first, is instructive. Here the taxpayers had no business plan, either before they started buying Paso Finos or after their farm was in operation. They relied on their own limited expertise or occasionally relied on a questionable expert for assistance. They kept records but did not use those records in a way that could have helped them increase the profitability of their operation. They did not sell any horses for several years and then sold only to cull their herd.

It is tempting to see the second example as proof the IRS will recognize enjoying your horse activity and running it as a business as mutually exclusive, but that is not always the case. The Tax Court was careful to explain that deriving personal pleasure from an activity is only one of nine relevant factors and does not preclude a profit motive. It is clear, though, that IRS recognition of a profit motive depends on having all your ducks in a row, with a sound and flexible business plan, either personal or outside expertise, comprehensive record-keeping procedures, expert assistance in the business aspects of the operation, and an ongoing (and demonstrable) commitment to turning a profit.

Appearances do matter. If your horse activity looks like a business to an outsider, it is more likely to be treated like one if there is a tax audit.

ACTIVE OR PASSIVE?

Even if your horse activity is conducted with the requisite profit motive, and you convince the IRS that it is a "business," your ability to deduct losses from the operation against other income may be limited if you do not "materially participate" in the horse activity. If there is no active participation in a business by a taxpayer, losses from the business can be used to reduce taxable income from other "passive" activities. It cannot be used to reduce taxable income from non-passive sources such as salaries, interest income, or income from any other activity in which the taxpayer has material participation.

These so-called "passive losses" may be carried forward to be used against passive income in subsequent years, and a taxpayer can deduct passive losses in full in the year in which the passive activity is sold or otherwise disposed of.

The passive loss provision is contained in Section 469 of the tax code, and it came into being as part of the Tax Reform Act of 1986. Often the word "reform" attached to legislation indicates someone thinks someone else is getting too good a deal on something. That was the case in 1986 when legislators responded to the perception that absentee horse owners had access to a significant and enjoyable tax shelter. Addition of the passive loss provision to the tax code generally is credited with being a major contributor to a lengthy downturn in the economic health of the horse business.

This provision of the tax code clearly presents potential problems for some horse owners. If you are a limited partner in a partnership that races or shows horses, for example, the IRS will consider your partnership interest to be passive because limited partners take no part in the management of the horse activity. The same is true for any other business activity in which the taxpayer does not materially participate. This means that losses generated by the limited partnership, which often is the case with race and show horses, can only be used to reduce taxable income from other passive activities.

A few opportunities for creative tax planning remain, however. A limited partner in a loss-generating partnership might be encouraged to invest as a limited partner in another partnership that happens to be showing a profit, for example. In that circumstance the passive loss from one limited partnership can reduce the taxable income from the other.

The tax code defines material participation in an activity as involvement by a taxpayer that is "regular, continuous, and substantial." This seldom is a straightforward question, and as you might expect, the IRS uses several tests to determine whether a taxpayer's participation in an activity is "material."

1. Does the taxpayer and/or spouse work more than five hundred hours in the business?

If the answer is "yes," there will be material participation. This test creates a "safe harbor" and is the test taxpayers should strive to satisfy.

2. Does the taxpayer do most of the work in the business?

If the answer is "yes," there will be material participation. A taxpayer who operates a small horse farm as a sole proprietor and who has no employees can satisfy this test.

3. Does the taxpayer work more than one hundred hours a year in the business and no one works more hours?

If the answer is "yes," there will be material participation.

4. Does the taxpayer have several passive activities in which he or she participates more than one hundred hours each, for a total of more than five hundred hours in the tax year?

If the answer is "yes," there will be material participation.

5. Did the taxpayer materially participate in the activity for any five of the ten preceding years?

If the answer is "yes," there will be material participation.

6. Did the taxpayer materially participate in a personal service activity for any three prior years?

If the answer is "yes," there will be material participation. Personal service activities include the fields of medicine, law, engineering, architecture, accounting, performing arts, and consulting, and this test has little application to horse activities.

7. Do the facts and circumstances indicate the taxpayer is materially participating?

If the answer is "yes," there will be material participation.

If you spend at least five hundred hours on your business during a tax year, your participation will meet the IRS test for active participation. If you spend less than one hundred hours on the business during a year, your participation generally will not satisfy the IRS threshold.

If you spend more than one hundred hours on your business in a year but less than five hundred hours, you still may satisfy the IRS test, depending on the facts and circumstances of your specific business. Taxpayers should keep a detailed log of the time spent on the business. Less than two hours per week will satisfy the one hundred-hour threshold, and ten hours per week will meet the five hundred-hour presumption of material participation. You also should consult an attorney or accountant for advice about what specific activities satisfy the material participation test.

TWO, FOUR, SIX, EIGHT, HOW DO WE DEPRECIATE?

Section 162 of the tax code allows taxpayers operating a business to deduct from gross income "ordinary and necessary expenses" to determine taxable income, even if those deductions create a loss. Many deductible expenses are for items that are quickly used up, such as hay and grain, fuel, wages to employees, and utilities. Most big-ticket items, such as farm buildings, farm machinery, vehicles, and horses, have a useful life longer than one year, however. They are not considered expenses but investments of capital. A taxpayer still can deduct the purchase price of these things, but the tax treatment is somewhat different.

Rather than taking an immediate deduction for the entire cost of the asset, a taxpayer must apportion a certain amount of the price to each year of the item's expected useful life. The process is called depreciation. There is an important distinction between horses that are homebreds and horses that are purchased. A horse bred by the taxpayer cannot be depreciated; only horses purchased for the business are subject to depreciation deductions as reasonable and necessary business expenses.

The useful life of depreciable farm property varies, as established by the IRS, and only coincidentally bears any relation to how long an individual item might actually last in the real world. Racehorses more than two years old and breeding stock more than twelve years of age are depreciated over a three-year period; racehorses two years old or younger and breeding animals less than twelve years old are depreciated over a seven-year period. Show horses and any other horses not addressed specifically by the rules are depreciated over a seven-year period.

Most farm vehicles are depreciated over a five-year period, while most farm equipment and fencing are depreciated over seven years. Non-residential agricultural buildings are depreciated over ten or twenty years, depending on the type and use of the structure.

The most common ways to compute depreciation are the simpler "straight line method" and the more complicated "declining balance method." The former provides for a depreciation allowance in equal amounts during the property's useful life; the latter provides for accelerated depreciation during the first years after depreciable property is placed in service. The declining balance method is more attractive for investors because it allocates a higher percentage of the cost to the early years of the property's useful life.

The IRS requires taxpayers to use the declining balance method for most farm property. Deductions are calculated by using 150 percent of the straight-line depreciation rate initially and then switching to straight-line rates toward the end of the item's useful life.

Consider a $20,000 light-duty farm truck placed into service on January 1, 1995, and depreciated over the required five-year period. Using straight-line depreciation, the taxpayer deducts one-fifth of the total cost ($4,000, or 20 percent) each year for five years. Using a declining balance method, on the other hand, the straight-line rate (20 percent) is multiplied by 150 percent (as is the case for horses and most other depreciable farm property), and the resulting depreciation rate (30 percent) is applied each year to the unrecovered balance to determine the depreciation allowance for that year.

Under the declining balance method, the depreciation allowance will be greater than the straight-line allowance of $4,000 for the first two years, but less thereafter. At the point when it becomes economically favorable to do so, a conversion to straight-line depreciation is made.

Depreciation seldom is this straightforward in practice. Not all property is eligible to be depreciated, and the calculations become more complicated when property is acquired and put into use during the tax year rather than at the beginning. Also, the IRS does not follow the usual convention of assigning all horses a January 1 birthday. For tax purposes a horse becomes more than two years old on the first day *after* twenty-four months from the day the animal was foaled. Questions also may arise about when a horse actually was placed in service.

To complicate matters further, Congress occasionally makes temporary changes in depreciation schedules to encourage investment. For example, in response to the terrorist attacks on September 11, 2001, legislation was passed allowing "bonus" depreciation that allowed even greater concentration of depreciation deductions in the years immediately after property was acquired and put into service. Some, but not all, horses were included under the temporary legislation.

Section 179 of the tax code also gives taxpayers the option of writing off, or "expensing," the entire purchase price of horses and other equipment during the year of purchase, up to a specified amount. If expensing is chosen as an option, the item is not depreciated. The general maximum that can be expensed is $25,000 per year. For the tax years 2003 through 2007, however, the maximum was increased to $100,000, indexed upward annually for inflation. Unless Congress acts to extend the $100,000 maximum, the amount that can be expensed will return to $25,000 after the 2007 tax year.

Keeping in mind that the amount that can be expensed is subject to various restrictions, consider the following simple example. An Arabian breeder purchases a ten-year-old broodmare for $75,000 in 2006. When preparing his federal income tax return for 2006, the breeder has two options, either depreciate the horse over seven years or "expense" the entire purchase price during the tax year in which the mare was purchased. The option that is better cannot be decided in isolation and will depend on the taxpayer's overall tax situation.

CASE STUDIES

The following two case examples appear factually similar, at least on the surface: two Thoroughbred operations posting an unbroken series of loss years without ever showing a profit. The outcomes are different, however, and the reasoning of the two courts in reaching those conclusions is instructive. Although these two examples are Thoroughbred activities, the principles are applicable to any horse operation.

Kuberski v. Commissioner of Internal Revenue, 2002 Tax Court Memo LEXIS 206 (US Tax Court 2002)

The Kuberskis owned Caduceus Thoroughbreds, a breeding farm in Arizona. They reported the following gross income and losses to the IRS for the farm:

Year	Gross Income	(Loss)
1980	$0	($1,825)
1982	$0	($435)
1984	$136	($22,690)
1986	$5,375	($44,320)
1987	$13,832	($46,440)
1988	$5,935	($39,684)
1989	$3,434	($38,602)
1990	$2,306	($33,662)
1991	$14,388	($89,355)
1992	$33,280	($106,041)
1993	$39,662	($96,738)
1994	$40,485	($62,142)
1995	$19,824	($80,205)
1996	$26,630	($67,605)
1997	$24,931	($95,432)
1998	$52,492	($63,492)
TOTAL	$282,710	($888,263)

Following a tax audit, the IRS disallowed loss deductions for the years 1994, 1995, 1996, and 1998, and assessed additional taxes totaling $96,896. The Kuberskis argued that they were conducting a business during the years in question, and the matter wound up in tax court. The court found the following facts to be true:

During the years in question, Thomas Kuberski was a physician. He and his wife reported combined annual income ranging from approximately $287,000 to approximately $342,000.

From 1986 through 1996, the Kuberskis operated Caduceus Thoroughbreds in partnership with Sun State Farm, a separate operation where the Caduceus horses were boarded. During that period the Kuberskis deducted board bills totaling more than $400,000 as business expenses.

The Kuberskis wrote a business plan in 1995 that was adapted from a business plan originally drafted for Sun State in 1987. The original business plan included projected annual expenses of $93,100 and projected annual income of $102,600, but the 1995 supplement stated only that the "potential for profit would increase."

"Petitioner believed that he could breed a better-than-average thoroughbred (sic) horse because of his medical background and his understanding of physiology and statistical analysis. Petitioner is a licensed trainer and owner, as well as a certified horse appraiser. He has taken annual classes on taxes, business, shoeing horses, veterinary problems, animal husbandry, and sales preparation. Petitioner wrote several articles for the thoroughbred horse industry, including one explaining the dosage system, a horse breeding theory, and others related to various medical problems in the racehorse industry. Petitioner sent out bills every month, knew all the mares on the farm, and knew why particular mares were bred with his stallion.

"Petitioners characterize the thoroughbred horse industry as a 'loss' industry and contend that statistically it is possible to make a profit only once every 25 years. Petitioners have never made a profit from their Schedule C horse breeding and racing activity."

The tax court considered the nine factors set out by the IRS and found four to be most significant.

Factor 1: Although it sounded as if the Kuberskis were doing many things right, the tax court found otherwise. The court stated that the "petitioners' arguments appear to have been copied from the tax guides for horse owners that they presented at trial and have little support from the evidence. Their briefs do not cite the record, and, in most instances, there is no support in the record for their assertions." The court also noted that the "evidence presented at trial does not persuade us that petitioner maintained records for the purpose of 'cutting expenses, increasing profits, and evaluating the overall performance of the operation.' Petitioner testified that 'all the records in the world, or business plans in the world are not going to make a difference on whether you make a profit in this.' A businesslike operation, however, would include analyses on why large losses recurred over a long period and whether any possibility of recouping them existed."

Most important for the court, it seemed, was that the record keeping appeared to be for show only, and that the Kuberskis did not use the records to improve their chances of making a profit. It generally will be a hard sell for a taxpayer to convince the IRS that a profit motive exists if the operation makes no changes in the face of mounting losses.

Factor 6: The court did not automatically assume that a series of loss years indicated the lack of a profit motive, especially if the losses occurred during the first years of operation. The court recognized the usual start-up period for a horse operation is five to ten years, but noted that the loss years at issue were "well beyond the period customarily necessary to bring similar operation to profitable status."

The court also noted that the Kuberskis attributed some of the losses to unforeseen events such as "lawsuits against the business, downturns in business, changes in the purse structure at races, a decrease in Breeder's awards, and death or problems with important horses." Unforeseen problems can be an excuse for a series of loss years, but in this case the court found no evidence presented at trial corroborated the claims.

Factor 7 and Factor 8: The court explained: "Petitioner has never made a profit in his horse activities, although they have generated generous tax savings in the form of depreciation deductions and net losses that offset his substantial income as a physician ... Petitioners' level of income permitted them to continue the horse activity without a profit. If they had regarded the activity as a business, they would have focused more on the financial aspects and ways to cut their losses. Only their other income allowed their continued pursuit of losing operations."

In the end, the IRS was the winner. It is clear from this decision that record keeping for its own sake is less important than using the records to try and correct problems in the horse operation. It also should be obvious that self-serving statements made without evidence to support them will be given short shrift by the court. Finally, it should be noted that the Kuberskis decided to represent themselves in tax court. Although it is dangerous to generalize, a review of tax court cases shows that taxpayers who appear without representation by counsel almost always lose.

Dishal v. Commissioner of Internal Revenue, 1998 Tax Court Memo LEXIS 399 (US Tax Court 1998)

The Dishals, like the Kuberskis, had a Thoroughbred operation that posted a series of loss years without ever showing a profit:

Year	Gross Income	Total Expenses	(Loss)
1992	$62,770	$167,912	($105,142)
1993	$19,565	$99,633	($80,068)
1994	$11,446	$106,130	($94,684)
1995	$29,734	$81,810	($52,076)
1996	$28,618	$103,728	($74,120)
TOTAL	$152,133	$559,213	($406,090)

The IRS disallowed loss deductions for the years 1992, 1993, and 1994, and assessed additional taxes of $141,118.

The tax court made the following findings of fact:

Sidney Dishal was an "extraordinarily successful" businessman prior to his retirement in 1992.

Between the years 1988 and 1996 the Dishals owned between twenty and thirty horses, nearly all homebreds. The Dishals did not own a farm and boarded their horses at outside farms or with trainers. Their horses were the only assets used by the Dishals in their horse operation.

"On a regular basis, petitioner personally visits the facilities where his horses are boarded and trainer in order to inspect the condition of the horses and to consult with the caretakers and trainers. Including the time spent driving between his home and the horse facilities, petitioner normally spends at least 4 hours a day, 6 days a week, inspecting his horses and conversing with their handlers. Petitioners usually attend races in which their horses are participating."

(Although the question of material participation was not before the court, it is clear that Mr. Dishal's participation gave him the benefit of the five hundred-plus hours per year safe harbor.)

The Dishals' horses were successful at the racetrack, and the owners regularly improved the quality of their breeding stock.

"Several horses have had their racing careers, and in some instances their lives, ended by unforeseen and unfortunate circumstances which were beyond the petitioners' control. Petitioners' horses, Super High Pockets, Miss Super Natural, Glorious and Bold, Nipsey's Sundance, and Rusty's Lady all died in accidents at the racetrack. The horse Miss Nipsey Ann died after producing a foal. The horses Ann's Veil and Lexi's Dream developed tendon problems which ended their racing careers. Ann's Bold Lady fractured her knee and Super Clan developed a flesh-eating disease."

The Dishals did not have a written business plan, but they consistently followed a policy to "race the horses that are healthy, retire the females for breeding when they can no longer compete successfully on the racetrack, and race the males until they are claimed, sold, or given away."

The Dishals did not maintain their own records of their horses' earnings, but those figures were kept by the trainers and state breeders organizations. The Dishals did maintain complete records of expenses.

Neither of the Dishals rode.

The tax court considered the nine IRS factors and ruled in favor of the Dishals.

Factor 1: The court determined that the Dishals "were very serious about their horse activities and operated them in a businesslike manner." Their records were "extensive" and "complete" and their business plan, although unwritten, was apparent from their consistent actions and attempts to upgrade their operation. This factor favored the Dishals.

Factor 2: The court noted that the Dishals employed a successful trainer and boarded their horses at a farm with an experienced manager. This consultation with experts convinced the court of a profit motive.

Factor 3: The court noted that Dishal devoted "a substantial amount of time to the horse activities." He spent a lot of time visiting the racetrack and consulting with his trainer, and the farm manager testified that Dishal "examines all of his horses and feeds some of them, doctors them, cleans water troughs, and picks up rocks." This factor favored the Dishals.

Factor 6: The IRS argued that the record of consistent losses was proof of the absence of a profit motive, but the court disagreed. "The losses petitioners sustained, however, were in part due to unforeseen and unfortunate circumstances beyond their control which abruptly ended the racing careers, and in some instances the lives, of several of their horses … Furthermore, petitioners are capable of making up their losses from prior years since their horses are now entered in high stakes races." This factor favored the Dishals.

Factor 7: The court determined that occasional profits can indicate a profit motive and noted that the "opportunity to earn a substantial ultimate profit in a speculative venture may be sufficient to indicate a profit motive." The court noted the Dishals had two horses entered in Breeders' Cup races with purses of more than $1 million each. This factor favored the Dishals

Factor 9: The court determined that personal pleasure or recreation was not a motive in the Dishals' horse activity. This factor favored the Dishals.

The court concluded the Dishals were operating their horse activity with a profit motive. In this case the court credited the taxpayers with good record keeping that also served a purpose, allowing them to alter their horse operation in an attempt to make it profitable. This willingness to change course in response to losses was important to the court. The consistent use of well-qualified advisers and the substantial amount of time spent in the activity by the Dishals also were important considerations.

Finally, the Dishals, unlike the Kuberskis, were represented by counsel in tax court.

CAPITAL GAINS

A taxpayer also may be entitled to special tax treatment if a horse is purchased, held for a specified period of time, and then sold for a profit. If the horse qualifies, any gain from the sale may be taxed as a capital gain at a rate generally lower than the taxpayer's regular tax rate.

To qualify for capital gains treatment, the horse must be held by the taxpayer for twenty-four months if used for breeding or sporting purposes (including racing and showing). The usual holding period for other property to qualify for long-term capital gains treatment is twelve months. Also, the taxpayer must not keep the horse for the primary purpose of selling the animal to clients. If there is a loss on the sale of property that qualifies, that loss can offset other long-term capital gains, and if there is a net long-term capital loss, up to $3,000 can be deducted against ordinary income.

Capital gains treatment of gains and losses is a complex matter well beyond the scope of this book and the advice of a tax professional is essential.

RESOURCES

The American Horse Council strives to keep horse owners abreast of tax developments with two publications, the comprehensive *Horse Owners and Breeders Tax Handbook*, written by Thomas A. Davis and updated on a regular basis, and a *Tax Bulletin* that comes out more frequently. The AHC can be contacted at 1616 H Street NW, 7th Floor, Washington DC 20006; (202) 296-4031; horsecouncil.org.

Available from the Russell Meerdink Co. is *The Official IRS Tax Guide to Auditing Horse Activities*. (800) 635-6499; www.horseinfo.com.

The official IRS Web site, irs.gov, is somewhat difficult to navigate but offers a wealth of information on every imaginable tax topic. The IRS Web site does not provide legal or accounting advice to taxpayers.

EMPLOYMENT

The vast majority of horse operations, like most businesses, are divided into two camps: bosses and workers. The two groups have some common interests, getting the work done, for example, but they also may have some competing interests that create friction in the workplace. Questions about benefits, time off, working conditions, and pay can disrupt a generally smooth-running business.

Disputes between employers and employees often are the result of misunderstandings about the rights and obligations of the parties. This chapter discusses those rights and responsibilities in the multiple contexts of hiring practices, employment at will, the pros and cons of written employment contracts, illegal discrimination, sexual harassment and violence in the workplace, independent contractors, and minimum wage. There also is an overview of safety in the workplace and worker's compensation.

EQUAL OPPORTUNITY

Employers have a legal duty to avoid discrimination in the workplace, and workers have a right to expect fair and equal treatment. This is one of the most fundamental guidelines of employment law. Fair treatment does not mean that employers must hire everyone who applies for a job, however, nor does it mean that employees never can be fired. It does mean that individuals in some specific groups, called "protected classes," have legal protection against discrimination.

Title VII of the **Civil Rights Act of 1964** marked the first major attempt by Congress to prohibit discriminatory practices by private employers. In a nutshell, Title VII prohibits discrimination by an employer on the basis of a job applicant's or employee's race, color, religion, gender, or national origin. Discrimination on the basis of pregnancy and the problem of sexual harassment in the workplace are addressed under the general prohibition against discrimination based on gender. Sexual preference, however, currently is not covered by Title VII, although some states have enacted laws that expand the protection afforded by federal statutes.

Since Title VII was enacted, Congress has addressed other forms of employment discrimination, including bias based on age and disability, and many jurisdictions have enacted similar legislation. When state anti-discrimination laws provide more protection than their federal counterparts, a business operating in that state must comply with the more stringent state requirements.

Title VII, for example, applies to employers who are engaged in a business affecting interstate commerce, with fifteen or more workers employed during a specified period. Kentucky's counterpart, KRS 344.100, on the other hand, defines a covered employer as a person or entity with eight or more employees during a specified period. Kentucky's law thus applies to many smaller businesses that would not fall under the umbrella of Title VII. Anti-discrimination laws in a majority of other states also apply to employers that are not covered under Title VII due to the number of employees.

Because the nature of state anti-discrimination laws and their application may vary somewhat from jurisdiction to jurisdiction, employers should familiarize themselves both with federal requirements and with the law in their own locale. Keep in mind, though, that an employer with only a few workers does not have free rein to discriminate, even if he or she does not fall under the statutory definition of "employer." The spirit, if not the letter, of this kind of legislation applies regardless of the size of a business and impermissible discrimination is fertile ground for a lawsuit under a variety of common law legal theories.

The following brief summary of federal anti-discrimination laws is not intended to be exhaustive. Rather, it highlights some of the potential problem areas for unwary employers and encourages them to become familiar with federal laws that may affect the way they deal with employees. Most states have similar legislation and the application of both federal and state law to an employer's horse business should be discussed with an attorney.

Title VII of the Civil Rights Act of 1964 makes it unlawful for an employer to "fail or refuse to hire, discharge or otherwise discriminate against any individual with respect to compensation, terms, conditions or privileges of employment because of such individual's race, color, religion, sex or national origin." An employee who thinks that he or she has been discriminated against on the basis of one of the listed grounds has the option of either filing a charge with the Equal Employment Opportunity Commission or, after receipt of a "right to sue" letter from the commission, bringing a lawsuit against the employer in state or federal court.

Remedies available to a successful civil litigant (the person initiating the lawsuit) include reinstatement to the position, back pay, and compensatory and punitive damages. (Unlike compensatory damages, which are awarded to make up for lost opportunities, punitive damages are awarded to punish the wrongdoer.)

The **Age Discrimination in Employment Act of 1967** (AEDA) makes it unlawful for an employer to "fail or refuse to hire, discharge or otherwise discriminate against any individual with respect to his/her compensation, terms, conditions or privileges of employment because of such individual's age." The AEDA protects workers ages forty and older and can be enforced by an employee in a manner similar to the enforcement procedures of Title VII. Remedies for a successful civil litigant can be substantial, including back pay, front pay, reinstatement, promotion, awards of seniority, and liquidated monetary damages.

The **Equal Pay Act of 1963** (EPA) makes it unlawful for an employer to discriminate on the basis of an employee's gender in the payment of wages

AT A GLANCE

- Title VII of the Civil Rights Act of 1964 prohibits discrimination by an employer of an employee's race, color, religion, gender, or national origin.
- Employers should always require a prospective employee's references and check them.
- Employees covered by worker's compensation in their workplaces must use that program to recover medical costs when injured on the job.

for similar jobs. In other words, the EPA requires that an employer pay a comparable wage to male and female workers who are doing the same job under generally similar conditions, such as male and female exercise riders or grooms.

The **Americans with Disabilities Act of 1990** (ADA) prohibits discrimination by private employers against workers with disabilities. The ADA protections include prohibitions against discrimination based on disability in job application and interview procedures, hiring, promotion, wages, training, and most other terms and conditions of employment. The ADA includes a broad definition of disability to include persons with a physical or mental impairment that "substantially limits" one or more of the individual's major life activities; a person with a history of such impairment; or a person who is perceived as having such an impairment.

Major life activities include performing manual tasks, caring for oneself, walking, seeing, talking, hearing, breathing, and learning. Covered disabilities include physical and mental impairments, cosmetic disfigurement, learning disabilities, and infectious or communicable diseases (including HIV infection and AIDS). A history of alcoholism is a disability, as is prior drug use in a person who has completed a rehabilitation program; current use of illegal drugs is not considered a disability, however, nor is ongoing alcoholism that prevents an employee from doing his or her job in an efficient and safe manner.

The ADA prohibits pre-employment medical tests but allows such tests during the period between an offer of employment and the time the worker starts on the job. Some employers require a pre-offer screening for illegal drugs, and there is dispute about whether this practice constitutes a prohibited "medical test." The ADA also prohibits an employer from asking a prospective employee if he or she has a disability but allows questions about the person's ability to perform job-related tasks.

It is possible and, given the level of complexity of federal and state law, even probable that an employer can discriminate against a job applicant or an employee without intending to do so. Current hiring practices, including questions that can and cannot be posed to job applicants, procedures for disciplining and discharging employees, wage plans, and all other facets of employer-employee relations should be discussed with an attorney. In the area of employment, an ounce of prevention in the form of discussion and planning with an employment attorney truly is worth a pound of cure.

THE INTERVIEW AND BEYOND

Employers and employees have somewhat different objectives during the hiring process. An employer wants to discover all relevant information about the employee while an employee wants to put his or her best foot forward in hopes of landing the job. If a potential employee has something to hide, those objectives become mutually exclusive.

One of the most valuable sources of potential information for employers is the list of references provided by the applicant. Employers always should require references from potential employees, and the references should be checked. If an employee's violent behavior on the job later becomes an issue, for example, the employer might be legally liable for negligent hiring if he or she knew, or reasonably should have known, about the worker's violent character.

Many employers are reluctant to give out anything other than basic information on a former employee, fearing a bad reference will result in legal action by the employee. Nevertheless, employers should check the references as thoroughly as possible.

Some employers also conduct background checks on potential employees. Most cities have one or more private investigative agencies that for a reasonable cost can retrieve police and court records, and some information is available, either for free or for a fee, on the Internet. Also, if an employee will be driving a farm-owned vehicle, a valid driver's license and a clean driving record should be mandatory.

The next step in the actual hiring process — after information about an open position has been made available to potential hires and applications and references are reviewed — usually is a personal interview with job applicants. The interview can be as formal or as informal as the employer thinks appropriate, with the goal being to learn as much pertinent information about the prospective employee as possible within the bounds of the law. This is an important caveat because the various anti-discrimination laws discussed earlier impose serious restrictions on the types of questions that can be asked of a job applicant.

Interview questions cannot legally address issues that might give rise to illegal discrimination on the part of the employer. A list of possible interview questions should be developed in consultation with your attorney *before* the interview. If this sounds like too much trouble, consider the possible consequences of running afoul of the law, among them a discrimination lawsuit that could put you out of business — even if you win.

For example, the Equal Employment Opportunity Commission, the federal agency responsible for enforcing the ADA, recommends that questions similar to the following *should not* be asked of a job applicant:

"Have you ever been hospitalized? If the answer is yes, for what condition?"

"Have you ever been treated by a psychiatrist or a psychologist? If the answer is yes, for what condition?"

"Do you suffer from any health-related problems that would prevent you from doing the job?"

"Do you have any physical defects or disabilities that would prevent you from doing the job?"

"Have you ever been treated for drug addiction or alcoholism?"

While the answers to these questions might reasonably provide information that an employer would like to know about a job applicant, they all run afoul of the ADA because they seek information about disabilities that could form a basis for discrimination. Better options might be:

"Can you perform all the functions required by the job?"

"Can you meet the attendance requirements?"

"Do you currently use illegal drugs?"

The differences between the two sets of questions can be subtle. Those in the latter group ask for general information without being directed at an applicant's possible disability. (Current use of illegal drugs is not a covered disability; past drug use that is not continuing is covered by the ADA.) Even if a job applicant volunteers information about a disability in response to a legal question, an employer still cannot discriminate because the applicant is in a protected class. Interview questions addressing an applicant's age, race, gender (including whether a female applicant is married or plans to become pregnant), and national origin raise similar concerns.

A vexing problem for job applicants is how to respond to what appears to be an illegal interview question, especially if the answer would reveal the applicant is in a protected class when that information is not obvious. There may not be a good solution. Simply answering truthfully might leave the applicant feeling as if he or she was forced to reveal private information with no real recourse.

Informing the employer that the question is illegal and refusing to answer might guarantee that the employee is not hired. This action may be discriminatory in its own right, but the only option at that point for the applicant is a costly and time-consuming lawsuit. Questioning the legality of the inquiry then answering truthfully, on the other hand, may earn an applicant points for honesty but might lead to discrimination if there actually is a disability. Telling a falsehood in a job interview never is a good idea.

Preparation for a job interview is important for both employers and job applicants. Employers should draft questions that do not violate the law, and applicants should prepare responses to appropriate and inappropriate interview questions.

One initial decision facing an employer when deciding to hire someone is whether to formalize the employment agreement in a written contract. Although the use of written contracts almost always is sound business practice, there has been slow and reluctant acceptance of such formal agreements in the horse business. Horse dealings traditionally have been conducted with a handshake, and that trend continues today in all aspects of the industry. The decision whether to use a written employment contract or to rely on an oral agreement between the parties is a personal one, but the decision should be made with the advice of legal counsel and with an understanding of the potential consequences.

There are pros and cons to the use of written contracts in the employment arena. Reducing an oral agreement to writing forces the parties to be certain they both understand and agree on the important terms of the contract and the written document can reduce misunderstandings if there is a dispute. On the other hand, employers enjoy more freedom dealing with employees if there is no written agreement.

No one hires an employee anticipating the worker will create a problem and will have to be fired. Such situations develop with alarming frequency after the fact, however, and an employer's ability to discharge an employee depends, in part, on whether there is a written employment contract. In most states a worker who is hired without a written employment contract for a specified term of employment is considered an employee "at will."

Status as an at-will employee traditionally meant that the worker could be fired at any time, for any reason, or without any reason at all. The employee literally worked at the will and whim of the employer. Clearly, this was not in the employee's best interest.

More recently, statutory protections against various forms of discrimination enacted at the federal and state level have curtailed an employer's ability to discharge an at-will employee. As noted earlier in this chapter, an employer cannot fire an employee, even a worker without a written employment contract, based on the employee's race, national origin, gender, religion, or, in many instances, disability.

This does not mean that an employee in a protected class never can be fired. Anti-discrimination laws only prevent an employer from taking action against an employee in a protected class *because of* the employee's status. There may be legitimate reasons to fire an employee that are unrelated to the employee's status as a member of a protected class, and an employer is not required to keep an employee who cannot do the job. The law does prevent an employer from using poor job performance or some other reason as a pretext, or excuse, to discriminate against an employee in a protected class.

Another recent trend is to provide some protection for at-will employees whose discharge violates a fundamental public policy. This can be difficult to define but probably includes firing because the employee exercised a statutory or constitutional right, refused to perform an illegal activity, or was a "whistle-blower" about an employer's illegal or improper practices. Beyond these restrictions, however, an at-will employee has few protections against discharge. Caution should be exercised when firing an at-will employee, however, to avoid a wrongful discharge lawsuit.

An oral contract of employment for a specified period, like a written contract, sometimes can modify the at-will status of an employee. There also are occasions when a court will decide that an employment contract exists between the parties based simply on the fact that the parties act as if there is an agreement. The difficulty with such oral and implied contracts is, first, proving their existence, and, second, establishing the relevant terms.

The situation becomes somewhat more complicated when there is a written employment contract. An employee serving under an employment contract for a specified period still can be discharged prior to the termination of the contract. The employer must establish negligence, lack of skill, gross inefficiency, dishonesty, or some other legitimate cause for the firing, or possibly face a lawsuit brought by the disgruntled ex-employee.

A contract employee also can be discharged if his or her position is eliminated due to legitimate economic business conditions. A farm deciding to stop standing stallions as a result of a downturn in the market for breeding seasons would be a legitimate reason to discharge the stallion manager, for example, even during the life of a valid employment contract. The principal restriction, again, is that the alleged economic condition cannot be a bad faith pretext for firing the employee.

The foregoing may sound like a good reason not to have a formal employment contract because doing so restricts the freedom of an employer to discharge workers. Generally, though, the benefits of a written agreement with employees far outweigh the problems that such an agreement causes, by setting out in detail the rights and obligations of each party. An attorney can help draft an employment contract appropriate for your individual situation.

It may be possible for an employer and an employee to be bound by a contract even if that result is not intended. The use of an employee handbook is one example.

Employers generally are not required to distribute an employee handbook to workers. If employee handbooks are used, employers should be aware that courts sometimes interpret affirmative statements in the manual as creating an employment contract, even if that was not the employer's intent.

That potential problem aside, the advantages of an employee handbook probably outweigh the disadvantages, by reducing the risk of misunderstandings between employers and workers. The employee manual should include all relevant conditions of employment, such as expected work hours, duties, policies about overtime and sick pay, health and worker's compensation insurance benefits, any other benefits, and circumstances that can be expected to lead to dismissal.

The employee handbook also should make it clear that there is a zero-tolerance policy for violence, discrimination, and sexual harassment, as well as a "no firearms" policy. If foreign nationals are employed, all written material should be provided in a language that can be understood by the employees. Finally, employees should be required to indicate in writing that they have received a copy of the handbook and that notice of receipt should be kept in the worker's personnel file.

SEXUAL HARASSMENT AND VIOLENCE

Sexual harassment, as noted earlier, is covered under Title VII and various state laws. The problem merits a separate section because it is so pervasive. Some reports suggest that as many as nine out of ten female workers and two out of ten male workers have experienced or will experience some type of sexual harassment in the workplace during their employment.

The Equal Employment Opportunity Commission states:

> Unwelcome sexual advances, requests for sexual favors, and other verbal or physical conduct of a sexual nature constitute sexual harassment when submission to or rejection of this conduct explicitly or implicitly affects an individual's employment, unreasonably interferes with an individual's work performance or creates an intimidating, hostile or offensive work environment.

This is a very broad definition of offensive conduct, one that includes both job-related demands for sexual favors (the legal term for this is quid pro quo sexual harassment) and the creation of a hostile work environment. In the former, the aggrieved worker only has to prove one instance of harassment; for the latter, a pattern of offensive conduct generally must be proved.

Employers also may be liable if an employee is sexually harassed by a non-employee, such as a client or vendor who comes to the farm. Employers should establish a policy against sexual harassment (and other forms of discrimination), make the employees aware of the policy, and enforce it if there are violations. Employers also should establish and enforce a policy of confidentiality for employees who report incidents of alleged harassment.

Having a stated and enforced policy against sexual discrimination will not absolutely protect an employer from a lawsuit, but failure to have such a policy will look incriminating to a jury. An attorney, preferably one familiar with employment law, can help draft an effective policy that protects both employers and employees.

Protestations of mail carriers aside, the phrase "going postal" has entered our vocabulary as shorthand for an employee who goes berserk and injures or kills fellow employees or others. Keeping in mind that anti-discrimination legislation limits somewhat the types of questions employers legally can ask a potential employee in a pre-employment interview, there still are things that can be done to protect employees and customers from potentially violent employees.

Experts agree that one of the best predictors of violent behavior is a history of violence. One question that should be asked in any job interview is whether the applicant has any prior criminal convictions. Keep in mind that while convictions are fair game for questions, arrests may not be because a person is presumed innocent until proved guilty, and innocent persons sometimes are arrested. If the job prospect has a history of violent crimes, that could be a valid ground for an employer's refusal to make an offer of employment.

In addition to limiting the types of questions an employer can ask during a pre-offer job interview, the ADA also may limit an employer's ability to require a pre-offer drug screen because such tests may be regarded as medical tests, prohibited at that stage of the hiring process. Medical tests, including drug screens, are allowed during the period between the time when a job offer is made and when the employee actually starts work, however. Once the person is offered a job, an employer legally can make employment contingent on the employee passing a drug test. If the person fails, the job offer can be withdrawn at that point without liability on the part of the employer. It is important to require all employees for similar positions to take the same test to avoid charges of discrimination.

Although helpful, pre-offer investigation and pre-employment drug tests will not disclose all potentially violent employees. The best time to spot violent tendencies is after the employee starts working, and all employers should establish and strictly enforce a policy of zero tolerance for violence in the workplace. This provision can be included in an employment contract, in an employee handbook, or both, and employers should emphasize during the hiring process that *any* violent behavior toward other employees, clients, or animals will result in immediate dismissal.

It always is better to be safe than sorry when the issue is violence in the workplace.

WORKER'S COMPENSATION

Worker's compensation is an insurance program that is funded by employers to protect employees who suffer job-related injuries. Worker's compensation provides the *exclusive* remedy through which a covered employee who is injured on the job can recover his or her medical expenses. This means that an employee who is injured on the job and who receives money from a worker's compensation program cannot also sue his or her employer in an attempt to recover damages resulting from the injury.

In theory, at least, worker's compensation benefits both employers and employees. The mechanics and application of worker's compensation programs vary somewhat from state to state. Generally, the programs require a covered employer to obtain insurance to cover his or her employees in the event of injury or occupational disease, with the premiums varying based on the number of workers and other factors.

Through participation in the program, an injured worker gives up the right to sue the employer, making worker's compensation payments to the employee the only remedy for a work-related injury. The injured worker then gains the right to recover through the system without having to show fault on the part of the employer for an injury, as would be the case in a lawsuit. This means that an injured worker's medical bills will be paid fairly quickly with little or no money coming out of the employee's pocket. The employer, who pays the worker's compensation insurance premiums, is insulated from lawsuits.

Whether employers will be required to participate in a worker's compensation program is a matter of state law. Many states require coverage for all employees, while other states exclude agricultural workers.

In Kentucky, for example, although most workers are included in the worker's compensation program by statutory mandate, those individuals employed in agricultural businesses are not. A variety of state court decisions have determined that the agricultural exemption in the worker's compensation program includes horse farms and operations that condition and exercise racehorses that have been at the track but have been returned to a farm for rehabilitation due to injury. Businesses that board and breed horses also are exempt.

Trainers at racetracks, however, are not exempt. So, depending on the nature of the business and where it is located, employers may be required to participate in the state's program.

Even if an employer is not required to participate in a state's worker's compensation program, most jurisdictions allow employers not otherwise covered to participate voluntarily. The owner of a sport-horse breeding farm with several employees may, for example, purchase the required insurance and elect to join the state's worker's compensation program voluntarily even though participation is not required by law. By so doing, the employer has insulated himself or herself from lawsuits by injured employees, while at the same time creating an attractive enticement for prospective workers.

MINIMUM WAGE

With passage of the Fair Labor Standards Act of 1938, a minimum wage of $0.25/hour was established. At this writing, the federal minimum wage is $5.15/hour for non-supervisory, non-farm, private sector employees, with some support in Congress for an increase above that figure in the near future. The minimum wage for workers in agriculture is less, based on statute. It is worth noting that since the last increase in the minimum wage, in 1996, lawmakers in Congress have bickered about increasing the minimum wage while voting cost of living raises for themselves of more than $30,000 each.

Most states adopt the federal minimum wage standards by reference. Some states have minimum wage standards set higher than the federal minimum, a few have a lower minimum wage than the federal standard (in which case the higher federal minimum applies), and a very few states have no minimum wage at all (federal standards apply here as well).

Employers should be able to determine the minimum wage for farm workers with a telephone call to the state wage and hour department, or to the U.S. Department of Labor's Wage and Hour Division. As always, if there are questions, employers should consult an attorney to determine the minimum wage for a particular business. An attorney also can advise employers whether they are required to post an informational poster that outlines employer-employee rights and obligations of the parties.

Finally, employers should keep in mind that a minimum wage establishes a floor, not a ceiling, for what they pay their employees, and that a legally mandated minimum wage is not necessarily a living wage.

SAFETY IN THE WORKPLACE

The Occupational Safety and Health Act (OSHA) of 1970 represented an attempt by Congress to provide comprehensive regulation of health and safety issues in the workplace. The law imposes a general requirement on virtually every private employer to provide a workplace free of dangerous tasks and conditions. Many states have adopted their own occupational safety and health programs, which, if approved by the federal government, assume front-line responsibility for enforcement of workplace safety standards.

Kentucky's Occupational Safety and Health Program received final federal approval in 1985. It mirrors federal legislation in most respects and is typical of many similar state plans.

State law imposes on every employer both a general and specific duty. First, each employer "shall furnish to each of his employees employment and a place of employment which are free from recognized hazards that are causing or are likely to cause death or serious physical harm to his employees." Second, employers must comply with any specific safety standards relevant to their particular businesses issued under the state program.

Employees also have legal rights and duties. Each employee has a right to expect a workplace free of recognized health and safety hazards and a legal duty to comply with all relevant occupational health and safety standards and applicable rules and regulations.

OSHA regulations also require every employer to keep records of occupational injuries and illnesses, post a summary of those statistics for the information of employees, and maintain the records for five years.

Finally, an employer cannot discriminate against an employee who reports a possible violation to authorities or who requests an inspection of the place of employment.

There appear to be few specific safety standards or regulations directly applicable to horse farms although some of the general agricultural standards might be applicable, depending on the actual nature of the business. The possibilities for violations of the general obligation to provide a safe workplace on a horse farm are virtually endless, however. Problems could result from poorly maintained or dangerous farm equipment; improper storage of fertilizers, insecticides, and other commonly used chemicals; hazardous conditions in a hayloft; or possibly even keeping an unmanageable stallion.

Penalties for violations can be severe. For a willful or repeated violation, for example, a civil penalty of $5,000 to $70,000 may be assessed if the violation is determined to be serious; a maximum penalty of $7,000 may be assessed for a violation determined not to be of a serious nature.

The world of employer-employee relations is a complex one, with myriad opportunities for problems. The value of a written contract should be obvious in this context; by allowing both parties to begin the employment relationship with a clear understanding of what each expects, the chances for misunderstandings are substantially reduced.

IMMIGRATION

Always complex, immigration matters have become even more complicated since the terrorist attacks on the World Trade Center and the Pentagon in 2001. The Immigration and Naturalization Service was swamped with bad press when, six months after the fact, the agency approved student visas for two of the dead foreign nationals who were involved in the attacks. Congress initiated an overhaul of the agency, which in March 2003 became part of the Department of Homeland Security and morphed into the U.S. Citizenship and Immigration Services (USCIS).

Anyone who doubts that the employment of foreign nationals has become essential to the success, and some might argue the economic survival, of the horse business need only stroll though the backstretch of a racetrack or the stable area of a horse show, or visit any one of the majority of horse operations in the country. Foreign nationals play a vital role, but along with their growing numbers in the workplace have come increased demands on employers.

A foreign national who is working in the United States can be deported by the government if he or she is found to be without a green card or government authorization to work in one of a number of specified employment categories. Until the mid-1980s, however, the employer of an undocumented alien faced neither criminal nor civil liability for having hired a foreign national who did not have employment permission from the government. Employers traditionally could hire illegal aliens without fear of repercussion.

That situation changed with passage of the Immigration Reform and Control Act of 1986 and the Immigration Act of 1990. The former, particularly, fundamentally changed the way employers must deal with foreign nationals by shifting the enforcement burden for policing the country's immigration laws to private employers. The full impact of this legislation is far beyond the scope of this book. Questions about the various alternatives open to an employer who intends to bring foreign nationals to the United States for either permanent or temporary work, including an explanation of the different visa categories, should be directed to an immigration attorney or to the USCIS.

Employers must verify both the authorization to work and the identity of each person hired, either before a final job offer is made (the preferable option) or within three days after employment starts. This verification must be made for *every* employee, not just employees an employer might think are foreign nationals. Verification is accomplished through completion by both the employer and employee of federal Form I-9. The employee must provide either a single document that establishes both identity and authorization to work or separate documents. Originals must be provided.

I-9 forms are not filed with the government. The employer must retain the forms for three years after the date of hire or for one year after employment is terminated, whichever date is later. The forms should be kept either in each employee's personnel file (which may be impractical if there are a large number of employees) or in a central location and should be accessible within three days to satisfy a request by the USCIS for inspection.

Single documents that establish both identity and authorization to work, so-called "List A" documents, include a U.S. passport (either current or expired), a Certificate of U.S. Citizenship, a Certificate of Naturalization, or an unexpired Temporary Resident Card or Employment Authorization Document. Documents that establish identity alone, "List B" documents, include a driver's license with photograph or identifying data, a government identification card, a school identification card with photograph, or voter registration card. Documents that establish only eligibility to work, "List C" documents, include a U.S. Social Security card or an original or certified copy of a birth certificate issued by a state, county, or municipal authority in this country. (This list is not inclusive. A complete listing of acceptable documents, along with detailed instructions for completion of Form I-9, is available from the USCIS.)

The employer must state under oath and penalty of perjury that he or she has examined the offered documents, that the documents appear on their face to be genuine, and that the person presenting them is eligible to work in the United States. Employers cannot request "more or different" documents than are required nor can they refuse to honor documents that appear to be genuine. Good faith compliance with the verification requirements by the employer is a defense to a violation.

Finally, it is worth repeating that I-9 verification procedures are required for *all* employees, not just employees who obviously are foreign nationals.

If an employer discovers that an employee may not be authorized to work in the United States, the USCIS recommends that the employee be given

CASE STUDIES

Munday v. Churchill Downs, Inc., 600 SW2d 487 (Ky App 1980)

John Joseph Munday, a jockey, was injured when he fell from his mount during a race at Churchill Downs in Louisville, Kentucky. Munday applied for worker's compensation, but the claim was denied after an agency finding that he was an independent contractor and thus not covered by the program. Munday appealed the decision and argued that worker's compensation was appropriate either because he was an employee of the horse's trainer or that he was an employee of Churchill Downs. The Kentucky Court of Appeals disagreed.

The court explained:

Munday was given pre-race instructions by Hancock, the owner/

trainer, to stay close and win if he could … The claimant [Munday] is a member of a licensed occupation and was employed and paid by the job as a freelance jockey, as opposed to a contract jockey. He solicited trainers and operated by himself or through an agent. A contract rider is one who works under an agreement with a particular trainer … Hancock's right of control over Munday's work was extremely limited. The instructions of Hancock did not amount to a control of the details of the jockey's work. A jockey is required by the Rules of Racing … to ride the horse as to win, or finish as near as possible to first, and to demonstrate the best and fastest performance of which the horse is capable. The admonition by the owner prior to the race was only a repetition of the jockey's professional obligation.

The court also found that Munday was not employed by the racetrack:
There is no reason to believe from the evidence that Churchill Downs could be considered as the employer of the jockey. Jockeys receive no riding instructions from any track official. The jockey is paid [his or her share of purses won] once a week on a gross basis with no deductions being made for taxes or social security. The track furnishes each jockey with an annual 1099 form for tax purposes … Supervision of the racing is in the hands of the stewards. Churchill Downs does not control the arrival or departure of jockeys or pass on their qualifications. Payment through the track office is not enough to create an employment relationship.

Not surprisingly, resolution of the rider's employment status turned on the level of control exercised by the employer. Because there was little or no control, Munday was determined to be an independent contractor.

Goetzinger v. Wheeler, unpublished case, 2002 Iowa App LEXIS 438 (Iowa App 2002)

The employment status of Nancy Wheeler became an issue when she was injured while showing a horse for Ronald Goetzinger. Wheeler worked part-time for Goetzinger during the week and on weekends training and showing horses. She was injured during a weekend horse show and the state worker's compensation board determined that she was an employee of Goetzinger's and thus entitled to worker's compensation.

Goetzinger contested this determination. He admitted that Wheeler was an employee during the week, when she kept track of her hours and was compensated for them, but that she was an independent contractor on weekends when she neither kept track of her hours nor reported them to Goetzinger.

The Iowa Court of Appeals sided with the worker's compensation board. Wheeler testified that the purpose of her work during the week was to prepare Goetzinger's horses for weekend horse shows. She stated, "Well, usually when you put a trainer or somebody in the barn to take care of your horses, the end results (sic) is to show them. I mean, you don't get something ready just to stand in the barn for individuals to look at." The court determined there was sufficient evidence in the record to support the determination that Wheeler was an employee of Goetzinger's during the week and during the weekend.

a second chance to provide acceptable documentation. If that cannot be done, the employment must be terminated.

It is against the law for an employer to hire workers the employer either knows or has reason to know lack authorization to work in the United States. The penalties for violations can be severe and may include both fines and a prison sentence.

INDEPENDENT CONTRACTORS

This chapter so far has addressed employees, but there is another classification of workers called independent contractors. Employing an independent contractor is much simpler than hiring an employee because there is far less paperwork. Employers must pay their share of employment taxes (including Social Security, Medicare, and federal and state unemployment taxes) for employees and also must withhold federal and state income taxes and the employee's share of employment taxes from each employee's gross pay. An employee's gross and net wages must be reported each year to the government, and a W-2 form must be provided to the employee.

There are no corresponding requirements for the employer of an independent contractor. The only reporting requirement for an employer of an independent contractor is the filing of a Form 1099-Misc if more than $600 is paid to the independent contractor in a year. A copy of the 1099 also is provided to the independent contractor.

Federal and state anti-discrimination laws generally do not apply to independent contractors, which means that an independent contractor cannot file a discrimination lawsuit against an employer. Also, independent contractors are not included in state worker's compensation programs.

Considering the relative freedom accorded an employer when dealing with independent contractors, it may be tempting for an employer to treat *all* workers as independent contractors. That would not be a good idea, however. An independent contractor has a legal status determined by law, which requires more than a label applied by an employer. An independent contractor agrees to perform certain specified work at his or her own risk, with no intermediate control exercised by the employer.

While the IRS utilizes a multi-part test to determine the status of a worker, the overriding consideration is the amount of control, if any, the employer exercises over the worker. If an employer directs how, when, and where a worker does the job; provides materials, tool, uniforms, and training; sets the worker's schedule; and pays the worker on a regular basis; it is likely that the worker is an employee and not an independent contractor.

Regardless of whether an employer calls a worker an employee or an independent contractor, the final determination will be made by the IRS if a question arises. If an employee has been mischaracterized as an independent contractor, the employer may be subject to federal and state penalties that can include back taxes that should have been withheld, as well as interest and penalties.

Courts in many states have wrestled with the question of whether a particular worker, or class of workers, is an employee or an independent contractor. The question usually arises in a worker's compensation case or in a lawsuit in which a worker claims that a farm owner is responsible for injuries.

Farriers and veterinarians generally are considered to be independent contractors, as are workers hired for particular construction projects, while grooms and other regular farm workers typically are considered employees. Courts are split on whether jockeys and exercise riders (at the track and sometimes on the farm as well) are employees or independent contractors. A public trainer who conditions horses for several different owners almost certainly is an independent contractor while a trainer who works for one owner exclusively likely is an employee.

RESOURCES

The U.S. Equal Employment Opportunity Commission Web site provides employers and employees with information and guidance about fair practices in the workplace: www.eeoc.gov.

To obtain information about compliance with the Occupational Safety and Health Administration standards, visit the Web site at www.osha.gov.

For information of hiring foreign nationals, visit the Web site of the U.S. Citizenship and Immigration Services at www.uscis.gov.

13

ESTATE
PLANNING

Death and taxes. Both are inevitable and both should be the subject of substantial advance planning.

This chapter, like the earlier chapter on tax issues, addresses estate planning in a selective and very general fashion. This is done out of necessity. Effective estate planning, probably more than any other area of legal practice, depends on the facts, circumstances, and goals of the individuals involved. A good estate plan for one family might be a disaster for another, and individualized advice must come from professionals experienced in the field, not from a book. With that caveat, some general information can be valuable when considering an estate plan.

WILLS

The mainstay of any estate plan is a will, and everybody should have one. A properly drafted will, one that satisfies the legal requirements of the state in which the maker of the document (the testator) lives, can accomplish several things.

A will sets out how a person's property will be distributed after the testator's death. This is an important consideration because the property of a person who dies intestate (without a valid will) will be distributed according to state law. Inheritance laws represent a legislature's best guess about how a person might want his or her property divided, but it is rare if state law mirrors exactly the distribution an individual might desire.

Consider a man who in partnership with his wife owns a small Arabian breeding farm and show stable. The couple has one adult child, who has no interest in the farm, and a nephew who wants to be in the Arabian business. The man might leave the farm and horses to his wife and the nephew, while setting aside a sum of money for the child to use in a non-horse related business. This distribution could easily be accomplished through a properly drafted will.

Without a will, however, most state laws would provide for distribution of all the man's property (including the farm and horses) to his wife and child, with the nephew totally out of the inheritance picture. The surviving family members probably could eventually shuffle things around to meet the deceased's intentions, but that complication could have been avoided with a will.

Other benefits of a will include but are not limited to the following:

• A guardian for a minor child can be designated in a will.

• The testator can identify an executor for the estate in a will and eliminate the need for a monetary bond to be posted by that person.

• Charities and non-family members can be designated as beneficiaries.

For some individuals, a basic will that can be prepared by an attorney for a few hundred dollars will be sufficient.

POWERS OF ATTORNEY

Many people are familiar with health care surrogates and living wills. They are documents prepared ahead of time that tell family and doctors what medical choices an individual wants made on his or her behalf in the event of a terminal illness. This information is vital if a person cannot inform the appropriate individuals at the time a decision needs to be made. State laws vary regarding health care surrogates and living wills, and advice from an attorney is necessary to prepare a document that will actually accomplish what it is supposed to do.

Not all injuries or illnesses are life threatening, however, and it is important to ensure that someone else has legal authority to act on an individual's behalf in other situations. In part, this will depend on how a business is organized and run. A corporation or partnership where management duties are shared, for example, may have options not available to a sole proprietorship, where the individual owner *is* the business.

Whatever the business structure, it is important that someone have the legal authority to order feed, write checks to pay bills and employees, and generally direct the operation. Under many, but not all, circumstances a spouse can act on behalf of the other spouse. But what if the situation is one where that would not be possible?

Often the simplest way to give someone else legal permission to act for you is to appoint another person as attorney-in-fact, to act on your behalf. This frequently is called giving someone power of attorney. There are several ways to do this. It is important for you to know what kind of power of attorney is given and to choose the person to act for you very carefully.

General Power of Attorney

Also simply called a "power of attorney," this form is available in all states and generally allows another person to do everything for you that you could have done for yourself. It does not take any power away from individuals to act in their own behalf. A general power of attorney takes immediate effect. When someone acts as attorney-in-fact, he or she usually must inform other parties that the attorney-in-fact is acting for someone else, by signing checks or other documents, for example, as "Martin Page, attorney-in-fact for Mary Green" or "Martin Page, POA for Mary Green."

A show horse trainer who spends substantial time on the road might use a general power of attorney to authorize a trusted individual to pay bills, buy feed, and deal with veterinarians and farriers in the trainer's absence. "Trusted" cannot be overemphasized, because the holder of a general power of attorney can do anything that the grantor can do, including empty out checking and savings accounts.

The general power of attorney does not extend into periods of the grantor's disability, however. If a general power of attorney is used, it generally requires that someone get court permission to act in your stead if you become disabled.

AT A GLANCE

- Everyone should have a properly drafted will.
- Power of attorney allows you to appoint someone to act on your behalf legally in business affairs.
- There is little uniformity in states' statutes regarding trusts for the care of animals.
- Animals are the personal property of their owner and are subject to the provisions of their owner's will.

Durable Power of Attorney

This form of power of attorney is identical to the general power of attorney, except that it also continues through periods of disability. It should contain a clause specifically giving authority to act during periods of disability. It also may include a description of the evidence necessary to establish disability in the grantor of the power. This is probably not necessary with this form of power of attorney, however, as the attorney-in-fact has power to act immediately.

Springing Power of Attorney

This form of power of attorney comes into effect *only* when the grantor becomes disabled. It must specify the method in which disability is to be determined. Many people like this because they worry about the other forms giving the attorney-in-fact too much power too soon. This form is not recognized in all states, however, because statutes may not provide for it and courts can be reluctant to accept that the grantor really would have made this same choice at some nebulous point in the future. It seems easier for courts to accept the notion, as with the durable power of attorney, that a person you trust to act for you at the time the power of attorney is executed also would be someone you would trust to act for you in periods of disability.

Limited or Special Purpose Power of Attorney

Unlike the other powers of attorney, this form gives one person power to act on another's behalf only in specific circumstances or for a specific period. This avoids giving someone too much power or giving it too soon, but it also requires a new power of attorney for any act not within the scope or outside of the time limits of the first document.

TIME IS OF THE ESSENCE

Generic fill-in-the-blank will forms available on the Internet and at office supply and stationery stores almost certainly are not a perfect fit for anyone in particular, and they also may not satisfy the requirements of state law. Even with a properly drafted will, however, provisions should be made for the care of animals immediately after the owner's death.

It takes time to have a funeral, locate a will, get to court to have the will probated, and have the court appoint the executor. In the meantime, the horses and pets need food, water, and maybe veterinary care at the very least. Plan now to have them cared for immediately in the event of your death.

LETTER OF LAST INSTRUCTIONS

Care for animals after the owner's death is an issue because a power of attorney no longer has effect once the grantor of the power dies. While it might be tempting to assume that only one spouse will die, leaving the other to handle the details, all too often spouses die together, or the health of the surviving spouse is too poor for that person to be able to deal with immediate personal or business details.

Obviously, if a business is such that there are other people around to provide short-term care for the animals, this may not be a problem. It frequently is a problem, however, especially for very small business operations and for horse owners who are not in business at all but who have pleasure horses.

One of the best ways to deal with the problem is to prepare a letter of last instructions. This will handle the period between death and the time a will is probated. In addition to providing information about any funeral arrangements that may have been planned or the deceased's wishes about a funeral service, the document should name someone as interim caretaker for the horses. It should contain enough information to allow those acting on the basis of the letter to determine how to contact the owners of boarded horses. Depending on the circumstances, it also may be necessary for the letter to give permission for someone to go onto the deceased's land to care for the horses.

A letter of last instructions is useful only if it can be accessed quickly after the death of the writer. One option is to provide copies to the individuals identified in the letter. This is somewhat problematic, however, because drafters of such letters often change their minds about something and decide to write a new letter of last instructions.

Another option is to secure the letter in a safe, fireproof place. In some communities, ambulance and other emergency personnel are trained to look in the freezer for medical information about elderly persons. Nearly everyone has a refrigerator, it is usually easy to find, and it is unlikely to be destroyed in a fire. This would be an ideal place for such a letter, if double wrapped in a sealable freezer bag. The freezer is preferable to a bank safe deposit box, at least in states where such boxes are sealed until a representative of the state taxing authority can attend the first post-death opening.

Depending on the nature of the business, it may not be sufficient to identify people to care for the animals immediately after the owner's death. If there are horses boarded on the farm, for example, agreements or contracts with owners of boarded horses should explicitly specify not only the amount of payment, the services provided, etc., but also whether the contract terminates in the event of the sudden death of the business owner(s) and how the transition will be handled.

TRUSTS

Various kinds of trusts also can be valuable estate planning tools, although trusts probably are not the cure-all for probate problems they sometimes are advertised to be.

Revocable Trusts

Revocable trusts also are known as "living" trusts. Such trusts take effect and can be modified or completely revoked during the lifetime of the maker of the trust. This flexibility makes them ideal for certain circumstances.

If horse owners use a revocable trust, they can place ownership of the horses and funds for the care of the animals in the trust. They will have to name a trustee, who will have a fiduciary duty to manage the trust assets for the economic benefit of the beneficiaries. A successor trustee also should be named who can take charge of the trust if the first trustee is unable or unwilling to serve.

A revocable trust takes effect immediately and will not go through the probate process at the death of the grantor. A revocable trust ideally is suited to provide a means for continued operation of a family farm or business. The trust is a separate legal entity and will file its own income tax returns through the trustee, who as noted above acts as fiduciary.

Life insurance policies often are included in trusts as sources of funds, but some readily available cash also should be added. It takes time to receive the proceeds from a life insurance policy, and funds should be provided to care for the animals during the waiting period.

A horse owner also can act as trustee of a revocable trust and thereby retain the right to sell the horses or acquire others in trust during the trustee's lifetime. Spouses can act as co-trustees, and the trust can be written so that either can act alone as trustee or as survivor trustee should only one of them die. Because the trust is revocable, they can change their minds at any time.

If the trust still exists at the death of the trustee, or trustees, the property in the trust will go to the named beneficiary or beneficiaries. A letter of last instructions is important, because it can take some time to transfer legal ownership of the horses and other trust property, even though the living trust avoids the probate process.

Although the revocable or living trust can provide for the care of a grantor's horses without the delay of the probate process, such a trust will not reduce the size of the taxable estate, for estate tax purposes. The Internal Revenue Code contains several sections pertinent to trusts. Only placing assets into a trust over which the trust maker holds no strings will reduce the size of the individual's federal taxable estate.

Because a revocable trust leaves the maker of the trust with the power to alter the terms of the trust or to revoke the trust entirely, such a trust would remain part of a decedent's federal taxable estate. Anyone considering a revocable trust should check with their legal and financial advisers to find out how their state treats revocable trusts.

Irrevocable Trusts

A horse owner also can establish an irrevocable trust. Like a revocable trust, an irrevocable trust avoids the delay of probate. If, however, a horse owner decides to create an irrevocable trust, the grantor will not, as maker of the trust, be able to remove ownership of a horse from the trust. Nor will the grantor be able to remove funds from the trust unless the grantor appoints himself or herself as trustee. A grantor can serve in that capacity, just as with a revocable trust. As trustee, a grantor can exercise all the powers given to the trustee under the terms of the trust. These terms may include, among other things, selling a horse.

But remember those strings in the Internal Revenue Code?

If a grantor acts as his or her own trustee, even though the trust is irrevocable, the grantor will be said to have retained power. In that situation the value of the property held by the trust will be included in the grantor's federal taxable estate. A horse owner should seek professional advice to help decide whether reducing the size of the taxable estate is more important than the flexibility of acting as trustee.

Trusts for Animals

Probate administration is strictly a matter of state law, and as with most things discussed in this book, there often is little uniformity in states' statutes. As a result, the success of a trust for the care of an animal will depend on two things: whether the grantor's state recognizes such trusts and, if so, whether the trust satisfies the requirements of state law.

The National Conference of Commissioners on Uniform State Laws is a national body that drafts model laws on a variety of subjects and promotes the adoption of those laws by the states. The idea is an admirable one, uniform laws throughout the states, but the results have been mixed. The National Conference of Commissioners on Uniform State Laws works in an advisory capacity only, and states are not required to adopt any of the group's uniform laws. Some have been adopted; others have not.

Among the uniform laws promulgated by the National Conference of Commissioners on Uniform State Laws are the Uniform Probate Code and the Uniform Trust Code. Both have been modified in recent years to address concerns of animal owners who want to provide for the care of their animals after the death of an owner.

Section 2-907, authorizing trusts "for the care of a designated domestic animal or pet animal," was added to the Uniform Probate Code in 1990. A similar provision, found at Section 408 of the Uniform Trust Code, was added in 2000 to authorize a trust "to provide for the care of an animal during the settlor's lifetime."

To date, some two dozen states have adopted either the Uniform Probate Code or the Uniform Trust Code provisions, while several other states have similar legislation on their books. Drafting a trust that satisfies a state's statutory provisions or that satisfies a state's general probate laws is a complicated task best left to an estate planning professional. The language used in the trust is crucial, especially in states without specific statutory provisions for animal trusts.

Testamentary Trusts

A tempting alternative may be to provide care for horses and other animals by setting up an honorary trust in the owner's will. This type of trust is called "testamentary" because it comes into being after death, as a provision of a deceased's will. Section 2-907 of the Uniform Probate Code specifically authorizes such testamentary trusts, but in states that have not adopted that provision or that lack similar statutory authorization, there may be problems.

Difficulties may arise if a probate court views testamentary trust language providing for the care of an animal as "precatory," meaning that the will provisions merely express what the decedent hopes will happen. If a court refuses to enforce the trust provisions, the recipient of the horses and funds may not be required to care for the animals or even spend the money on their care.

This happens most often when the will of the decedent violates either a statute or some important matter of public policy. Because our entire legal system, including the probate systems of the states, is essentially a system of balances and counterbalances, the court may not honor the intentions expressed in your will if it violates public policy. This can happen even though courts generally give great weight to the intentions expressed in a will.

A rather dramatic example of a situation in which a court might not honor the terms of a trust created in a will might be a document that left funds and assets to care for a horse, while providing little or nothing for a handicapped child. In a situation such as this, an argument could be made that the testator was not in his or her sound mind, invalidating the entire will.

A more likely problem is the potential for violation of some less well-known principle of law. One example is the "rule against perpetuities," an arcane legal principle that has confounded generations of lawyers. This rule makes any testamentary provision invalid if the gift allows the trust property to be used for longer than 21 years after the death of some relevant "life in being" at the making of the trust provision.

Animals generally don't count as lives in being for purposes of satisfying this rule, although Section 2-907 of the Uniform Probate Code authorizing trusts for animal care suggests a similar 21-year limit for the duration of the trust. This is perilous ground for non-lawyers — and for many attorneys as well — and animal trusts should be carefully drafted to avoid potential problems.

Absent violation of statute or some principle of public policy, many courts will at worst declare that an "honorary trust" exists for the care of the animals. In essence, when a court recognizes an honorary trust, it means that the testator hasn't created a legally enforceable trust, but if the named trustee agrees to care for your horses in the manner specified in the trust, the court will allow this to happen.

A final option is simply to give the animals and funds for their care to someone else as a provision in the owner's will. Animals, remember, are the personal property of their owners and are subject to the provisions of a valid will. This can be accomplished without a trust. The will should state that the decedent would like the money or proceeds from a life insurance policy used for the care of the horses while giving the beneficiary of the animals and funds complete and unrestricted power to decide how to spend the money. In this way, a court is likely to interpret that the will provides for a simple gift rather than an honorary trust. It should go without saying that the recipient should be chosen with great care.

The instructions regarding care of the horses impose a moral but not a legal obligation on the recipient. This is an example of precatory language mentioned earlier in this chapter.

SURVIVAL OF THE BUSINESS

Can a horse business continue after the death of the owner or owners? The answer depends on how the business is owned. Corporations generally continue after the death of one of the directors or officers, while many sole proprietorships unfortunately die along with their owners. A partnership may continue after the death of one of the partners, depending on the terms of the partnership agreement.

Depending on the intent of the owner or owners, planning for the continuity of a business is an essential part of estate planning. The federal Small Business Administration (SBA) estimates that 90 percent of all U.S. businesses are family owned. That probably is a reasonable figure for horse businesses as well. Of those family-owned businesses, the Small Business Administration estimates that only 30 percent will survive into a second generation and that only 15 percent will continue operating into a third generation of the family.

TAXES

One of the goals of estate planning usually is reducing the amount of taxes paid to the federal and state government. Estate tax planning is far beyond the scope of this book and should be left to professionals.

RESOURCES

The Humane Society of the United States offers an information kit about including animals in their owners' estate plans. The information, which includes sample language for wills may be found at www.hsus.org/petsinwills.

When Your Pet Outlives You: Protecting Companion Animals After You Die, by David Congalton and Charlotte Alexander, Troutdale, Ore.:NewSage Press, 2002. www.newsagepress.com.

Information about the National Conference of Commissioners on Uniform State Laws may be found at www.nccusl.org.

APPENDIX

State	Agister's Lien Statute	Equine Activity Liability Statute	Animal and/or Pet Trust Valid
Alabama (Ala. Code)	§35-11-70	§6-5-337	
Alaska (Alaska Statutes)	§34.35.220	§09.65.145	§13.12.907
Arizona (Ariz. Rev. Stat. Ann.)	§3-1295	§12-553	§14-2907
Arkansas (Ark. Code Ann.)	§18-48-101	§16-120-201	§28-73-408
California	§3080.01 (Cal. Civ. Code)		§15212 (Cal. Probate Code)
Colorado (Colo. Rev. Stat.)	§38-20-202	§13-21-119	§15-11-901
Connecticut (Conn. Gen. Stat.)	§49-70	§52-557p	
Delaware (Del. Code Ann.)	Title 25, §3901	Title 10, §8140	
Florida (Fla. Stat.)	§713.65	§773.01	§737.16
Georgia (Ga. Code Ann.)	§44-14-406	§4-12-3	
Hawaii (Haw. Rev. Stat.)	§507-1	§663B-2	§560.7-501
Idaho (Idaho Code)	§45-805(b)	§6-1801	
Illinois (Ill. Rev. Stat.)	Chapter 770, 40/50	Chapter 745, 47/1	Chapter 760, 5/15.2
Indiana (Ind. Code)	§32-38-8-1	§34-31-5-1	§30-4-2-18
Iowa (Iowa Code)	§579.1	§673.1	§633A.2105
Kansas (Kan. Stat. Ann.)	§58-207		§58A-408

State	Agister's Lien Statute	Equine Activity Liability Statute	Animal and/or Pet Trust Valid
Kentucky (Ky. Rev. Stat.)	§376.400	§247.401	
Louisiana (La. Rev. Stat. Ann.)		§9:2795.1	
Maine (Me. Rev. Stat. Ann.)	Title 10, §3352	Title 7, §4101	Title 18B, §408
Maryland (Md. Code Ann.)	Commercial Law, §16-401		
Massachusetts (Mass. Gen. L.)	Chapter 255, §24	Chapter 128, §2D	
Michigan (Mich. Comp. Laws)	§570.185	§691.1661	§700.2722
Minnesota (Minn. Stat.)	§514.18		
Mississippi (Miss. Code Ann.)	§85-7-103		
Missouri (Mo. Rev. Stat.)	§430.150	§537.325	§456.4-408
Montana (Mont. Code Ann.)	§71-3-1201	§27-1-725	§72-2-1017
Nebraska (Neb. Rev. Stat.)	§54-201		§30-3834
Nevada (Nev. Rev. Stat.)			§163.0075
New Hampshire (N.H. Rev. Stat.)	§448:2	§508:19	§564-B:4-408
New Jersey (N.J. Rev. Stat. Ann.)	§2A:44-51	§5:15-1	§3B:11-38
New Mexico (N.M. Stat. Ann.)	§48-3-7	§42-13-1	§45-2-907
New York (N.Y. Law)	Liens, §183		Estates, Powers, & Trusts Law, §7-8i
North Carolina (N.C. Gen. Stat.)	§44A-2(c)		§36C-4-408
North Dakota (N.D. Cent. Code)	§35-17-01	§53-10-01	

State	Agister's Lien Statute	Equine Activity Liability Statute	Animal and/or Pet Trust Valid
Ohio (Ohio Rev. Code Ann.)	§1311.48	§2305.32.1	
Oklahoma (Okla. Stat.)	Title 4, §191	Title 76, §50.1	
Oregon (Or. Rev. Stat.)	§87.152	§30.687	§128.308
Pennsylvania (Pa. Stat. Ann.)	Title 37, §81		
Rhode Island (R.I. Gen. Laws)	§34-48-1	§4-21-1	
South Carolina (S.C. Code Ann.)	§29-15-60	§47-9-710	§62-7-408
South Dakota (S.D. Codified Laws Ann.)	§40-27-1	§42-11-1	
Tennessee (Tenn. Code Ann.)	§66-20-101	§44-20-101	§35-15-408
Texas (Tex. Code Ann.)	Property, §70.003	Civil Practice, §87.001	Property, §112.037
Utah (Utah Code Ann.)	§38-2-1	§78-27b-101	§75-7-408
Vermont (Vt. Stat. Ann.)	Title 9, §2075	Title 12, §1039	
Virginia (Va. Code Ann.)	§43-32		§55-544-08
Washington (Wash. Rev. Code Ann.)	§60.56.010	§4.24.530	§11.118.005
West Virginia (W.Va. Code)	§38-11-4	§20-4-1	
Wisconsin (Wis. Stat. Ann.)	§779.43	§895.481	§701.11
Wyoming (Wyo. Stat.)	§29-7-101	§1-1-122	§4-10-409

NOTE: Although every effort was made to ensure the accuracy of these references, old laws change and new laws are added, sometimes with an alarming frequency. These references are for informational purposes only, and anyone affected by these laws, or by any others, should refer to current versions of their state statutes.

GLOSSARY

ABSOLUTE INSURER RULE — A rule adopted by most horse racing jurisdictions and horse show organizations that makes a trainer responsible for the condition of horses in the trainer's care. When a horse tests positive for a prohibited medication, for example, the rule shifts the burden of proof to the trainer, who must show that he or she neither administered the drug nor allowed it to be administered.

ACCEPTANCE — An essential part of contract formation, acceptance means that a party has agreed to the terms and conditions of an offer.

ACCRUAL METHOD ACCOUNTING — Accounting method in which income is recorded when it is earned and expenses are recorded when they are incurred.

AFFIDAVIT — A statement made under oath and penalty of perjury.

AGENCY — The relationship between two parties, an agent and a principal, in which the agent has the authority to act on behalf of the principal, and can obligate the principal to take some action.

AGENT — An individual who has the authority, either actual or implied, to act on behalf of another.

AGREED VALUE POLICY — A mortality insurance policy in which the value of the insured animal is established by agreement between the owner and the insurer when the policy is purchased. The agreed value cannot change during the term of the policy.

AGISTER'S LIEN — A farm owner's security interest in a horse being boarded to secure payment of the board bill by the animal's owner.

AGRICULTURAL LIEN — A security interest pursuant to Article 9 of the revised Uniform Commercial Code that is available in some, but not all, states.

ALTERNATIVE DISPUTE RESOLUTION (ADR) — A collective term for non-judicial ways to resolve disputes, including mediation and arbitration.

AMERICAN RULE — A general rule requiring each party to pay his or her own attorney fees in a lawsuit.

ANIMAL RIGHTS — Generally used in reference to efforts aimed at altering animals' current status as property through establishing legal rights for animals, including recognition of animal "guardians" rather than "owners."

ANIMAL WELFARE — General term expressing a concern for the health and welfare of animals within the existing legal framework, emphasizing adequate food and water, shelter, veterinary care, companionship, owner education, and enforcement of anti-cruelty laws.

ANSWER — The first pleading filed by the defendant in response to a complaint. The party filing an answer either acknowledges or denies the allegations made in the complaint.

APPELLATE REVIEW — The process by which a trial court judgment is reviewed for errors by a higher court. Appeals generally are based on alleged mistakes of law or fact and not on a party's dissatisfaction with the outcome of the trial.

APPRAISAL — An assessment of value by an impartial third party.

ARBITRATION — A type of alternative dispute resolution in which an impartial third party, the arbitrator, listens to both sides of a dispute, then makes a decision.

ASSETS — All property, both real and personal, owned by an individual or by a business.

ASSUMPTION OF THE RISK — A legal doctrine preventing an individual from recovering damages for an injury suffered during a dangerous activity if the injured person knew of the danger and voluntarily took part in the activity knowing the risk.

ATTRACTIVE NUISANCE — A dangerous condition on a landowner's property that is likely to attract children who, because of their age, lack the ability to recognize the danger. The landowner has a legal duty to take reasonable measures to protect such children from the harm, even if they are trespassers to whom no duty generally is owed.

BAILMENT — A transaction in which one party, the bailor, transfers possession of property (such as a horse) to a second party, the bailee, for safekeeping. The bailee generally has a duty to exercise reasonable care to prevent harm to the property.

BILATERAL CONTRACT — A transaction in which the parties to a contract exchange mutual promises to do or not to do something.

BUSINESS — For federal income tax purposes, a business is an activity that is engaged in for profit.

"C" CORPORATION — A corporation organized under Chapter C of the IRS tax code.

CAPACITY — The ability to understand and enter into a valid, legally binding contract.

CAPITAL — For accounting purposes, the amount of money invested in a business.

CARE, CUSTODY, OR CONTROL INSURANCE — Insurance that protects a farm owner from injury to horses owned by someone else while the animals are in the farm owner's care.

CASH METHOD ACCOUNTING — Accounting method in which income is recorded when it is received and expenses are recorded when they are paid.

CAVEAT EMPTOR — "Let the buyer beware."

CIVIL LAWSUIT — A judicial proceeding initiated by one private party against another private party, seeking damages for violation of some right.

COMPENSATORY DAMAGES — A common form of damages awarded to the winning party in a civil lawsuit. Compensatory damages do not punish the losing party but instead restore the winning party to his or her position before the injury.

COMPLAINT — The pleading filed by a plaintiff to initiate a civil lawsuit. A complaint states the claims made by the initiating party and may or may not specify the amount of damages sought.

CONSENSUAL SECURITY INTEREST — A security interest resulting from an agreement between the parties in a transaction.

CONSIDERATION — An essential part of a valid contract, consideration is that which each party gives up during negotiations to obtain something in return. Consideration can convert a gratuitous promise into a valid, enforceable contract.

CONTRACT — An agreement between two or more parties that creates a legal obligation on their respective parts either to take some action or to refrain from doing so. The non-breaching party can enforce the terms of a valid contract in court if there is a breach of the agreement.

CONVERSION — The civil version of criminal theft. Conversion occurs when one party takes unauthorized possession of another party's property and can be the basis for a civil lawsuit.

CRIMINAL PROSECUTION — Legal action initiated by the state against an individual or business for violation of a law.

DEDUCTION — An item of expense that is used to reduce a taxpayer's gross income.

DEFAULT JUDGMENT — A judgment in favor of the plaintiff when the defendant does not respond to a civil complaint within the required time limit.

DEFENDANT — The party against whom either a civil complaint or a criminal charge is directed.

DEPRECIATION — An accounting method that spreads the cost of an asset over the asset's useful life. When an asset must be depreciated, a taxpayer is allowed a deduction for only a portion of the asset's cost each year.

DUTY — A legal or moral duty either to act or not to act. Breach of a legal duty can be the basis for a civil lawsuit or a criminal charge.

EMPLOYEE — A worker over whom the employer exercises control regarding when, where, and how a job is to be done.

EXCULPATORY CLAUSE — A contract clause in which one party attempts to disclaim any liability for harm to another party.

EXPRESS WARRANTY — A warranty created by the affirmative statement of a seller regarding the quality or performance of the goods being sold.

FAIR MARKET VALUE — The price that would be paid in a transaction involving a willing buyer and a willing seller.

FAIR MARKET VALUE POLICY — A mortality policy that pays the fair market value of a horse at the time of the animal's death. The fair market value at the time of death may be different from the animal's value when the policy was purchased.

FELONY — A serious crime, with punishment for a term of more than one year in prison.

FIDUCIARY DUTY — A duty imposed on one party to act in the best interests of another party, even at the expense of the first party's personal interest.

GENERAL PARTNER — A member of a partnership who is jointly and severally liable for the debts of the partnership.

GRATUITOUS PROMISE — A promise made by one party without consideration from the other party. A gratuitous promise is not a valid contract and cannot be enforced in court.

GROSS INCOME — The total of all income received by a taxpayer, including income from illegal sources.

HOBBY LOSS PROVISION — Found in Section 183 of the Tax Code, the hobby loss provision allows a taxpayer to use a loss from an activity (including a horse activity) to reduce taxable income from another activity only if the activity generating the loss is a business "engaged in for profit."

HONORARY TRUST — A trust that for one reason or another is not legally valid and thus cannot be enforced by a court. In states without specific laws validating them, some trusts for the care of animals may be deemed to be honorary by probate courts.

I-9 — Documentation required by the U.S. Citizenship and Immigration Service (formerly the Immigration and Naturalization Service) where an employer verifies an employee's identity and authorization to work in the United States.

IMPLIED WARRANTY — A warranty that arises through the operation of law and does not depend on any action by the seller. Typical implied warranties are the warranty of title, warranty of merchantability, and warranty of fitness for a particular purpose.

INDEPENDENT CONTRACTOR — A worker who contracts to do work over which the employer exercises control regarding only the final product or result.

INTESTATE — To die without a will.

INVITEE — A person who enters onto another person's land by invitation, in connection with the property owner's business, with a resulting benefit to the property owner or to both parties.

JOINT AND SEVERAL LIABILITY — The legal principle that makes each general partner in a partnership individually responsible for all the debts of the partnership.

JOINT VENTURE — A business entity similar to a partnership, generally established for one transaction only.

JUDGMENT CREDITOR — The winner of a monetary judgment in a civil lawsuit. A judgment creditor is entitled to have the judgment enforced in court.

LEASE — An agreement between two parties in which the lessor transfers right of possession and right of use of property, but not ownership, to the lessee for a period of time.

LIABILITY — Either the obligation to repay a debt or financial responsibility for injury to a person or to property.

LIABILITY WAIVER — An agreement, usually in writing, by an individual to assume the risk of injury resulting from an activity. Liability waivers may or may not be enforced by a court.

LICENSEE — A person who enters onto another person's land by permission of the landowner, without any direct benefit to the landowner.

LIEN — A security interest in property to secure payment of a debt.

LIMITED PARTNER — A member of a partnership whose liability is limited to his or her investment and who has no personal liability for the partnership debts. Limited partners generally have no role in management of the partnership.

LIMITED PARTNERSHIP — A partnership consisting of one or more general partners and one or more limited partners.

LIVE FOAL — As generally used, a foal that stands and nurses.

LOSS OF USE POLICY — Insurance coverage that pays when a horse becomes injured or incapacitated and permanently unable to perform.

MEDIATION — A type of alternative dispute resolution in which an impartial third party, the mediator, listens to both sides of a dispute and then attempts to facilitate an agreement between the parties. Unlike an arbitrator, a mediator does not make a decision.

MEETING OF THE MINDS — The mutual agreement to the terms and conditions of a contract by the parties.

MINOR — A person who because of his or her young age lacks the legal capacity to enter into a valid contract. In most states a person's status as a minor ends at age eighteen.

MISDEMEANOR — A criminal offense less serious than a felony, generally punished with imprisonment for less than one year.

MORTALITY INSURANCE — Insurance coverage that pays when the insured horse dies. Full mortality insurance covers death by any cause; limited risk mortality covers death by specified causes.

NEGLIGENCE — Failure to exercise reasonable care under the circumstances of a situation.

OFFER — A proposal to do something, such as buy a horse, that a second party can accept or reject.

OCCUPATIONAL SAFETY AND HEALTH ADMINISTRATION (OSHA) — The agency, either federal or state, responsible for developing and enforcing workplace safety regulations.

PARTNERSHIP — A business owned by two or more individuals that is not organized as a corporation or limited liability company.

PASSIVE ACTIVITY — An activity in which the owner has no material participation, as defined in Section 469 of the Tax Code.

PASSIVE INCOME — Income generated by a passive activity.

PASSIVE LOSS — A loss generated by a passive activity. A passive loss generally can be used to reduce only the taxable income from other passive activities.

PERSONAL PROPERTY — All property other than real estate.

PET TRUST — A trust established for the care of an animal, generally during the owner's lifetime. Such trusts are valid in many, but not all, states.

PLAINTIFF — The party initiating a civil lawsuit.

POWER OF ATTORNEY — A written document giving one person the legal authority to act on behalf of another person.

PRE-PURCHASE EXAM — A veterinary examination performed on a horse prior to purchase.

PRINCIPAL — In an agency relationship, the individual on whose behalf an agent acts.

PROTECTED CLASS — One of several distinct groups of individuals protected by federal and/or state anti-discrimination. It is illegal to discriminate against a person because of the person's race, color, national origin, religion, or gender.

PROXIMATE CAUSE — The event that directly produces an injury, without any intervening event.

PUFFING — A statement made by a seller that is so outrageous or unbelievable that no reasonable buyer would rely on it.

PUNITIVE DAMAGES — Damages awarded by a court in a civil lawsuit to deter future wrongdoing and to punish the losing party.

REAL PROPERTY — Land and anything growing or built on the land.

REPOSITORY — A service offered by some sales companies allowing consignors to provide radiographs, records of endoscopic examinations, and other veterinary information in a central location for review by potential buyers.

RESERVE PRICE — The lowest price at which a consignor is willing to sell a horse.

RISK OF LOSS — The financial responsibility for harm to a horse.

"S" CORPORATION — A corporation organized under Chapter S of the IRS tax code.

SALES TAX — A state or local tax, generally a percentage of the purchase price, levied when goods are sold.

SECURITY INTEREST — An interest in property to secure payment of a debt.

SERVICE OF PROCESS — Delivery of a complaint and summons to a defendant, giving notice that a lawsuit has been initiated.

SHAREHOLDER — A person or entity that owns stock in a corporation.

SMALL CLAIMS COURT — Court that provides a relatively informal forum for the resolution of disputes with small amounts of money at issue. Parties are encouraged and in some states may be required to proceed without an attorney.

SOLE PROPRIETORSHIP — A form of business ownership in which one person, the sole proprietor, owns all the assets of the business, makes all business decisions, and is personally responsible for all business debts.

SPLIT SAMPLE — Standard procedure when testing blood and urine samples from competition horses for prohibited substances is to divide the sample into at least two parts, allowing a second test to confirm an initial positive result.

STATUTE OF FRAUDS — Legal requirement that some types of contracts must be in writing to be enforced in court. They include contracts for the sale of real property, contracts that cannot be performed within one year, contracts to guarantee the debt of a third party, and contracts for the sale of goods for more than $500.

STATUTORY LIEN — A security interest that arises as the result of a statute and that does not depend on an agreement between the parties. Agister's liens are examples of statutory liens.

SUMMARY JUDGMENT — A judgment in favor of a party prior to a trial, based on a determination by a judge that there are no issues of fact in dispute and that the winning party is entitled to the judgment based solely on the law applicable to the case.

SUMMONS — In a civil action, the document delivered along with a complaint to the defendant notifying him or her that a lawsuit has been filed; in a criminal prosecution, the document notifying the defendant that he or she has been charged with a criminal offense and directing the defendant to appear in court.

SYNDICATION — The sale of fractional interests in a horse, usually a breeding stallion, to several buyers.

TAXABLE INCOME — A taxpayer's gross income minus the allowable deductions.

TESTAMENTARY TRUST — A trust established after a person's death, as part of a will.

TORT — A private injury that can be the basis for a civil lawsuit, such as personal injury or breach of contract.

TRESPASSER — A person who enters upon the land of another person without legal authority to do so.

TRUST — A legal entity created by an individual (the grantor) for the benefit of someone else (the beneficiary). In some states a trust can be established for the care of an animal.

UMBRELLA POLICY — An addition to an insurance policy that increases the upper limit of coverage, without providing any new coverage that did not exist under the basic policy.

UNIFORM COMMERCIAL CODE (UCC) — A body of law that governs commercial transactions and has been adopted in some form in every state.

UNILATERAL CONTRACT — A contract in which one party makes a promise that can be accepted through performance by the other party to the agreement, unlike a bilateral contract that involves promises from both parties.

USE TAX — Similar to a sales tax, a use tax is collected by a state for purchases of goods made in another jurisdiction and brought into the home state.

WARRANTY — A promise, either express or implied, that goods offered for sale are actually what they are held out to be.

WARRANTY OF FITNESS FOR A PARTICULAR PURPOSE — Implied warranty that arises when a seller knows that the buyer intends the goods to be used for a particular purpose and knows that the buyer is relying on the seller's expertise to provide goods suitable for that purpose.

WARRANTY OF MERCHANTABILITY — Implied warranty that goods sold are generally fit for the purpose for which the goods are sold.

WARRANTY OF TITLE — Implied warranty that the seller has the legal right to sell the goods being offered, reflecting the basic principle that sellers cannot legally sell what they do not own.

INDEX

About the Author

Milton C. Toby, J.D., practices law and mediation in Georgetown, Kentucky, near Lexington. In addition to his law practice, Toby teaches equine law at Midway College in Midway, Kentucky, and at Bluegrass Community and Technical College in Lexington. He also is developing an online equine law and taxation course for Midway College.

Toby has enjoyed a lifelong involvement with horses. He exhibited American Saddlebreds in shows and competed in hunter, combined training, and dressage events. He served as a steward for the American Horse Shows Association (now United States Equestrian Federation) and as a director of the Kentucky Horse Council. He also has worked as a journalist and photographer.

In addition to *The Complete Equine Business & Legal Handbook*, Toby is the author of *Understanding Equine Law* and *Understanding Equine Business Basics* (co-written with former law partner, Karen Perch); *Ruffian* in the Thoroughbred Legends series; and *Col. Sager, Practitioner*, which recounts the experiences of the late Col. Floyd Sager, one of the country's most prominent equine veterinarians.

Toby lives in Georgetown, Kentucky.